INDIAN FEDERALISM
Emerging Issues

INDIAN FEDERALISM
Emerging Issues

Editor
S.K. Jain

KALPAZ

First Published 2017

Published by

Kalpaz Publications
C-30, Satyawati Nagar,
Delhi - 110052
E-mail: kalpaz@hotmail.com Ph.: 9212142040

Printed at : G. Print Process, Delhi

Cataloging in Publication Data--DK
Courtesy: D.K. Agencies (P) Ltd. <docinfo@dkagencies.com>

National Seminar on "Indian Federalism: Emerging Dimensions and Issues" (2013 : New Delhi, India)
Indian federalism : emerging issues / editor, S.K. Jain.
pages cm
Includes bibliographical references.
ISBN: 9789351282631 (HB)

1. Federal government--India--Congresses. I. Jain, Sumitra Kumar, editor. II. Shaheed Bhagat Singh Evening College (New Delhi, India), organizer. III. India International Centre, host institution. IV. Title.

JQ220.S8N38 2013 DDC 321.020954 23

Dedicated to

My father Sri Surendra Kumar Jain

who has been always an inspiration for me in my academic persuit against all the odds of life.

Contents

Foreword

India's federal democracy has developed through successive phases of growth, combining centralism and federalism in varying doses. The major motors for the transition from one phase to the other have been changes in the balance between these forces, in the party system as well as in the political economy of the federal system. The current phase began some twenty-five years ago and is characterised by two major trends: the federalisation of the party system and the salience of federal coalitions as a form of federal governance.

The resilience of the federalised party system contributes to the persistence of coalitions due to multilevel electoral contests. Coalitions no longer merely address deficits in numbers in the Lok Sabha. They also cater to the need for allies in the states in order to reach the required numbers in the Rajya Sabha and for the more effective implementation of national policies in the states. They have become essential to carry forward the legislative agenda of the party in power at the Centre.

This collection of essays looks at the issues that have emerged from this changed constellation of forces in the context of sustained economic growth and enduring inequalities. Many of the problematic issues addressed are a legacy of previous phases, such as the persistent neglect of certain regions and sections of society.

The neo-liberal phase of globalised economic growth has aggravated the spatial and individual differences in levels of income, growth and prosperity.

The previous phase of India's federal development was marked by the stunted growth of institutional devices designed to meet the needs of cooperation and coordination. It is important to recall that the original design vested substantial legislative powers and responsibilities in state governments for key developmental activities. Financial limitations of the states as well as a centrally driven model of development led to the proliferation of central schemes and national missions. In the current phase, these features of the division of powers and responsibilities have assumed renewed importance after the enhanced devolution of financial resources to the States by the Fourteenth Finance Commission.

The federal dialogue between the Centre and the states is often pre-empted by central administrative and policy decisions taken unilaterally. The Centre often decides on a particular course of action and only thereafter, if at all, does it seek inputs from the states. Consensus building in many policy cases is after the decision, not before. This mode of decision-making is being increasingly contested. In the emerging context of assertive states' rights, mere formal consultation may not suffice. What is needed is a more proactively inclusive decisional process. From this perspective, it would be useful to study the process through which the GST Council has established itself as a major player in the scheme of intergovernmental fiscal relations.

Related to the quest for a more responsive and participatory federal democracy is the notion of asymmetric federalism. As political and economic asymmetries get accentuated, demands are bound to grow for statutory asymmetric arrangements. In India, the inequality of states, and of regions within states, has commonly generated tensions and dissatisfactions. Asymmetrical federalism and special status provisions, including special fiscal regimes and incentives, have helped address these problems to only a limited extent. More studies are needed to work out the kind of asymmetrical federalism that would really make a dent in this area.

Greater reliance on market allocation of capital investments has given rise to competition among states, a competition that they are unequally equipped and endowed for. This has given rise to a lop-sided competitive federalism in which a level playing field has yet to be created. The impact of competition for attracting investments to the states is to be understood at two levels. On the one hand, states are under pressure to provide good governance and to manage their finances with prudence. On the other hand, they are faced with the possibly negative impact of many of the reform measures they are asked to implement.

These are some of the issues that deserve further investigation in the light of new trends towards centralised federalism, and in the absence of a robust institutional framework for cooperative federalism. It would be useful to explore through what legal devices the Centre manages to impose its will on the states in matters that are essentially within their domain of competence. There are many unfunded mandates issued by the Centre where refusal to implement may not even involve financial sanctions, since central funding is not involved. When the Centre errs, do the states not have both a right and a responsibility to stand up and oppose wrong policies, by using the powers at their command? This was done during the Emergency when states refused to implement central censorship rules. When the Centre regresses, the states can remain progressive. The advantages of a federal structure can come into play in such situations. This has been referred to as 'progressive federalism'. The rise of cultural intolerance poses yet another regressive threat to the delicate fabric of our pluricultural federal democracy, where progressive federalism could give some relief.

The logic of democratic development in a federal democracy allows several experiments in governance to take place simultaneously, provided they respect the basic values and features of the Constitution. The capacity of the system to generate alternative paths of development through experimentation by the states has however to be tested in order to discover its limits.

The tendency to rely on central instruments for delivery of public goods and services directly to citizens, thereby bypassing the multilevel federal structure, is another trend that deserves attention. Central instruments like banking, currency, national highways, posts, petroleum, railways and airways are a few of the channels that can be used to effectively carve out a unique centralised space. They permit the implementation of policies without the mediation of state governments, as opposed to an earlier phase where both levels competed with each other to capitalise electorally on benefits financed by one level and delivered by another.

Indian federalism thankfully continues to develop, raising new issues at each stage and hopefully revealing new ways to address fresh challenges.

Balveer Arora
Chairman
Centre for Multilevel Federalism
Institute of Social Sciences,
New Delhi

13th March 2017

Acknowledgements

The present work is the outcome of the National Seminar on "Indian Federalism: Emerging Dimensions and Issues" organised by Shaheed Bhagat Singh Evening College, University of Delhi on 8th and 9th March 2013, at India International Centre, Delhi. In the process of making the seminar successful and bringing out this book, I am thankful to several people and institution.

First of all, I am thankful to ICSSR, New Delhi for the financial assistance to organise the seminar without which it was not possible. I am also thankful to Shaheed Bhagat Singh Evening College for partial financial assistance and particularly Dr P.K. Khurana, Principal for his encouragement to enhance the academic activities of the college. I am thankful to all the speakers, paper presenters particularly, Zoya Hasan, Prof. Balveer Arora, Prof. M.P. Singh, Prof. Rekha Sexena, Prof. Asha Sarangi, Prof. Harihar Bhattacharya, Prof. G.M. Gulwani, Prof. Gopa Kumar, Prof. John Sema, Prof. Ajay Kumar Singh, Prof. Ujjwal Singh, Prof. Ruchi Tyagi, Prof. Subendhu Raj, Dr B.K. Pandey, Prof. Himanshu Roy, for their participation and presentation in the seminar. I am also thankful to other paper contributors, Prakash Singh, Sukhjit Singh, Dr G.S. Arora for their extended cooperation for the book. I am thankful to all my colleagues' friends and more particularly our students to make the seminar not only successful but more lively and meaningful. I am also thankful to my father and family members for their constant support in my all endeavour and academic pursuit. Finally, I am grateful to my publisher "Kalpaz Publications" to get the book published with minimum time and printing error. I would also like to thank all those who could not figure here but certainly not forgotten for their direct or indirect contribution towards the completion of this work.

S.K. Jain

List of Contributors

B.K. Pandey and M. Saravanan - Senior Consultant for M.H.R.D and Rastriya Uchatar Shiksha Abhiyan.

G. Gopa Kumar - Vice-Chancellor, Central University of Kerala, Kerala.

G.K. Arora - Principal, Dr Bhim Rao Ambedkar College, University of Delhi.

Gull Wani - Director, Centre for Kashmir Studies, Kashmir University, Srinagar.

Harihar Bhattacharyya - Professor, Department of Political Science, Burdwan University, West Bengal.

Himanshu Roy - Fellow, Nehru Memorial Museum and Library, Teen Murti, New Delhi.

John Sema - Associate Professor, Central University of Nagaland, Kohima.

M.P. Singh - Former Professor, Department of Political Science, University of Delhi and Senior Fellow, Centre for Multilevel Federalism, New Delhi.

Prakash Singh - Former Director General of Police, U.P and B.S.F.

Ruchi Tyagi - Associate Professor, Kalindi College, University of Delhi.

S.K. Jain - Associate Professor, Shaheed Bhagat Singh Evening College, University of Delhi.

Subash C. Kashyap - Eminent Constitutional Expert and Former Secretary General, Lok Sabha.

Subhendu Ranjan Raj - Associate Professor in Political Science, PGDAV College, University of Delhi.

Sukhjit Singh - Assistant Professor, P.G. Department of Political Science, Khalsa College, Amritsar.

Introduction

S.K. Jain

Federalism is best understood as a method of promoting self rule and shared rule and of balancing the interest of a nation with that of its region. This is done for a dual purposes that of limiting the possibility of a tyranny of the majority and of generating strength through union. A durable federal design thus aims at the contradictory goals of reconciling freedom with cohesion, and a diversity of political cultures and identities with effective political action. A federal system is the constitutional arrangement that gives federalism its institutional form.[1]

Throughout history, India has been characterised by diverse, cultures, languages, religions and regions. Indian federalism serves the second largest population in the World with multiple diversities and ethnicities. The federal system has served well for India in terms of promoting democracy, strengthening the national unity and achieving the fair level of economic progress. Though Indian federalism is not among the world's oldest federal political system, it is nevertheless, steadily emerging as a key feature of its political system and also an interesting example of the innovative potential of federalism.

The history of federalism and centre-state relations in India remains characterised by political mobilisation and intermittent struggle towards a more meaningful federal set up.[2] Alarmed at the volatile turn of events preceding the birth of free India and the partition of the country, the framer of Indian constitution opted for a Union of States. However, there were number of amendments moved in the constituent assembly to call it a "federation" instead of "union of states". Dr B. R. Ambedkar, Chairman of the drafting committee had his own explanation and justification for this. He said, "though India was to be federation, the federation was not the result of an agreement by the states to join in a federation and that the federation not being the result of an agreement, no state has the right to secede from it. The federation is a union because it is indestructible. Though the country and people may be divided into different states for convenience of a administration, the country is one integral whole, its people a single people living under a single imperium derived from a single source. The Americans had to wage a civil war to establish that the states have no right of secession and that their federation was indestructible. The drafting committee thought it was better to make it clear at the outset rather than to leave it to speculation or the dispute.[3]

Whether India is a federation at all has long been debated by scholars and experts, who hold different view while interpreting the federal nature of the Indian constitution. Some scholars described Indian federalism as "administrative federalism" and some others holding "together federalism" unlike coming together federalism of United States. Paul A. Appley[4] observed that "India is most federal in so far as centre is weak and depends upon its units for the execution of several developmental programme and projects. Other call it "cooperative federalism", an amicable union (Austin 1966)[5] K.C. Whear (1953)[6] characterised it as "quasi federal", something between a unitary state and a federation.

However, Indian democracy and federalism in its working of more than six decades, though suffered from numerous shortcomings, has nevertheless remained the most successful and stable democratic federation among post-colonial states. With the exception of Emergency (1975-1977), India has been governed by democratic institution with routinely electorally mandated transfer of power peacefully.

One of the factors that supported parliamentary federalism, as conceptualised by the framers of the constitution was what is popularly described as the "Congress system". In the initial years of independence, Indian federalism worked without any serious problem due to the Congress party's dominance. After the transfer of power, the Congress quickly became India's central political institution more important than parliament, bureaucracy or any other formal institution of the state. In the first two decades of federal experiment in India, the leaders both at the centre and the states faced two sets of compromises in order to bring about national integration. There were compromises which could lead to easing the centrifugal pressures by allowing the state borders to coincide either before or after independence with predominantly linguistic, tribal, or racial characteristics and the second compromise was to develop a national language as a means of linking together the diverse people. This "accommodative federalism and effective leadership" period was also supported by some contextual factors. During this period the Congress party was in power not only in the centre but almost all the states as well. Intra-party cleavages did not threatened its hegemony. The charismatic stature and unquestionable leadership of Nehru favoured the climate of the Centre's political dominance over the states. Moreover during this period, the state governments were able to enjoy a measure of autonomy within a broad framework of their constitutionally delimited jurisdiction. The operational constraint for the states could mainly be attributed to the factor of resource inadequacy rather than to any major redefinition of restructuring of centre-state relations.[7]

There was no organised attempt to destabilise the governmental leadership at state level during Nehru-Shastri era. There was always accommodation and mutual adjustment of centre-state relations mainly because the centre in general did not take unilateral non-negotiable position. A part of this explanation lies in the persistence of earlier consensus system.[8] The Congress till this time had not completely abdicated its role as a party of national movement, the history of which was a continuous process of accommodation and reconciliation of various interest and point of view. This was also possible because of relatively homogenous elites both at national and regional levels. Thus, all this contributed to smooth functioning of India's delicately balanced federal constitution in the first two decades after independence.

India's federal system started experiencing tension from the late 1960's. Such tension was almost non-existent during the first generation of India's federalism (1950-67). During the second generation following the death of Prime Minister Lal Bahadur Shastri, rise of Indira Gandhi as a powerful leader of the Congress party and the emergence of dissent inside the Congress party led to a greater emphasis on centralisation within the party. At the same time however, economic development had helped to produce new political elites from rural areas who benefited from the "Green Revolution" of the 1960's. These new elites challenged the professional and industrial elites who had long controlled the Congress party, the national government and many state governments. They demanded decentralisation, greater state autonomy and tolerance to state based opposition parties.

In the post-1967 period for the first time, the non-Congress parties made a determined bid to emerge from the role of "Pressure Politics" to a role of democratic opposition parties with actual or potential possibilities of their forming alternative governments. A shift from dominance to competition was indeed brought about although it was only an existing situation and not a stable party system.[9] The post-1967 witnessed the creation of a significantly different political milieu, an environmental change that profoundly influenced the India's federal polity. India during "Indira Gandhi era (1967-84) was the phase of "confronted leadership and distorted federalism" because federal compromise was achieved with great difficulty. There was lack of party discipline, confrontation occurred in economic policy and misuse of Article 356 (President Rule) affecting the smooth functioning of Indian federalism. Soon after Nehru's demise, the Congress system started breaking down.

From 1969 onwards, Indira Gandhi, when faced with increased opposition strength rejected the principle of consensus in favour of majoritarian principle.[10] Indira Gandhi believed that if she centralised power in her hands, her influence would penetrate more effectively into regional and sub-regional arenas. On the contrary, attempt to centralise power at the national level increased rather than reduced the disparities between the national, state and local level. She thought, she was regimenting and homogenising politics in the various states by drawing power into her hands during emergency.

The reality however was radically different. Indeed the natural heterogeneity of the various states increased considerably during emergency and after that.[11] The gradual erosion of inner party democracy during Indira Gandhi's leadership and the increasing recourse to centralising institution device led to crisis of governance and federalism in India. The deinstitutionalisation of the Congress party contributed enormously to the erosion of India's federal system by dismantling the party's federal structure. Not only this decay led to the massive concentration of power in the central leadership but it also deprived the party of seasoned leadership at the national and state levels. During the period 1969-77, centre-state relations were practically nonexistent and unitarism triumphed under the aegis of the strong state whose power controlled by a ruling party which relied exclusively on its leaders for its survival. The 1975-77 emergency was probably the most serious affront to federalism for it led to the consolidation of a puissant centre presiding over a federation of thoroughly enfeebled states.[12]

The coming of Janta Party government in 1977 did not witness much change in the attitude of central government for federal structure of India. The Janta Party government led by then Prime Minister Morarji Desai under the influence of then Home Minister Charan Singh dismissed the nine Congress rule state governments on the pretext of loosing the faith of the people in the Lok Sabha election. Many Governors appointed by Congress government were also replaced with party loyalist of new dispensation. All this left the Janta Party government in poor impression for federal polity of India.

Indira Gandhi's coming back to power in 1980 after another split of the Congress (1978) and the brief gap of Janta Party Government (1977-79) witnessed further emasculation of power in her hands. By this time centralisation had become inevitable for her and for the Survival of the Congress party. This however resulted into a political conflict as the states ruled by the opposition demanded more power and autonomy to states. It was during the Indira Gandhi regime (1967-84) when President Rule (Art 356) was used as many as 71 times compared to Nehru-Shastri period (1950-67) of 11 times.[13] This reflected the erosion of liberal values and intolerant view of the Congress leadership fashioned by Indira Gandhi. Thus, during this period, Indian federalism became a victim of crude centralisation, which led to the rapid erosion of federal system of India.

The Indian politics in the post-Indira Gandhi era brought the change of the guard in the Congress party with Rajiv Gandhi as a successor. The cruel assassination of Indira Gandhi and ascendance of Rajiv Gandhi at the centre stage gave the Congress party an overwhelming majority (400/542) in the 1984 Lok Sabha election. The brute majority that the Congress party garnered was mainly due to the sympathy wave of Indira Gandhi's assassination. It appeared as a return to the earlier politics of conciliation and consensus, when the then Prime Minister Rajiv Gandhi announced his commitment to the essential values of democratic values in politics in his address to the Congress centenary session in December 1985 at Mumbai. Initially Rajiv Gandhi allowed a variety of opinions to support on the major national issues and insisted on carrying the opposition parties with him. He was initially tolerant to the states led by the opposition political parties.

However, Rajiv Gandhi's such politics became short lived due to the emergence of regional forces. The regional elites used the post-Indira Gandhi period to strengthen their position through bargaining. Rajiv Gandhi by now changed his earlier conciliatory politics and reverted to the political culture practiced by Indira Gandhi. Regular elections of the Congress party were not held. Rajiv Gandhi's increasing intolerance for dissent and his longing for personal dominance in the party organisation led to the revival of earlier practice of running the party through nominations. Fourteen State Congress chiefs were being replaced through nominations rather than elections. The chief ministers of several Congress ruled states were named at New Delhi rather than elected on the floor of the assembly of the states. In the face of election reverses in Andhra Pradesh, Karnataka, Assam, West Bengal, Punjab, Kerala, the Bofors Scandal and the increasing erosion of Rajiv Gandhi's credibility both as a leader of the nation and as a vote mobiliser of the Congress party, the initial direction he gave to the federal relations disappeared and a drift towards confrontation took place.[15]

This was reflected in his reply to the opposition sponsored no confidence motion against the government in the Lok Sabha on December 1987, where he warned that if any state government was found taking anti-national direction, he would dismiss it regardless of majority if enjoyed.[16] The seven non-Congress state chief ministers decried his observation against the spirit of federalism and straining centre-state relations. However, Rajiv Gandhi's centralised authoritarian functioning as party leader and head of the government with the overwhelming majority in the parliament weakened Indian federalism.

Indian politics witnessed from the 1980s onwards a growing assertion of states and regional identities in the forms of seeking more autonomy for states and restructuring of centre-state relations. By the beginning of the eighties, there emerged a different political complexion in the country. During this period the relationship between Congress ruled centre and non-Congress ruled states became strained. Two political trends were apparently discernible.

First, most of the regional parties that came to power like Telgu Desam in Andhra Pradesh, Janata Dal led by R.K. Hedge in Karnataka, DMK/AIDMK in Tamil Nadu and Pondhichery had wide social base and regional emotions. Similarly Samajwadi Party (SP), Bahujan Samaj Party (BSP), in U.P. Rashtriya Janata Dal (Samata party and later Janata Dal (United) in Bihar and Assam Gan Parisad (AGP) in Assam became strong regional parties in their respective region to capture power in nineties and after.

Secondly, there occurred a convergence of opposition political forces along with regional parties in the form of conclave politics. Such a high alignment of the political forces wooed the demands of regional autonomy. The Bengaluru conclave (1983) of four southern state chief ministers, the

Vijayawada conference (1983) of opposition leaders of 14 political parties, the Srinagar conclave (1983) of 18 opposition political parties drew the attention of the country, on the issue of the state autonomy and restructuring the centre-state relations.[17]

The period between 1989 - 2014 could be characterised as an era of "Regional Leadership and Electoral Federalism" because of assertion of regional parties on national politics and their increased strength in Lok Sabha elections. This period did not return any single political party with majority to rule at Centre. The election instead ushered in a phase of minority/coalition government at Centre with diverse regional and state parties sharing the power.

The emergence of coalition governments at Centre from 1989 to 2014 (with exception of minority Congress government led by P.V. Narashima Rao 1991-96) reconfirmed the growing regionalisation of Indian Politics at the national level. What began in the provinces in post-1967 era with the capture of power by state-based parties became a well entrenched now at national politics although there was no concretised pattern. Voters seemed to favoured the coalition government in Centre endorsing the multiplicity of interest. This was exemplified by the major coalitions of parties brought under one umbrella, where ideology did not appear to be as significant as generally construed. The poll outcome unequivocally endorsed the increasing importance of a multiparty system as integral to India's democratic federal governance and contestation.[18]

It was beyond doubt till 2014 general election, the growing importance of regional parties in the formation of coalition governments by accelerating the process of federalisation of India's parliamentary system of governance since 1989, which during the Congress system, was bordered on Centre's hegemony that disregarded regional interest to a large extent.

However, the coming of Narendra Modi led NDA government with majority of Bhartiya Janata Party in Lok Sabha after 2014 election, promised to usher in a new era for Indian federalism, on the idea that a state leader's vision from below would transform India's federal polity.[19]

The process of progressing towards cooperative federalism envisaged by Prime Minister Narendra Modi is reflected in the policy initiative like fourteenth finance commission recommendation to increase in the share of divisible tax pool from 32 per cent to 42 per cent and transferring 68 per cent divisible pool to the states. The larger transfers to the states are accompanied by the significant reduction in the central schemes and rationalisation of remaining schemes to give greater flexibility and control to the individual states.

The establishment of NITI (National Institution for Transforming India) Aayog occupied the resource allocation space vacated by the planning commission as a socialist hangover having no role in market economy. The most important responsibility of NITI Aayog relates to promoting cooperative federalism through structured support initiative and mechanism with the states on a continuous basis.[20] However, the effectiveness of the NITI Aayog in transforming India will depend upon the clarity in the functions assigned, the status and power given and the quality to the people who will steer the institutions.

The promise of "cooperative federalism" however suffered a jolt by imposing the President Rule under article 356 in Arunachal Pradesh (2015) and Uttrakhand (2016) by Narendra Modi led BJP government ignoring completely the Sarkaria Commission recommendation and Bommai judgement of Supreme Court. It came as a set back to Modi Government when Supreme Court intervention restored the dismissed Congress led previous governments in respective state. However, Prime Minister Narendra Modi led BJP government that insists on "Cooperative federalism" must resist the temptation to use the sledgehammer of President Rule to grab power in state for restoring the federal spirit.

By reviving and convening the Inter-state council (Art 263) in July 2016 for cooperation of states in tackling challenges to internal security is an indication of close centre- state relationship by Modi government. The BJP led NDA governments main focus is to promote federalism be it cooperative or competitive federalism.[21] But a key element in fostering cooperative federalism is the respect for the mandate of elected governments, even run by opposition parties. In an era, where the party system is fragmented along federal lines, the need is still felt by BJP to include state parties in federal coalitions in post-2014 general election even though technically it was not necessary. However, the way alliance partners are treated will become an important element in federal functioning. For working India's federal system, one has to go beyond brute parliamentary majority and grapple with the multi-level government opposition matrix which constitutes the architecture of federal power sharing.[22]

The time has come to take a stock of the prevailing situation. Should India remain Union of states as at present or should we have United States of India? It is therefore important to look at the constitution with an approach of pragmatic evolution rather than treat as a sanctified static documents. Federalism too will need to expand beyond its rigid boundaries lest the prevailing tensions between Centre and states exacerbate to a point beyond constitutional sanction. The ruling establishment, of whatever ideology, background or hue would have to learn the steering the ship of the nation with adequate flexibility, striking constructive compromises in the spirit of give and take. It is here that the model of cooperative federalism that has been discussed could be one of the guiding principles in the evolution of redistribution of powers and responsibilities between the union and states.

There are 14 chapters in this volume by the experts in the field which dwell on the new and emerging trends in the working of Indian federalism in the larger context of political, social and economic changes taken place in India.

In the first chapter **"Centre-state relations: Towards a fresh balance of power"** Dr Subhash Kashyap, an eminent constitutional expert, provides an historical review of centre state relations and the factors for shaping federal democratic system in India. To him, India's constitution has been variously described as quasi federal, federal with strong unitary bias etc. Reasons for this unique unitary federal mix are found in the constitutional history of India, the sheer size of the country and the nature of her complex diversities based on religion, language, region and culture. Highlighting a conflict resolution mechanism to built a new balance of power in centre state relations, he argues that the constantly evolving federal structures and innovating devices have proved to be very powerful. He concludes by saying that a great deal of reforms needed in our politics within a constitutional framework by strong political will. However, only in the rare cases constitutional amendments can be carried out without violating the basic structure of the constitution.

Prakash Singh in his chapter "**Impact of police reforms on insurgency and the structure of Indian federalism**" traces the police reforms in India and argued that all the recommendation by various commissions on police reforms received only cosmetic treatment. The police structure therefore does not show any substantial change. Hence the intended police reforms have hardly any impact on the insurgency situation in different parts of the country. Though India has a federal structure but the constitution has nevertheless pronounced unitary features. The founding father of the constitution could foresee separatist and secessionist tendencies in parts of the country and therefore they so designed it. The states definitely need full autonomy in respect of subjects falling in the state list. However, they need to extend full cooperation to the federal government in respect of subjects which, though technically in the state list, yet spill over and acquire inter-state or even international ramification.

G. Gopa Kumar in his paper "**Globalisation, Federalism and Democracy in India**" tries to examine the changing and challenging nature of Federal Democracy in the specific context of India's tryst with globalisation. The author tries to analyse the brief history of liberalisation and globalisation, and its deep impact on the social, economic and federalist character of the country in the last two decades. The author argues that as a policy, globalisation was not against decentralisation process but its strategies include strong neo-liberal approach towards decentralised governance. The paper concludes that the federal democracy in India is changing phenomenally taking cues mainly from the framework of globalisation.

Harihar Bhattacharya in his chapter "**West Bengal against the Centre. Continuity in Anti-centrism in Indian Federal Politics**" highlights the behavioural aspects of federal politics in India, that is how federal politics is conducted, operated its language, terms used to engage in 'federal bargain', the social and cultural repertoire used to buttress a political argument in favour of either the federation or the state's right. The case of West Bengal, a post-partition (1947) creation is discussed here as a major illustration. The author argue that West Bengal anti-centrism is deeply rooted in her history and culture, the experiences of successive state contraction as a result of administrative fiats and partitions: its perception of acute neglect despite being overburdened with millions of post-partition refugees the restlessness of a highly educated and socially and politically conscious elite known as the Bhadralok" to define and defend a homeland space in a land which was constantly subject to changing borders, and resultant loss of ethno linguistic brethren.

John Sema in his chapter "**Inequality of Indian Federalism: Issues and problems with special reference to North-Eastern states**" argues that ever since the framing of constitution of India, there has been controversy among the scholars as to whether the constitution of India can be truly described as federal or not. Although Indian federalism has some federal features in structure but most of its characters are unitary in nature, over and above there is inequality of representation in both the house of parliament, this means the state with large number of population has got more number of member of parliament having more voice and influence than the state with less population and member of parliament like North Eastern states. This ignored the principle of equality before law whether big or small states. Thus, it could not able to represent and satisfy the political aspirations of diverse multi-culture, ethnic minority groups, language and region.

Sukhjit Singh in his paper "**Indian Federalism, Sikh Identity and Akali Demand for State Autonomy**" underlines the importance of a true federal set up to provide a sense of security to the minorities. The working of Indian federalism, with a tinge towards centralised political set, has only accentuated the demand for state autonomy by those regional political parties which represent minority assertions in their respective region of influence. Akali Dal which always looks Sikhs as a distinct community, having their own separate culture, religion and language conceived highly centralised Indian political system as detrimental for the separate and unique identity of the Sikhs. Akali Dal fears that microscopic minority like Sikhs might lose their distinct identity as the party identifies centralised political setup as the rule of Hindus who always tried to assimilate Sikhs within the fold of Hinduism. Akali-Dal therefore, believes that only a true federal set up in India can produce a conducive environment for the religious, cultural and linguistic identity of the minorities especially Sikhs in India.

Gull Wani in his paper "**Self Rule and Autonomy: Politics of Contestation in J and K**" argues that India and Pakistan have traditionally pursued policies on Kashmir around their concerns regarding territoriality and sovereignty. In recent years more so during general Musharaf's tenure as Pakistan president, dialogue and peace process helped the stakeholders to make an incremental shift towards people centric approach. The people to people contact, trade and flow of new ideas have made it possible to evolve new and innovative approaches to conflict resolution. In December 2006, General Musharaf offered out of box options to Kashmir conflict and specified that Kashmir will have some borders and regions their self governance. In J and K, it renewed debate on autonomy, self rule within and between parties particularly two regional parties (National Conference and People's Democratic Party) which forms the subject matter of the paper. Both National Conference and People's Democratic Party have come out with documents to buildup the public opinion and also offer solution to the vexed issues.

G.K. Arora in his paper "**Statehood Demands in Globalising India: Retrospect and Prospect**" examines the issues of rising statehood demands in India while considering the historical context, factors that matter in the formation of states and globalisation with other socio-economic political changes taking place in an inter-connected manner in India's multicultural and democratic federal economy.

B.K. Pandey and M. Saravanan in their paper "**Centre State Fiscal relations in the New era of NITI Aayog and the Bygones Era of Planning Commission**" makes an attempt to examine the then existing arrangements of fiscal relation between the union and states governments in the context of the presence of the planning commission and how the relations have changed post-fourteenth finance commission and the setting of NITI Aayog. It also briefly delineates the fiscal imbalances between the central and state governments and also the inter-state and intra-state imbalances.

Himanshu Roy in his paper "**Regional Business and Federalism in India**" presents an analysis of the role of regional business, collectively represented by the trade associations and different regional chambers of commerce and industry in the creation of linguistic provinces in the pre and post-independent India. It also indicates the emerging subterranean trend of gradual marginalisation of regional parties in the social milieu of globalisation that propels scandalised attributes of market in the regions.

Subhendu Ranjan Raj in his paper "**Regional parties in Indian Federalism after the 2014 election**" argues that last few decades have been one of constant political change and the most significant is the changing nature of party system in India. From unipolarity of the Congress system of the yesteryears, bipolarity has ensued a contest between two alliances, the United Progressive Alliance (UPA) led by the Congress and the National Democratic Alliances (NDA) led by the BJP. Indeed the last decade and half has witnessed a polarised polity with multi-polarised context in many states. It has also led the emergence of small and regional parties. These federal parties have become the designer of politics in any Indian election. Since the fourteenth Lok Sabha election, the vote share of regional parties has hovered around 29 per cent of the total votes in all elections. These parties have popular support and have redefined the matrix (matrices) of electoral and coalition politics. However, the 2014 general election has changed the situation by giving majority to BJP. The paper focus on the performance of the regional parties in this election and argues that "it is too early to say that regional parties seem to have lost their importance because the total vote and seat share of regional parties remains exactly the same as it was in 2009 election i.e. 46.7 per cent and 212 seats. So a rethink on regional parties is necessary.

Ruchi Tyagi in her paper "**Federal Decentralisation in the era of Globalisation and Coalition Politics**" argues that since 1992, 73rd and 74th constitutional amendments have achieved a degree of democratic decentralisation which has compulsorily superimposed various tiers of local government on the federal structure. These amendments established India as a responsive multilevel federation in which local government is part of constitutional governance. They mobilised the power of people at local level effecting change most notably in relation to the involvement of women and of disadvantaged communities. The 1990's can be viewed as a defining transition for India's polity. New modes of participation and decision-making emerged through the mechanism of federal coalition. Globalisation has added a new dimension to the polity with economic reforms assigning new roles and responsibilities to the local bodies and despite various limitations federal decentralisation has ushered a new era of new role and responsibilities at grass root level.

S.K. Jain in his paper "**Indian Federalism: An empirical study of people's perception**" argues that it is only the first ever empirical study in India to capture the public perception on the various issues of Indian federalism. Due care has been taken to generate an all India perspective by selecting five states on Zonal basis. The study clearly shows that federalism is one of the cherished values of Indian people. Data reveal that people show strong preference for decentralised federalism and proactive role of the state. India has grounded potential to evolve as a matured federal nation and federal state.

The last paper is the **Valedictory address by Professor M.P. Singh** which has taken into accounts the historical process of development of Indian federalism from British Indian Government under the Government of India Act 1935 to appointment of M.M. Punchi commission in 2010 on centre-state relations. He concludes his observation where do we go from here? He opines that in the last 20 years or more, there has been decline and deinstitutionalisation in some cases but other organisations and institutions have either regenerated or have become reincarnated themselves in an activist role. The judiciary, National Human Right Commission, Election Commission, Vigilance Commission, Comptroller and Auditor General of India have demonstrated greater vigor and activism and this balance the situation.

REFERENCES

1. Mitra, S.K. and Marte Pehl "Federalism" in the Oxford companion to politics in India (edit) Niraja Gopal Jayal and Pratap, B. Mehta Oxford University Press, N. Delhi, 2010.
2. Roy, M. 2011, Federalism, Party system and structural changes in India, New Delhi (Sage Publication).
3. CAD, Vol. VII, p. 43.
4. Appleby, P.H. (1957), Public Administration in India: Report of a survey 1953, N. Delhi, Cabinet Secretariat, Government of India.
5. Austin, G. 1966, "The Indian constitution: cornerstone of a nation, Oxford Clanderson Press.
6. Where, K.C. (1953) – federal government, London, Oxford University Press.
7. Jain, S.K., Party Politics and Centre State Relations in India, Abhinav Publication, New Delhi, 1994, p. 35.
8. Kothari, Rajni, The Congress system in India, Asian Survey, 1969, Vol. 4.
9. The problem seminar December 16, 1969.
10. Chatterjee, R., "Democracy and opposition in India" E.P.W April 23, 1988.
11. Zins, Maxlean, "The Emergency 1975-77" in Hasan Z, Jha S N, Khan R (edit) The State, Poltitical Process and Identity, Reflections on modern India, N. Delhi, 1989.
12. Kaviraj, Sudipto," On the crisis of political institutions in India", contribution to Indian Sociology", Vol. 18, 1984.

13. Jain, S.K., "Article 356 and the Congress party" Mainstream, April 10, 1999.

14. Ray Amal and Kincaid John, "Politics, Economic Development and second generation strain in India's federalism" Publius The Journal of federalism, Philadelphia, May 1988.

15. *Ibid.*

16. The Hindu, December 11, 1989.

17. Jain, S.K., Party Politics and Centre State relations, Abhinav publications, 1989, p. 60.

18. Chakravarti Bidut, "Forging power: coalition politics in India, "Oxford University Press, 2001.

19. Arora, Balveer, the Hindu, May 22, 2015.

20. Rao, Govindam, Role and Functions and NITI Aayog, E.P.W. Jan 24, 2015.

21. Raj Nath Singh, Home Minister – Times of India, July 2016.

22. Arora, Balveer, The distant goal of cooperative federalism, The Hindu, May, 22, 2015.

1

Centre State Relations: Towards a Fresh Balance of Power

Subhash C. Kashyap*

The nation today is passing through critical times. Our polity is under a severe strain. Faith of the people in the quality, integrity and efficiency of governmental institutions stands seriously eroded. Security, unity and integrity of the nation are threatened. Problems and conflicts abound. One of the most difficult areas of concern is the Union-State relations. The question is, to what extent the multi-farious conflicts can be seen as emerging from the relationship between the Union and its constituent units and the tendency of the so-called centre to centralise powers in its hands? Can rebuilding federal structures and balancing power sharing mechanisms help resolve conflicts?

---

* *Courtesy:* Federalism in India: Towards a Fresh Balance of Power, Rawat Publications, Jaipur, (2014).

Some Conceptual Clarifications

Federal polity usually refers to the political system in a country with a rigid written Constitution defining and delimiting the powers and functions of both the federal legislature and government, on the one hand, and local or state legislatures and governments on the other hand. In a classic federation like that of the United States, sovereignty is divided between the federal and the state institutions, both partaking of sovereign powers in their respective spheres.

A classic federation, literally and historically, is the result of an agreement. It is when two or more sovereign states resolve to surrender part of their sovereignty and join hands to constitute a new union, a federal polity is born. It is a union without the constituent units losing their own identities. In fact, in a classic federation, the federal government enjoys only those powers that are, by agreement, surrendered to it by the units. However, there are also instances of some large countries where an existing unitary system may decide to share powers with the units under an agreed system of devolution or distribution of powers, for the sake of administrative convenience or for meeting linguistic or ethnic demands. Canada and India are examples of such polities. However, in every case of federalism — classical or otherwise — (i) the Constitution occupies the supreme position. It is written and relatively rigid, that is, not easily amendable; (ii) there are at least two levels at which government functions. In other words, two separate governments — federal and state — coexist; and (iii) as the arbiter of any disputes between the federation and the units as also between the units themselves, the highest judiciary — federal court or Supreme Court — enjoys a great authority and prestige.

Many countries that do not strictly fit in with the definition of a federal polity and yet have many of its features are variously described by scholars as some kind of a federation or a polity covered by some variant of federalism. Today, one hears of all kinds of 'innovative' federalisms — cooperative, executive, emergent, responsible, parliamentary, populist, legislative, competitive, fiscal, restructured, reluctant or quasi-federalism among others. 'Federations without federalism' is also mentioned.

The Western mind is anxious to reduce everything to a model or to fit every phenomenon into one of the models of its own conception. The tyranny of models and paradigms, however, may be dangerous.

Federalism today is basically an integrative device intended to keep different communities or divergent religious, linguistic, racial, tribal or other group identities together united under one nation—state. Problems of social pluralism are sought to be resolved by an arrangement or agreement to arrive at a balance in sharing political power. Irrespective of any variant of federal polity, federalism is relevant only in a situation where pluralism is territorially based, where particular groups are concentrated in separate territorial units or where the societal diversities are territorially identifiable, definable and separable. Federalism, as a political system, can be a meaningful performer only for a society faced with territorial diversities. It is an arrangement between separate territorial entities to come together or to avoid break-up and stay united by sharing power through a free democratic will. In a pluralist society, and in large nations with a multiplicity of diversities, feder-alism is the only way to genuine democracy.

India's Constitution has been variously described as quasi-federal — federal with a strong unitary or pro-centre bias, federal in structure but unitary in spirit, federal in normal times but with possibilities of being converted into a purely unitary one during the Emergency, etc. The fact is that it is difficult to put our Constitution in any strict mould of a federal or unitary type; it has features of both. It cannot be considered unitary because it provides, for example, the distribution of executive and legislative powers between the Union and the states and provisions affecting the powers of the states or Union-State relations cannot be amended without ratification by the states. It cannot be considered strictly federal both because the residuary powers vested in the Union and territorial identities of the states can be varied by Union Parliament through an ordinary legislation. The Supreme Court once called it amphibian.

Reasons for this unique unitary-federal mix are to be found in the constitutional history of India, the sheer size of the country and nature of her complex diversities based on religion, language, region, culture etc. There is perhaps no other comparable example of a classic plural society and a massive federal polity that is representative, republican and parliamentary, uniting and protecting under its umbrella numerous religious, linguistic, regional and other diverse identities. As has been well said India is a continental federal polity constituted into a single territorial sovereignty as a result of historical forces.

The Constitution describes India as a 'Union of States'. A separate part is devoted to 'Union-State Relations' meaning that it is about relations between the whole and its constituent parts and not between the centre of authority and its peripheries. The Constitution-makers avoided the use of words such as 'federation' or 'centre'. Actually- 'central government', 'central legislature' and centre law are an unfortunate hangover persisting the days of the centralised government during the colonial rule. A great deal of mischief has been caused by the wrong use of these words. Sources of conflicts in federal polities can be traced to differences based on ethnicity, religion, language, territory, and culture. Single most important source of conflicts in federal societies is the tendency of the Union to dominate the units, to make them dependent and to treat them as subordinates, not as equal partners in government and to work for the centralisation of authority under a top-down model.

We glibly talk about the 'transfer of power to the people' or `decentralisation of power to the grassroots' as if the power legitimately belonged to the bosses in Delhi or the so-called 'centre' and now they were condescending to transfer some of the power to 'we, the people' at the grassroots. In a democracy, all the sovereign powers belong to the people and it is for them at the grassroots to hand over some of these to higher tiers in the wider interests of a larger society and national and individual security. Democracy must begin at the local levels and to be safe and lasting, it must be crowned with a federal polity.

Moving towards building a new balance of power in intergovernmental relationship requires a conflict resolution (CR) mechanism. In recent decades, CR has developed into a distinct discipline in the academia and policy studies discourses. In specific situations, the nature of conflicts may vary; strong disagreements may emerge on grounds of ideologies, principles or differences in perception. Also, there may be areas beset with a genuine conflict of material interests. The notion of CR may be distinguished from prevention aimed at creating an atmosphere as a preventive measure, management involving a gradual incremental change through continued efforts and settlement on an ad hoc basis. All these may be stages in CR or independent goals. CR involves dealing with uses of the conflict and eliminating them once for all through necessary systemic changes and restructuring institution and relationships aimed at an honest balance of power between the union and the units.

In the context of Indian federalism, it is important to revisit the areas of conflict in intergovernmental 'relations and secure a proper balance of power sharing between the Union and the units. The constantly evolving federal structures and innovative devices have proved to be very powerful. CR and power sharing mechanisms have been integal to national integration, democracy and good governance. In fact, the Constitution of India itself has been the most potent CR mechanism — founded on the spirit of accommodation, adjustment and respect for diversity — ethnic, religious, linguistic and others. Whatever conflicts arose — and there were many major ones —were all sought to be resolved under the Constitution, for example, Tamil, Punjabi and North-East movements for secession or independence or demands for new states. Geographic boundaries of the states have often been reorganised. In 1956, they were organised on linguistic basis. Several states were then created as needed. Later, more states were formed, for example, Haryana, Himachal Pradesh, Nagaland, Manipur, Mizoram, Arunachal Pradesh and Goa. The ease with which the map of India has been redrawn and reorganisation of states effected during the last more than 60 years bears an eloquent testimony to the unique resilience and flexibility of the political system and efficacy of its CR mechanisms. In 2001, three large states were bifurcated to create three new states of Jharkhand, Uttarakhand and Chhattisgarh to respect and encourage the aspirations of the local people. Not all ethnic conflicts have been resolved. Movements continue for Vidarbha, Bodoland, Bundelkhand, and others. The process goes on. It is this dynamic process that is the source of the greatest strength to the system. The number of states which was 14 has doubled. As at present, the Union consists of 29 states and 7 union territories. Some unique solutions of regional councils, development boards, etc., have been attempted with varying degrees of success. We experimented with Bodoland Autonomous Council, Darjeeling Gorkha Hill Council, Jharkhand Area Autonomous Council, Leh Autonomous Hill Development Council, Tribal Areas Autonomous District Councils in Tripura, etc. India's Constitution is replete with CR and power sharing devices such as the Finance Commission, the Fifth and the Sixth Scheduled Reservations for SC/ST and Backward Classes.

Also, we have the CEC, CVC, AG, CBI, CRPF and the like. There are special provisions for adjudication of Inter-State Water Disputes, Inter State Council (Article 263), Article 370 for Jammu and Kashmir and Articles 371 to 371—I for Maharashtra, Gujarat, Nagaland, Assam, Arunachal and Goa.

Some scholars have suggested that India should be viewed as a civilisational state and not as a nation—state. Another suggestion is to call India a federal nation—state. We are, no doubt, a highly pluralistic society but our pluralism is not territory based. It is of a special kind. We have much diversity of various sorts, pulling us at once in the same or in opposite directions. The Indian society remains fragmented and segmented at every level on different grounds. Our-basic problem has never been one of territorially based diversities or pluralisms—Our diversities are within and cut across territorial units. In a sense, our diversities in themselves are plural and our pluralism is diverse both horizontally and vertically. However, what seems to divide also unites. In fact, our diversities are our greatest strength and a great cementing factor when it comes to national unity. Diversity is not division and unity does not mean uniformity or conformity. Also, unity of India and integrity of the nation as concepts are very different from national or political integration. When India achieved independence or what is called transfer of power in the midnight of 14-15 August 1947, unfortunately only the masters changed. The people did not feel the glow of freedom or transfer of power to their hands. The Constitution also continued the colonial model. Some people felt that they had been more free in their daily lives before independence and that they were being interfered with more and their freedom being taken away. For example, in the North-East, that feeling seemed to dominate.

We can look this matter from a different angle. The people have to function through their representatives. The state leadership is the closest representative of the people. Each state leadership deserves to be respected by the Union government. If the leadership does not deliver, it is for the people of the state to wake up and act. If the people of the state allow themselves to be exploited by their leaders — whether they are tribal leaders or caste or community leaders — they can only blame themselves. If the caste, community and tribal leaders come to have a vested interest in not developing and in exploiting their own people, then they become greater enemies of their people than anyone else. And, the solution has to be found by the people themselves in their own area. Many of the problems of the people and of polity — whether in the east or west, north or south — have to be solved in the area itself. In the North-East, before India's independence, the traditional institutions gave them more freedom and power to take their own decisions at the grassroots level. Problems arise and a feeling is generated when somebody takes away their freedom and independent identity.

The question is, where do we go from here. What is the way ahead?

Time has now come for a review of the Union-State relations and local governance institutions. More innovative federal structures need to be devised. It is necessary to address the deep-rooted sources of conflicts. We have to go for a different variant of the parliamentary system that is compatible with the new federalism, one which should build a united nation of a large number of autonomies considered not just as subordinates or subsidiaries, but also as federal and more importantly as equal partners at various levels, rooted in our culture, ethos and genius, and taking into account our weaknesses and needs of making the federal union an ever-developing and lasting reality. The honest and the practical way ahead for the Union is to lose its extra weight and shed its tendency to be the centre with a monopoly of power to dominate over the units and the people. In short, the only way to preserve 'India, that is Bharat' as a 'Union of States', is to work towards building it as a 'federal Union' with multiple tiers of government and sharing of powers from the lowest grassroot levels of panchayats to the Parliament and the Government of the Union. Incidentally, this would be the most rational and practical way of operationalising the Gandhian vision of a Constitution for India with the sovereign power vested within the people at the grassroots and building from below Gandhi conceived of public life as a mission of sacrifice and service and not as a lucrative profession. He advocated a less expensive election system linked with watchdog councils and separate elected chief executives at each local level. In the Gandhian model, the village is at the centre and all the power is posited at the grassroots and in a bottom-up (instead of the present top-down) approach; it travels upwards to the next tier of governance. There may be three or four tiers of governance represented by successive concentric circles with power at the highest level being limited to the minimum essential areas such as national security and external affairs. This also represents the quintessence of the subsidiarity principle in the European Union and Germany where those work that cannot be done at the lowest level are entrusted to the next higher tier.

Governance means dignity, development and growth of the individual to one's highest potential. This calls for power being ultimately vested with the individual citizen. Struggles for separate identities or greater federalism in pluralist societies are often not a fight for social justice, for the promotion of interests of the disadvantaged sections of the society or for protecting the rights of the units as against the Union. The real issue is not even that of separate cultural or ethnic group interests. The entire conflictual situation revolves around the issue of sharing the fruits of political power/Ethnicity, language and religion are politicalised to be used merely as the means to legitimise one's claims in the struggle for political power. For any CR to succeed, we must transcend vote bank politics built on corruption, casteism, communalism, black money power, crime and cabal rule.

While there is no dichotomy between a strong Union and strong states, the way Union governments have operated during the last more than 60 years have misused their powers blatantly for political and partisan ends, particularly under Articles 352 and 356 — proclamations of Emergency and imposition of President's rule in the states has weakened the case of the Union beyond repair.

Of late, the role and functioning of our Council of States, which was conceived by the founding fathers as a federal house consisting of the representatives of the states, has been considerably compromised on political, party and personal interest considerations of the rulers.

The Constitution Commission (2002) recommended (a) greater' consultation between the Union and the states through the Inter-State Council under Article 263; (b) establishment of an Inter-State Trade and Commerce Commission; (c) treating inter-state river waters as national assets and enacting legislation for dispute resolution; (d) appointing only persons of eminence with a detached outlook as Governors in consultation with the concerned chief ministers and respecting their five-year term; (e) using Article 356 only as a last resort after action under 256, 257, 355, etc., fails; (f) deciding questions of majority support only on the floor of the House and (g) in case of a hung house, election of the chief minister by the House.

The federal structure has come to stay and needs to be strengthened. The states are more and more asserting themselves through their political clout. They are demanding ever more space and extracting greater share of powers of governance and financial resources. However, the central problem today is not of Union-State relations, It is of greater decentralisation of economic and political powers. And instead of bottom-up approach, top-down approach should be applied. It is heartening and nothing short of revolutionary that after the 73rd and 74th Amendments coming into operation, India has 3.20 million elected rulers — over a million of them women. However, the states by and large seem unwilling to transfer power lower down and the MPs and MLAs feel uncomfortable and threatened by the new grassroot leadership. The Union and the states should concentrate on essentials following the subsidiarity principle. Economic liberalisation must come with decentralisation of political power and of management, while income tax, corporate tax and indirect taxes could be moved to the Concurrent List. Government at each higher level may be chosen by and remain answerable to the lower level. Government at a higher level should have no power to remove or supersede a duly elected government at a lower tier. If we are serious about providing a multi-tier governance and taking power to the doorsteps of the people at the grassroots, the Constitution should clearly provide for the distribution of powers between the Union, the states and the local governments, making the 11th and 12th schedules mandatory. It would do no harm either to the basic structure of the Constitution or the parliamentary system.

When the basic units of the federal Union at the grassroots become small and autonomous, most of the conflicts related to ethnicity and quest for freedom may get resolved and it may be possible to involve various groups in governance more closely and this may make the Union stronger and the nation more integrated, emotionally and culturally! There is every case for another *States Reorganisation Commission (SRC)* and creation of some 40-50 states of almost equal size and equal representation in one or both Houses of the Union Parliament. However, we should delink the ethnic aspirations from political demands for separate states. Apart from new states, substate and supra-state structures may be created to take care of common group concerns, which cannot be handled at the state level.' Combined with strong zonal councils, this would lead to greater stability, more accountability, stronger Union and better administered and more developed or fast-developing states. Norms for governor's appointments need revamping, Sarkaria Commission recommendations should be examined and implemented. Problems regarding Article 356 are only due to improper operation and interpretation of Articles 256, 257, 355, 356 and 365. These need to be read together.

It would be worth considering whether there should be a provision for President's rule or national government at the Union level also. One alternative worthy of further examination may be of having Lok Sabha constituencies as administrative units and subdistricts and tehsils may similarly coincide with MLA constituencies. That way, in a multi-tier system, it may be possible to involve various groups in governance and thereby making the nation more integrated, emotionally and culturally. Some such innovative multi-tier federal structures may have the potential to resolve many of the conflicts in our polity and arrive at a proper power sharing arrangement in Union-State relationship.

Apart from restructuring the federal Union set-up, we need administrative reforms, parliamentary reforms and overall reforms for good and clean citizen-friendly governance. No single reform can provide a miracle cure. Ideally, a simultaneous action on all fronts is required.

A great deal needs to be reformed in our politics, but most of the desirable reforms can be brought about within the constitutional framework by mere political will, executive action or through ordinary legislation. In rare cases only, constitutional amendments may be deemed necessary. These can be enacted under the Constitution itself without violating its basic structure. And, in any case, Constitution is also only a means. The end is the freedom and the well being of the people.

The ultimate way ahead would be to revisit Indian democracy and rebuild our federal polity on the foundation of an honest relationship between the Union and the units with governments at all levels providing good people-centric governance.

Today, public opinion is anxious for urgent changes. The time to act is now vested interests should not be allowed to come in the way. An early initiative may be of immense help in transforming the present national climate of doom and despondency to one of hope and harmony.

2

Impact of Police Reforms on Insurgency and the Structure of Indian Federalism

Prakash Singh

India has a federal structure. The Constitution has nevertheless very pronounced unitary features. The founding fathers of the Constitution could foresee separatist and secessionist tendencies in parts of the country, and therefore they so designed it. The states definitely need full autonomy in respect of subjects falling in the state list. However, they need to extend full cooperation to the federal government in respect of subjects which, though technically in the state list, yet spill over and acquire inter-state or even international ramifications.

India inherited a colonial police structure in the form of Police Act of 1861. The Act was legislated in the wake of Revolt of 1857, when the British felt the need of a force which would carry out their diktat, right or wrong, legal or illegal. The Act was specifically designed to raise a police which would be "politically more useful".

The Indian Police Commission of 1902-03, which reviewed the working of the police, found that the system had failed because the importance of the police work had been under-estimated and responsible duties entrusted to untrained and ill-educated officers recruited in the lowest ranks from the lower strata of society, that supervision had been defective, that the superior officers of the department were insufficiently trained, and that their sense of responsibility had been weakened by "a degree of interference never contemplated by the authors of the system".

Colonial Police Structure

At the dawn of independence, it was expected that a new role, a new philosophy would be defined for the police, that its accountability to the law of the land and the people of the country would be underscored in clear terms. But that was not to be and "the relationship that existed between the police and the foreign power before independence was allowed to continue with the only change that the foreign power was substituted by the political party in power". The colonial police structure remained unchanged.

As the years rolled by, there was unfortunately a qualitative change in the style of politics. The fire of idealism which had inspired the first generation of post-independent politicians and civil servants started getting dim. Power became an end in itself, and gradually a symbiotic relationship developed between the politicians on the one hand and the civil servants on the other. Vested interests grew on both sides and, as commented by the National Police Commission, "what started as a normal interaction between the politicians and the services for the avowed objective of better administration with better awareness of public feelings and expectations, soon degenerated into different forms of intercession, intervention and interference with *mala fide* objectives unconnected with public interest".

It was around mid-sixties that the political leadership injected the concept of 'commitment' in administration. It caused havoc. Officers were selected and given key placements in consideration of their affinity and loyalty to the ruling party and its political philosophy. The disastrous consequences of this were seen during the Emergency (1975-77) when, as observed by the Shah Commission, "the police was used and allowed themselves to be used for purposes some of which were, to say the least, questionable".

State Police Commissions

Several states appointed Police Commissions from time to time to review the working of police in their respective states and suggest necessary improvements. Police being a state subject, it was natural for the states to have taken initiative in the matter.

The following Commissions were appointed in different states:

(1) Kerala Police Commission (1959)

(2) West Bengal Police Commission (1960-61)

(3) Bihar Police Commission (1960-61)

(4) Punjab Police Commission (1961)

(5) Maharashtra Police Commission (1964)

(6) Madhya Pradesh Police Commission (1966)

(7) Delhi Police Commission (1966)

(8) U.P. Police Commission (1970-71)

(9) Assam Police Commission (1971)

(10) Tamil Nadu Police Commission (1971)

(11) Andhra Pradesh Police Commission (1984).

The State Commissions were, however, generally concerned with state-specific problems. They did not, as stated by C.V. Narasimhan, who was Member-Secretary of the National Police Commission, "address the fundamental changes in law to enable the police to function as impartial agents of law in a vibrant socialist democracy".

National Police Commission

In 1977, the Government of India appointed a National Police Commission as it felt that "far reaching changes have taken place in the country" since independence but "there has been no comprehensive review at the national level of the police system after independence despite radical changes in the political, social and economic situation in the country". The NPC submitted eight detailed reports between 1979 and 1981 which contained comprehensive recommendations covering the entire gamut of police working.

The Commission even drafted a model Police Bill which could be enacted. Its recommendations, however, received no more than a cosmetic treatment at the hands of the Government of India. The political leadership was just not prepared to give functional autonomy to the police because it had found this wing of the administration a convenient tool to further its partisan objectives. As for the bureaucracy, control over the police was - and continues to be - an intoxicant they have become addicted to and are just not willing to give that up. And so, the Act of 1861 continues to be on the statute book even after nearly 150 years – a millstone around the police neck.

Supreme Court's Directions

The Supreme Court, in a landmark judgement on September 22, 2006, in *Prakash Singh and Others Vs. Union of India,* ordered the setting up of three institutions at the state level with a view to insulating the police from extraneous influences, giving it functional autonomy and ensuring its accountability. These institutions are:

- State Security Commission which would lay down the broad policies and give directions for the performance of the preventive tasks and service oriented functions of the police;
- Police Establishment Board comprising the Director General of Police and four other senior officers of the Department which shall decide all transfers, postings, promotions and other service related matters of officers of and below the rank of Deputy Superintendent of Police and make appropriate recommendations regarding the postings and transfers of officers of the rank of Superintendent of Police and above to the State Government; and
- Police Complaints Authority at the district and state levels with a view to inquiring into allegations of serious misconduct by the police personnel.

Besides, the Apex Court ordered that the Director General of Police shall be selected by the state government from amongst the three senior-most officers of the Department who have been empanelled for promotion to that rank by the UPSC, and that he shall have a prescribed minimum tenure of two years. Police officers on operational duties in the field like the IG Zone, DIG Range, SP i/c District and SHO i/c Police Station would also have a minimum tenure of two years. The Court also ordered the separation of investigating police from the law and order police to ensure speedier investigation, better expertise and improved rapport with the people.

The Union Government was asked to set up a National Security Commission for the selection and placement of heads of Central Police Organisations, upgrading the effectiveness of these forces and improving the service conditions of its personnel.

The aforesaid orders were to be implemented by the end of 2006. The time limit was later extended to March 31, 2007.

Ten states have satisfactorily complied with the directions of the Supreme Court. The other states are however dragging their feet in the matter. Some states have passed Bills/Acts with a view to circumventing the implementation of Supreme Court's directions. The Thomas Committee, which was constituted by the Supreme Court to study the implementation of its directions by the various states, in its report submitted on August 23, 2010, expressed "its dismay over the total indifference to the issue of reforms in the functioning of Police being exhibited by the States".

The Supreme Court orders, if sincerely implemented, would have far reaching implications. They would change the working philosophy of the police. The Ruler's Police would be transformed into People's Police. The reforms, it needs to be understood, are not for the glory of the police - they are to give better security and protection to the people of the country, uphold their human rights and improve governance.

Impact on Insurgency

The country is witnessing insurgency in Jammu and Kashmir, in the North-East and in Central India.

In J and K, there was a significant decline in the level of violence during the year 2011. There is, however, no room for complacency with Pakistan continuing to stoke the fire of insurgency through non-state actors - the Lashkar-e-Toiba, Jaish-e-Mohammed and Harkat-ul-Mujahideen. According to an estimate, about 2500 terrorists are believed to be waiting in some 42 training camps across the border to infiltrate into India.

In the North-East, Nagaland has been having suspension of operations since 1997 but there has been no progress on the substantive issues. The NSCN (IM) has taken full advantage of the cease-fire period to augment its strength and build its finances. Manipur has about 15 militant groups operating in the Valley and the Hill districts. In Assam, the sharpness of ULFA has been blunted, thanks to Bangladesh's cooperative attitude; its leaders have shown willingness to negotiate with the Government of India and abandoned their insistence on recognition of 'sovereignty' as pre-condition for talks.

The Maoist insurgency is one of the biggest internal security threats to the country. Various groups subscribing to the Maoist ideology have pockets of influence in 182 districts across the country which are partially or substantially affected by the problem. Counter-insurgency operations by the security forces have made a dent, but the Maoist challenge remains formidable. There is unfortunately absence of clarity in Government of India's policy on the subject and lack of coordination between the Centre and the States and between the States themselves. Besides, the different Chief Ministers have been pursuing different policies as per their perception of the problem.

Police reforms even in states which are committed to carrying out Supreme Court's directions have not been implemented at the ground level. The other states have come up with all kinds of excuses to virtually maintain the status quo. The Supreme Court has been chary of wielding the whip by issuing contempt notices on the defaulting states. As a consequence, there is stalemate in the implementation of Court's directions. Under the circumstances, the question of reforms making any impact on insurgency in J and K, in the North-East, or in Central India does not arise.

Apart from the Supreme Court mandated reforms, there are several other aspects of police functioning which need to be reformed and reorganised. These concern building up the capability of the police forces. In the wake of 26/11 attack on Mumbai, Government of India took several steps to enhance the potential of its law enforcement apparatus. These included:

- NSG hubs were established at Regional Centres (Hyderabad, Kolkata, Mumbai, Chennai).
- Counter-Insurgency and Anti-Terrorism Schools (20) are being set up in different states.
- National Investigation Agency has been constituted.
- Police strength is being augmented.
- Modernisation of police is being given a push.
- Multi-Agency Centre (within IB) has been set up for effective intelligence sharing.
- Coastal security is being beefed up.
- Border security is being upgraded.

These measures have definitely augmented to some extent our capacity to deal with any terrorist attack or insurgency. However, a lot more remains to be done. There are huge deficiencies in the infrastructural set up. Thus, as stated by the Home Minister at the annual conference of DGPs/IGPs on September 15, 2011, there are over 5,00,000 vacancies in the State police forces. There is, besides, great shortage of IPS officers; as against the authorised strength of 4720 officers, there are only 3393 officers in position and it will take at least seven years to reach the optimum level. Other infrastructural deficiencies in weapons, transport and communication facilities also need to be filled up on a priority basis.

Indian Federation

Indian Constitution has pronounced federal features. The Constitution is supreme; it is written and is rigid insofar as the amendment process is quite difficult; the powers of the state and the centre are clearly defined; and there is an independent judiciary to interpret the Constitution and uphold its sanctity. At the same time, the Constitution has unmistakable unitary features also: India is a 'Union of States', which implies, firstly, that it is not the result of an agreement among the states and, secondly, the states have no freedom to secede or separate from the Union; the Governor, who is the constitutional head of the state, is appointed by the President; the states have unequal representation in the Rajya Sabha; important appointments like that of the Chief Election Commissioner, Comptroller and Auditor General are made by the Union Government; there are All India Services under the control of the Union; a unified judiciary with Supreme Court at the apex; and the President of India can declare emergency in the event of foreign aggression, internal armed rebellion or failure of constitutional machinery in a state.

Taking an overall view, the Constitution shows a distinct tilt in favour of the Centre, which has been assigned a dominant role. This was considered necessary by the founding fathers in view of the impending threats to the unity and integrity of the country.

The Union Home Minister, with a view to strengthening the country's counter-terrorism capabilities, announced at a conference of the Intelligence Bureau in December 2009, government's intention to set up an over-arching National Counter Terrorism Centre to perform "functions relating to intelligence, investigation and operations" for "preventing, containing and responding to terror attacks". The proposal led to a heated debate over the federal character of the Constitution and Union Government' alleged attempt to subvert it.

Several chief ministers objected to the NCTC on the ground that it violates the existing arrangement for the distribution of powers between the centre and the states. It attacks the federal principle enshrined in the Constitution, they alleged. The objection is valid only insofar as the proposed NCTC vests police powers to the body – powers which are exercised only by the state police, the CBI and the NIA. The Union Government should revisit this particular clause and withdraw it to avoid unnecessary controversy.

The 'federal' principle has however unfortunately become a convenient argument for the opposition parties to assail the central government on a wide range of issues – the Lokpal Bill, FDI in multi-brand retail, giving police powers to the RPF, BSF, etc. The state chief ministers seem to forget that they have to depend on the centre for even the most minor eruptions on law and order front – be it communal trouble, caste clash, *mela* arrangements, *rail roko* or any other agitation. Terrorist threat requires a much bigger and more comprehensive response. There are terrorist organisations which want to destabilise India politically, disrupt it economically and fracture it socially. There can be no getting away from greater central involvement in dealing with this international threat. The NCTC would have a pivotal role to play in combating the terrorist threat. This is however not to say, much less justify, that it should have powers which would be undemocratic. The country must have an NCTC – and a strong one at that – with comprehensive powers but not become a parallel police body armed with powers which may be misused.

Conclusion

Police reforms, as mandated by the Supreme Court, must be implemented. The executive must realise that these are absolutely essential for political stability and for sustaining the momentum of economic progress. Political stability of the country is threatened by the increasing infiltration of criminal elements in the legislatures and the parliament. The police must be insulated from political influences or else it would become an instrument of oppression and exploitation in the hands of unscrupulous politicians. Electoral reforms would also be necessary to debar persons with questionable background from becoming members of state assemblies or the parliament. The economic progress of the country would essentially depend upon good law and order in the country. Investments would not flow into the country if the investors are not assured of good returns under congenial circumstances. The wheels of production would grind at a fast pace only if there is peace and harmony in the industrial sphere. The stakes are thus very high. Police reforms are much too important and urgent to be delayed any further. A rejuvenated police force, freed from the shackles of politicians, would be able to deal with the problems of insurgency and terrorism far more effectively.

A reformed police would also contribute to strengthening the Indian federation. There should be no doubt that the country needs a strong federation to be able to deal with the various separatist and secessionist forces in the country. The states must have full autonomy in matters which are region-specific. In financial matters, perhaps they need a larger share of the pie. However, in matters which have a direct bearing on national security, the federal government must have over-riding powers and jurisdiction, and the states must be obliged to lend it necessary help and support.

3

Globalisation, Federalism and Democracy in India

G. Gopa Kumar

The transition of India towards democracy itself was a historical and complex process and this was further complicated by the arrival of globalisation and the neo-liberal policies that the country followed. Indeed, the nation accepted the new economic reforms in 1991 much ahead of its maturing of federal democracy. Many of the trends and discourses in the political system were altered once globalisation policies began influencing the various dimensions of the country—economic, social, environmental, cultural, educational, political and historical factors. The conventional competition in a federal system, viz. the centripetal and centrifugal forces that also dominated the discourse in Indian federalism has succumbed to the pressures of market forces. It also reduced the significance of the role attributed to state and national governments in regard to welfare and economic functions. New market forces attracted the entry of Multinational Corporations and national corporates in significant sectors of the economy and this had affected the incremental pace of economic growth.

The paramount role of agriculture in the Indian economy changed giving way to other sectors like manufacturing, construction, information technology, tourism, bio-technology, pharmaceuticals etc. Consequently, a new thrust was given to service sector and industrial sector and this shift was by and large accepted by the urban middle class in the country. The rural-urban divide, gender divide, digital divide, problem of effecting decentralised governance and other challenges of Courtesy –Foreign policy, Federalism and International Treaties (Book) by G. Gopa Kumar (Edited), New Century Publication, New Delhi (2011) development including low productivity in agriculture, overpopulation, widespread poverty, ignorance and illiteracy in BIMARU states (Bihar, Madhya Pradesh, Rajasthan and Uttar Pradesh) and North-Eastern region etc had sharpened the polarisation between emerging middle class and the poorer sections in the country.

The priorities of the corporates sidelined the welfare functions of the state and the approach of national and state governments underwent drastic changes. Major political parties at the national and the regional levels had limited options in the emerging context other than joining the official bandwagon of neo-liberal paradigm. Of course, negative reactions to these developments produced conflicting pressures from various sources. These include liberal as well as extreme reactions emerging from different sectors. The non-governmental organisations, human rights bodies and environmental activists constituted the evolutionary reaction whereas the rise of Maoist forces and religious fundamentalist forces highlighted the growth of political extremism. The predicament of the state in the emerging context is very clear. This paper attempts to examine the changing and challenging nature of federal democracy in the specific context of India's tryst with globalisation.

Of course, the early trajectory of globalisation, as a process, has been well documented in human history. But globalisation as an organised socio-economic activity and political process is rather a Twentieth Century phenomenon. The Western countries had accepted it during early 1980s and prompted the Latin American countries to follow it up. Mostly, Third World countries beginning with India accepted the neo-liberal process since 1991 at a time when bipolarism in global politics gave way to unipolarism led by USA. The formal disintegration of USSR on December 31, 1991 was a major watershed. The decline of Cold War actually started much earlier and intensified further in 1989 with the collapse of the Berlin Wall.

The dismembering of Soviet Union did not bring a peaceful transition towards liberal democracy as witnessed in the events in Eastern Europe and Central Asia. Although Francis Fukyama came up with the theory of the "End of History", taking few threads from Immanuel Wallenstein's critique of "World System Analysis", the global events marked conflicting developments. While ethnicity and religious fundamentalism intensified in many parts of the Third World, economic developments leading to a process of global integration could also be evinced in this context. The consensus evolved since the Mastrich Treaty strengthened the European Union whose membership went beyond Western Europe and accepted the fragile economies of Eastern Europe and Turkey.

Almost the same time when USSR was disappearing from the world map, India was facing acute Balance of Payment crisis and many western leaders predicted the bankruptcy of Indian economy. The country of course had limited option in the emerging situation and joined the neo-liberal world, accepting the dictates of World Bank and International Monetary Fund. This was a paradigm shift from India's conventional position in creating a welfare state with a socialist nature. The series of economic reforms that followed since 1991 opened up avenues for the private sector to enter in to the economy in a big way affecting the social values, attitudes, culture, profession, mobility and development. The mainstream India changed drastically since then.

Hardly there were very few areas India did not open up for private and foreign sectors. The neo-liberal reforms brought changes in the sectors like telecommunications, information technology, higher education pharmaceuticals, bio-technology, food and agriculture, tourism, education, healthcare, aviation industry, infrastructure, arts and culture, environment etc. Even in the area of decentralisation process, which the country had otherwise ushered through Constitutional reforms in 1993 (73rd and 74th Amendments), the globalisation policies contributed its own share of ideas and strategies. For instance, as a policy, globalisation was not against decentralisation process but its strategies included strong neo-liberal approach towards decentralised governance.

The corporatist forces find it convenient to approach local governments for expanding their markets and exploiting local resources. The "globalisation" theme has much to do with the neo-liberalist expansion of markets in the villages and urban pockets. Not only that, it facilitated the appropriation of indigenous knowledge to the global market, affecting the lives of the tribals and villagers. The union-state local governments could not develop a common strategy to counter the threat from corporatist forces. It is very clear in this context that not only the conventional nation-state had declined, affecting the national values and sentiments, the federal equation and balance (even if it was favouring an upper hand for the union government) also underwent a drastic shift, benefiting the new actors of globalisation process.

Perhaps one area that requires a serious discussion is the changing priorities in our foreign policy and perspectives towards international relations. As a tradition, two things are important here—the formulation of foreign policy was elitist through out, involving a small group of diplomats, strategic experts and foreign policy specialists.[1] Again, our conventional position towards newly independent countries, approach towards bi-polar conflict, relations with major powers, and the effective leadership we took for strengthening Non-Aligned Movement etc. had underwent transition. Indeed, both aspects are witnessing changes in the new context though not everything is moving in a negative direction. For instance, the controversy that followed the issue of Indo-US nuclear co-operation beginning with the CPI(M)'s strong objection brought the debate in to the national discourse.[2]

It could be possible that in future foreign policy issues would be debated more outside including in the fora of civil society, rather than restricting itself into an elitist discourse. Again, globalisation process had intensified international and cross-cultural migration and mobility in an unprecedented manner involving the concern of Indian states rather than leaving everything to the Union Government. Although foreign policy and foreign relations are items belonging to the Union List, in the contemporary situation states are equally interested and concerned. The Malayalee migration to West Asia is a strong case in point here. The bulk of gulf expatriates from India originates from Kerala state and it is natural that state government would influence the central government on many urgent issues. This trend received greater attention with the result a new minister for looking after Overseas Indian Affairs was appointed in 2006.

The LDF government in Kerala really complained that the centre is not giving security clearance to its project on Vizhinjam port in Trivandrum because the Build-Operate-Transfer (BOT) auction was won by a Chinese company, 'Tunes'. At the same time the LDF pointed out that the bilateral agreements are being signed by Government of India and Chinese Government. It highlighted that the central government has no hesitation in signing treaties with China but at the same time prevents Kerala state in allowing a Chinese company to start the working of the project for security reasons.

The border states in India are vulnerable to illegal migration and international terrorism which would demand better interaction between union and state governments for curbing the troubles and challenges across the border. Again, with the increasing level of foreign trade and investment, every state would be interested in formulating its share in foreign policy which would facilitate their economic and human security interests. It is well known that the concept of "Vibrant Gujarat" is linked to the substantial contribution and linkages of Gujarati expatriates settled in foreign countries. All these call for a fresh looks at Indian federalism.

Once we had practically abandoned Non-Alignment policy in the post-communist era, it also signalled a shift towards US and other western powers. The Pro-US shift began since 2000 and strengthened further with the civil nuclear agreement and defence treaties signed between India and the US. The shift also brought strong objection from states like Kerala and West Bengal for ideological reasons. Very soon the foreign policy leadership at the instance of coalition government at the centre, agreed to develop a policy in favour of multilateralism. This was also a product of our globalised policies in favour of trade, business and migration. The new trading class preferred to support the government in its "Look-East Policy", besides encouraging economic relations with Russia, France, UK, Japan, Brazil and countries in West Asia.

The economic growth witnessed in the country during the last two decades, the rise of India as 'soft power', contribution of Information Technology, professionals since Y2K issue, the predicted emergence of China as a potential super power by 2020 etc. had altogether shifted the external and internal dynamics. The potential market for the developed countries looking at the fast growing middle class (estimated at 360 million), was another factor in India's favour. Therefore, a multilateral policy even while keeping a pro-active tilt towards United States became the hall mark of the nation's foreign policy in the era of globalisation. Obviously, critics had noted the rise of market fundamentalism destroying the social security and welfare functions of the state in post-independent India. The new political discourse demanded for an "inclusive development" rather than falling an easy prey to the interests of corporatist forces and crony capitalism.

Globalisation and Nation State

It has been generally accepted that the impact and working of globalisation has considerably weakened the Westphalian concept of nation-state and state sovereignty. Viewed from this angle, globalisation process directly challenges national unity and the spirit of nationalism. The process of globalisation hinges upon inter-state treaties and international bodies and therefore we are caught between the dynamics of global integration and imperatives of identity.[3] The present wave of globalisation is contingent to the expansion of economic space beyond the nation state through global market mechanisms.[4] The continuous decline in the capacity of the state and the legitimacy of the government as a consequence to the increasing role of transnational institutions and global integration is promoting the politics of identity instead of citizenship based politics of nation building.[5]

The experience of India is not different we could notice not only the changing role of the State consequent to the economic reforms but also the rise of identity politics at the regional and local levels. On the other hand, powerful multinational enterprises are able to transfer investment across political boundaries, control the terms of technology transfer and enhance global business strategies through radical changes in information technology and telecommunication. These flows of investment, technology, communication and profit access across national boundaries are clear evidences of the global challenge for nation state.[6] As a contradictory phenomenon, globalisation is driven by the complex logic of geopolitics and capital and the apparent decentralisation of nation-states.[7]

Indeed there are many evidences to suggest regarding the set back and decline of nation states since the end of Cold War and the current march of globalisation. The nation state was put under pressure from two ends—the pressure for transcendence and amalgamation of nation states for economic goals (the European Economic Community and North American Free Trade Agreement are the best examples) and the pressure towards decomposition in to constituent linguistic, national, religious or ethnic components as witnessed in the decomposition of Soviet Union, Yugoslavia, Czechoslovakia, Ethiopia and Somalia. The consequent effect of the diminishing nation state would lead to the polarisation at two levels- democracies without empowerment and power inaccessible for democratisation.[8]

These are dangerous trends because the emerging world order will be controlled by the powerful sections without any humane national commitments. Given the social and cultural diversity of the Third World nation-states, the challenges have far reaching consequence. However, in the Indian case, an apparent consensus seems to have emerged although the social heterogeneity has made the reaching of concrete policy decisions difficult. Baldev Raj Nayar argues that political parties in India were forced to enter into alliance-building, which has moderated the extreme ideological positions of individual parties.[9] The centrist tendency generated in Indian political system is also a practical attempt to keep the balance between the appeals of globalisation and the demands and struggles exerted by the nationalist and regional groups. It acts as a safety valve to prevent the onslaught of globalisation on national values.

The contradictory forces of globalisation coupled with the pressures of post-communist world system had significantly affected the fortunes of democracy in the Third World. While scholars like Larry Diamond, and earlier Samuel Huntington, speaks about the rise of the fourth wave of democracy since 1991, the empirical scenario in Afro-Asian political systems were quite different. More than at any time in the history, issues like identity crisis, ethnic and military uprising and decline of national feelings were noted. This has led to the disintegration and failure of many Third World political systems.

Globalisation and Democracy

Did globalisation facilitate or hinder democracy? It is hard to find a scientific response to this question. Jagdish Bhagavathy, on the other hand, notes that successful and robust development in developing countries requires two strong pillars: democracy and market.[10] He feels that the effect of globalisation process on national sovereignty have an obvious relationship to the ability of the citizens to participate effectively in the democratic choice of policies with in the nation-state. Through trade, investment, foreign education, free mobility of people and expansion of the medium of television and flow of information, the quality of democracy has certainly improved.[11]

However, this analysis can be easily contested in a country like India where, despite the presence of a growing middle class, the status of Human Development Index has fallen (128th rank out of 178) and a huge majority of people live below poverty line. Further, the polling figures in national elections show a two point decline during the last fifteen years. However, some scholars attribute the rationale for the fractured verdicts, series of hung parliaments and the inevitability of coalition politics as the trend of increasing political awareness of the Indian electorate. Indeed, these developments had compelled the political elites to speed up economic reforms and maintain the tempo of inclusive development.

In the recent World Economic Forum (2011) Summit, the remarks made by the Deputy Chairman of Planning Commission of India, Montek Singh Ahluwalia and noted critique of globalisation, George Soros are worth stating here. While the former reminded the participants that political stability is crucial for the success of economic reforms and policy continuity, the latter commented that democracy is crucial for the globally integrated society. George Soros particularly compared China and India in this context. While China achieved higher economic growth without political reforms and democracy. India has been maintaining reasonably good growth rate while sustained democracy in her political system.

The political dimension of globalisation advocated for a "universal political culture" with a high priority to democracy and democratic institutions. The enthusiasts of globalisation championed the cause of democracy and viewed globalisation and democratisation to between the two sides of the same coin.[12] However, we cannot ignore the role and interests of market forces in this context. Actually, the whole idea of democratisation here is related to market democracy with emphasis on money, materialism, global capital, information flow, environmental issues etc. Traditional democratic concerns for human dignity and equal opportunity have been replaced by obsessions for managerial efficiency and product quality".[13] The citizenship values are replaced by the interests of share holders of a private company.

The negative results of this shift had resulted in the formation of anomie groups who believed and struggled for immediate reversal of the whole situation. These groups come from a complex background-environmentalist, human rights groups, other NGOs, religious fundamentalists and terrorists, causing uneven developments in domestic and international political systems. Indeed, the attempt to formulate globalised political culture under the agies of market forces produced dysfunctional results. This trend can also be seen in Indian political system. Therefore, a complex mix of responses, with some people adopting or adapting alternative ideas and joining global networks, while others reject competing universalisms in hostiles localised reactions can be vividly seen.[14]

Castel is (1997) views the relationship between state politics and transnational politics as paradoxical: "the more states emphasise communalism, the less effective they become as co-agents of a global system of shared power. The more they triumph in the planetary scene, in close partnership with agents of globalisation, the less they represent their national constituencies".[15] This apparent contradiction diminishes the potentialities of an emerging democratic system. The welfare state model with emphasis on centralised planning received a huge set back in India in the given context of economic reforms. The competing and conflicting demands of the states, the struggles of the communal organisations, the decline of nation-state sentiments, rise of localised struggles etc are clear reactions to the phenomena that emerged since 1991.

The changing role of civil society is worth discussing here. Unless civil society institutions emerge as effective mechanisms of citizen empowerment as well as regulators of state and market players, democracy with concern for the weak will not develop. Mere reduction of civil society to NGO's, with little regard for movements for people's rights is not at all a positive development.[16] The privileging of 'consumer' over the 'citizen' in matter of rights has far reaching implications for principles of democracy. Survival, sustainability, equity, democracy and social justice stand to lose out to consumer rights in case of a conflict in this kind of discourse.[17] In developing countries, the transition from the status of a citizen to consumer is not an easy process. Even before the basic imperatives of citizen empowerment has been completed, the new market forces are insisting for a shift in favour of consumers and further making the citizens as if they are share holders of a private sector. Thus, globalisation process widens the priorities and preferences between developing countries and developed countries and forces a typical polarisation which is not facilitating to the growth of democracy.

The Federal India and Democracy

Federal idea and federal systems are old but as democratic forms of government emerged, federal systems worked in harmony with modern political systems. Conventionally, the confederal idea was to organise diverse political systems under a common umbrella social as to face a common threat, or strive for particular political goals. Even today, confederal systems like the European Economic Union and Commonwealth of Independent States operate with a weak centre on the one side and strong states on the other. However, in major modern political systems, one of the two conventional features are prominent—the centripetal federal system and the centrifugal federal system. In the former, the federal trend is towards reaching a powerful centre where as in the latter, the system itself is trying move away from the centre. The United States which originally emerged as a confederation, before the 1789 Constitution was implemented, was a classical example of a centrifugal federal system. Most of the federal systems, particularly with parliamentary framework are clear cut centripetal systems. Canada, India, South Africa, Australia, Nigeria are the best examples. Switzerland, although a small country, remained as a confederal system with partial forms of direct democracy.

Ideally, huge and diverse political systems are suitable for federal forms of government. Most of the countries in the world lack homogeneity due to historical and contemporary factors. Hence, many of those countries qualify to be brought under federal systems. Conventionally, as argued, federal system is a political contrivance in which multiple layers of government are organised. Like an arch dam, the system is accepting pressures, eventually moving towards a centripetal or centrifugal pattern. Again, a federal system can easily accommodate diversity and differences. Especially in a democracy, diversity and accommodation are the hall marks of a federation. Regional, sub-regional and national interests are intertwined here. Cultural, social and economic integration are quite possible in this context by providing special rights and privileges in the Constitution.

For instance, according to the Constitution of 1982, Canada has given special veto power to five regions including Quebec Province in the law-making process. Quebec's distinct identity is protected through other provisions as well as including the provision for one-third members of the Supreme Court originating from Quebec province. As an economic imperative, in every federal system, sufficient checks are provided for the distribution of resources in a meaningful manner. Again, in a modern federal system, every citizen qualifies to be serviced by a variety of governments—local, sub-regional, regional, state and national. Now with the globalisation process, further diversity and accommodation has become contingent since market relations cut across horizontal and vertical dimensions. Both the citizens and variety of governments in the federal system are provided with numerous challenges and opportunities. This trend could alter the vertical governmental relationships in a significant manner.

Some of the federal scholars had argued that the sub-continent was strong and united under a strong centre. This was true even during the Ashoka period and once we compare with the Mughal period, it witnessed disunity and disruption. The colonial India was also centralised although, in theory, princely states enjoyed some elements of political and administrative freedom. The provisions of Government of India Act, 1935 also clearly leans towards a centripetal federal system. But once the goal of freedom was reaching closer, the confederal idea came up and sought for classifying Indian states into A, B and C categories. Probably India without the partition would have become a confederal state.

The impact of partition and the painful process of the integration of Indian states seem to have changed the attitude and approach of the makers of the Indian Constitution. Of course, integration of the former princely states was one of the major experiments in the history of nation building.[18] Despite many challenges, this process was completed more or less successfully. It was a remarkable achievement in the modern history of national unification.

Probably the second dilemma was the re-organisation of Indian states in the Union. The provisions of the Constitution particularly the dominance of the Parliament to enact various items in the Union List and Concurrent List, besides the possibility of shifting an item from the State List to Concurrent List had practically moved the system towards a centripetal federal system. The 'parliamentary-federal character' of the Indian constitution had made the federal system more centralised.

Even the existence of state boundaries, formation of new states, financial powers of the Union government, the prominence of All India Services, Emergency powers of the President of the Union, single citizenship, integrated judiciary with Supreme Court as the apex court had all practically made the system vulnerable to unitary features. K.C. Wheare had long back reviewed Indian constitution as 'quasi federal'. Even in the language policy, we can find several issues despite the fact the country is deeply multi-lingual and multi-cultural.

Of course, the state reorganisation process had more or less addressed these issues and India's record in shaping a linguistic federalism is satisfactory. There could be few more states and official languages coming through in the context of few years but the democratic process had successfully accommodated the diversities to a great extent.

The pre-globalisation period's economic policies and party system require further discussion, in this context. The nature of the Indian state was centralised and planning was officially organised from top to bottom. With a mixed economy, India-had given high priority to public sector to emerge as the commanding highlights of the economy. The creation of Planning Commission as statutory body with powerful provisions; planning, supervising and advising the Union cabinet, the significance of Finance Commission, a constitutional body, competent to decide on apportioning national revenues had drifted the federal status more towards the Union Government. The Indian welfare state model gave high prominence to the Centre and most of the centrally sponsored schemes plus the Community Development Plan energised the union government. The history of uneven development of the Indian states, economic the neglect and discrimination to certain regions had raised many issues-political, economic, ethnic and cultural. Over a period, this had affected the administrative and party system.

The centralised nature of the Indian state had two quick problems even from the beginnings: (1) the emergence of the 'licence raj' where the Indian bureaucracy sluggishly performed quota distribution and licence permits for all imports and exports, and (2) the slow pace of decentralisation process, although under Article 40 in the part relating to Directive Principles of State Policy of the constitution, provision for strengthening local governments were provided. Both these problems had significant impact in arresting development and social progress in the country. Critiques had attributed this to the existence of one party dominance system in the country besides the legacy of bureaucracy inherited from British power.

It is true that a post-independent polity like India could not quickly transform towards multi-party democracy. The Congress dominance was throughout, except Kerala, and few states for the first three decades. Yet the party was federal to a great extent until it was nationally split in 1969. Rajini Kothari (1965) conceptualised the 'Congress System' as democratic though not competitive. He analysed that dissent had become strong inside the Congress and therefore the scope of opposition is weak outside the Congress.[19] The non-competitive, non-authoritarian party system collapsed in the wake of Internal Emergency clamped on June 25, 1975. The sudden unity among major opposition parties and the over centralised misrule finally brought down the one party dominance system in 1977. Although Congress regained its popularity in 1980 and 1984, it was never the same again. Moreover, the second national split on January 1, 1978 further weakened the organisational base of the Congress party. Its typical shift towards 'High Command' politics in the subsequent years revealed the inner dynamics of a centralised political leadership as the best bet for rallying party unity and popularity.

The rise of regional and state centric national parties was also evident right from 1967 elections. States like Tamil Nadu, Kerala, Punjab, and Rajasthan, Jammu and Kashmir were examples to this phenomenon. Once the Congress suffered electoral setback and organisational schisms, the political space became much more competitive. In the federal discourse, this trend added another dimension when the non-Congress parties ruling few states alleged 'step motherly attitude' of the Centre towards the states. The demand for revising the Centre-State relations became prominent as series of non-Congress party conclaves demanded for strengthening the Inter-State Council, reducing the power and changes in the mode of appointment of governor, strict measures for preventing the misuse of Article 356, more allocation for the states by the Finance Commission etc. This trend was on the rise. With the arrival of globalisation process, a new form of caste and ethnic politics began to emerge. The fragmentation of multiparty system deepened in 1990's providing more avenues for the rise of identity politics. The neo-liberal age raised fresh challenges to parliamentary and federal system.

Shift towards Neo-Liberal State

The competing forces of nationalism, regionalism and globalism are working with divergent trends including antagonistic, overlapping and some times cooperative features towards each other.[20] This presents a very complicated profile of contemporary Indian polity. India's global integration is more in terms of information technology and open book printing, market and brain-drain than in economic and fiscal forms. The neo-colonial cultural and educational and information domination of the West is more threatening Indian cultural setting and ways of life than neo-colonial economic domination.[21] Therefore, the cultural impact of globalisation is attacking the basic values and traditional premises of the Indian society. It should be noted that one of the prominent factors of the unity of India is the existence of civilisational values including secularism and multi-culturalism. Despite the uneven nature of societal development, a broad civilisational unity was found in the country. Unfortunately, the cultural invasion of globalisation is attacking at the very root of the basic values of Indian society. The reaction emerges in diverse forms including the rise of political extremism and religious fundamentalism. In other words, the post-modern trends of globalisation produced dysfunctional results among some sections of the society.

In this context, it will be interesting to look at the impact of liberalisation in the federal structure of the country.

The flow of foreign direct investment (FDI), dismantling of 'license raj' system, competitive attitude of some of the states in India for attracting FDI and joining the bandwagon of global trade, the influence of Persons of Indian Origin (PIOs) in pressurising their foster land to help business and trade (especially' the case of states like Gujarat, Punjab, Maharashtra, West Bengal and Andhra Pradesh) in their motherland had deep impact in the hitherto federal balance and relations. Another aspect is the influence of World Bank, International Monetary Fund and the Washington Consensus groups support to strengthen decentralisation process and governance in the country. While the tradition of decentralisation and good governance was problematic, the neo-liberal setting provided an ideological and policy oriented setting for the promotion of these two goals. It may be coincidental that 73rd and 74th Amendments to the Constitution came in 1993 but the slow and steady pace of decentralisation process in some of the Indian states worked in harmony with the goals of neo-liberalism.

Lawrence Saez (2002), argues that liberalisation policy promoted a change in federal relations from intergovernmental co-operation towards inter-jurisdictional competition among the states. Although there witnessed a concentration of FDI in few states, the transformation from co-operative federalism to inter-jurisdictional competition had prompted states to compete each other for further flow of FDI. This development has increased the polarisation between states.[22] Nevertheless, a broad multi-partisan political consensus in favour of measured economic liberalisation has emerged. However, the gradual move to a market economy did not significantly alter the central governments financial relationship with the states.

The reforms had prompted some states to adopt major strategic and structural change towards internal development. State like Maharashtra, Gujarat, Tamil Nadu and Andhra Pradesh offered specific incentive packages for foreign investors. Saez concluded that political party realignment combined with the impact of foreign investment inflows has shifted the debates about federalism from inter-governmental cooperation to inter-jurisdictional competition. The transformation has several implications for federal relations. However, the role of inter-governmental institutions may become weak and it will weaken state capability because the state will be unable to either regulate or mediate inter-jurisdictional competition. In order to cope up with the emerging developmental challenges, he suggests the creation of strong inter-jurisdictional institutions to address the problem of horizontal integration of the states in India.[23]

The irony of Indian federalism in the age of globalisation was that it was accepting forces with divergent characteristics. For instance the strengthening of Inter State Council (initiated in 1990 lapsed during 1992-96 period) since 1996 points out the willingness of the Indian state for promoting intergovernmental jurisdiction and cooperative federalism. On the other hand the selective growth of some states making use of the virtues available in globalisation brought two results -the growth of inter-jurisdictional competition between states and the polarisation between performing and non performing states.

Thus, while a shift from vertical federalism to horizontal federalism becomes inevitable, the role of government becomes very much limited. The market friendly federalism has phenomenally reduced the role of inter-governmental institution. Again, the contemporary trends indicate the decline of centralisation process, due to the impact of market forces and the rise of political awareness in favour of decentralisation. However, in both these aspects, there is no homogeneity among the performance of states. Some states, especially BIMARU region, are still lagging behind making the work of "new federalism"really difficult and challenging.

In a sense, rigidity and formalism attached to operation of Indian federalism seem to have declined in the neo-liberal age. The country witnessed rapid political developments and realignment among political parties since 1989 and it is very evident that the new economic reforms had influenced the political parties. Although many of them were critics of globalisation (interestingly there was internal opposition inside the Congress party also), a broad consensus had developed compelling them to moderate in the new context. The contradictions proliferated when regional responses of national parties differed (look at the position of West Bengal unit of CPI (M) with that of Kerala until 2006) and the manner in which casteist and regionalist parties responded to globalisation. The DMK, a party in Tamil Nadu, committed for achieving social justice became the arch supporter of neo-liberalism. The Bahujan Samaj Party led by Mayawati, while promoting identity politics in Uttar Pradesh, was demanding for more foreign direct investment to flow in her state. The approach of Samajwadi Party led by Mulayam Singh was no different. Again, the major opposition party, BJP also changed its stance compared to its approach in 1991.

The Indian National Congress emerged as the chief architect of globalisation reforms in the country. By abandoning Nehruvian policies of planned economy, socialist ideas and self reliance, Congress was instrumental for shifting the conventional role of the state in India. However, it has realised the significance of 'inclusive development' after the NDA lost power with its pet theme of 'shining India' in the 2004 elections. Therefore, it is trying to perform a balancing act between large scale economic reforms in major sectors of the economy while in to uplift the vast majority of the poor through a series of popular policies like MGNREGS (Mahatma Gandhi National Rural Employment Guarantee Scheme) and National Rural Health Mission.

The CPI (M) has been a major critic of globalisation policies and all its frontal organisations took very clear ideological position regarding this. But it was supporting industrial and business development in West Bengal attracting strong criticism from its arch rival Trinamool Congress. The latter objected the development of car industry in Singur in favour of the settlement issue of the rural people. Eventually, the business lost to West Bengal was a gain for Gujarat. Similarly, in Kerala, the conventional anti-industrial policy of CPI(M) frustrated economic growth but in the new context, particularly since 2006, the LDF government modified and welcomed business and industry, though with caution. Indeed, it was a hectic struggle for CPI(M) to fine tune with economic growth and social justice. On the whole, the attitude of left parties underwent major changes during the neo-liberal era.

Parties with strong regional base like Samajwadi Party (Uttar Pradesh), Rashtriya Janata Dal (Bihar), Janata Dal-(United) (again, in Bihar), Biju Janata Dal (Odisha), Nationalist Congress Party (Maharashtra), Janata Dal-Secular (Karnataka) maintained twin imperatives in the context of their orientation towards reforms. First, they have the pressure for appear as pro-people and not pro-MNCs. Second, they have to produce conducive environment for the entrepreneurs for investment and employment generation.[24] It is a win-win formula of selective use of reforms and foreign investments and promotion of self-reliance but eventually there exists considerable confusion on issues like agricultural subsidies, privatisation of sectors like health and education, encouragement of FDI and increasing the cost of urban services.[25]

Baldev Raj Nayar (2004) finds out two major factors which brings BJP little to differentiate with Congress Party or United Front: (1) the centrist tendency of Indian politics in the context of country's immense social diversity and the institutionalised nature of its political framework of democracy and (2) the asymmetric yet interdependent world economy which assures substantial initiatives to participate.[26] There are many areas where BJP shifted from its conventional ideology of 'Swadeshi' or economic nationalism-Free, Trade Areas (in fact preferential trading areas), sale of equity of a PSE to benefit a strategic partner in the private sector to assume management control of the enterprise, patents policy and the Insurance Regulatory and Development Authority (IRDA) policy.[27] The centrist tendency generated by India's political system is the major explanation for the change in the BJP to a moderate economic policy and Nayar holds the view that "in an era dominated by economic globalisation, the acceptance of economic liberalisation is a manifestation of the centrist tendency in Indian politics".[28]

These are strong evidences to suggest how the major, medium and regional parties cutting across the traditional ideological positions of right, left and centre had modified its policies to suit the context of globalisation. Obviously, the decline of the centralised role of the Indian state is very much evident leading us to suggest that the conventional and unilateral tendencies of federalism are undergoing serious changes. In a parliamentary federal system, parties and their positions are extremely important. Given the above background, the increasing role of the international market is driving federalism in hitherto unexplored areas Paradoxically, though it may appear, decentralisation measures are also becoming stronger which again formulates new federal trends. The emerging role of Self Help Groups, other NGOs, new social movements, civil society etc. is to be noted with significance.

*The emerging interaction of national, state and local governments with foreign governments and corporations is not only redrawing state-market boundaries but also reconfigure federal institutions.[29] In the case of the first, financial sector reforms, assignment of regulatory, infrastructure reform and development are included while in the case of the latter, tax reforms, Centre-State fiscal transfer mechanisms and local government reforms are bringing new dimensions of political economy and issues of regional inequalities.[30] Differential growth across states and the continued inequalities across the states and regions are found during the last two decades of reform.

While some states were able to achieve independent growth, co-ordination between federal institutions in designing and implementing reform policies becomes most essential. On the whole Indian federalism is facing new challenges due to greater openness to world economy and growing regional disparities.[31]

Conclusion

The two decades experiences of economic reforms have brought significant changes in the country. A new middle class has emerged in the country that holds professional skills, higher and technical education, mobility and dynamism. The foreign policy initiatives underwent drastic changes. But, on the other hand, the decline of the welfare state has brought many negative results. It had widened inequality among people and regions, increased the poverty ratio, and weakened the social security network, created new power lobbies like Mining giants and land mafia groups. The rural-urban and digital divide has become more polarised

At the federal level new trends had emerged. The conventional, political-legal dimensions of the centre-state relations are getting increasingly outdated. Earlier, the arrival of 'cooperative federalism' strengthened the position of the centre even though the roles of states were becoming equally significant. It was not possible to implement pro-poor and popular policies without the joint effort of union and states. The emergence of a strong multi-party system and coalition politics in the backdrop of the decline of 'one-party system' facilitated the process. However, the effects of the new economic reforms since 1991 had changed the trends altogether and opened up fresh debates on the theory and practice of federalism.

Market friendly federalism is fast replacing parliamentary federal status in the country. Emphasis is more on trade and business relations, inter-state migration, approach of private sector and Non-Governmental sectors in directing neo-liberal agenda. The role of the Union and State governments is that of a facilitator to these reforms and efforts. The primacy of the new economic actors had overshadowed the conventional role of political leadership. Of course, the inter-state competition continues to drive the economy. Nevertheless, the political leadership could not prevent the growing inequality between states. Few states have emerged as the economic role models while many others on the other side are struggling to cope up with the challenges of ensuring basic elements of development like education, health, infrastructure, food security etc. This apparent inequality between performing and non-performing states or between developed and underdeveloped regions will produce friction and tension areas in Indian federalism. A recent estimate has also shown that 75 per cent of foreign direct investments is flowing to the five leading states of the country.

Critics had noticed the evolution of apolitical attitudes among people in the context of globalisation. While the environmental and economic effects of land mining are huge, in many states there did not witness any rapid protest movements. While the mainstream political forces had silently assimilated to the new process of development, there witnessed localised struggles led by marginalised groups and human rights movements. Thus, apolitical attitude of the middle class is 'creating a vacuum in the functioning of democracy. The response of the civil society especially in urban areas was notable'. One should also notice the rise of Maoist groups in more than seven states challenging parliamentary democracy and the neo liberal state, compelling the Prime Minister Manmohan Singh to state that political extremism of Maoist groups constitutes a major challenge to the country. The rise of inter-jurisdictional sidelining the centre-state and inter-state conflict marks another emerging trend in Indian federalism. The economic activities following the march of globalisation have shifted the dynamics of vertical federalism to horizontal federalism. This process was facilitated by the intense competition by the market forces cutting across the territorial aspects and sidelining the role hitherto played by state governments. Business and trade relations, demand for infrastructural developments, technological break through are beyond the geography of states; Internalised territorial dimension is becoming weak in this context. Infrastructural facilities needed in specific regions can bring a sea change in future. Once trade related developments take place, jurisdiction becomes wider and wider and this would impact upon federalism in newer forms. The impact of globalisation, in foreign policy of the country has been discussed. With the emergence of multilateral, polycentric world, India will actively engage with the host of countries including economies of South-East Asian region besides European Union and US. China is a strong competitor globally acknowledged, but India can initiate for fresh economic relations, there by cast an indirect influence over Pakistan. The relevance to this discussion is that the priorities of international relations are changing fast and many of these are determined by global developments in the move towards an integrated economy, new issues are emerging. Problems of illegal migration, interest of non-resident Indians (NRIs) in investing in the Indian economy, issues of (NRIs) in Middle East etc. have federal dimensions too.

Therefore, the Government of India, at the instance of some state governments, had initiated reforms and set up institutions to look after these affairs. International issues and developments are therefore going to create both national and state specific reactions. An alignment of domestic policies with international policies has become the order of the day. International terrorism, issues of human security and human rights, poverty, malnutrition etc require global and regional attention. All these are bound to impact on federalism in India.

While local democracy in India is growing in an uneven form, the influence of the neo-liberal agenda could also be noticed here. Some of the pet themes of World Bank and Asian Development Bank in regard to infrastructural development were borrowed by the state and local governments and used for infrastructural development. The increasing role of voluntary organisations and civil society movements in local governance is evidence in this direction. The support extended by outside agencies and their sponsored agencies is impacting local leadership through material and policy oriented guidance. The new form of "globalisation process", is changing the conventional parameters of democracy. Altogether, federal democracy in India is changing phenomenally taking cues mainly from the framework of globalisation.

NOTES

1. Prakash Karat, Indo-US Civilian Nuclear Agreement and the Strategic Relations: Whither Independent Foreign Policy and Strategic Autonomy?, *Journal of Parliamentary Studies,* Vol. 1, Issue 1, June 2010: 30.
2. *Ibid.*
3. Roberts, J.T and Amy Hite (2000). *From Modernisation to Globalisation,* London: Blackwell cited in Anand Kumar *Modernity, Nation Building and Globalisation: An Indian Anxiety,* in Kameshwar Choudhary (2007). *Globalisation, Governance Reforms and Development in India,* New Delhi: Sage Publications: 525.
4. Anand Kumar, *Ibid:* 526.
5. *Ibid:* 533-534.
6. Vidhu Verma, *Globalisation and the State in India in* Kameshwar Choudhary (2007). op. cit.: 470.
7. Kavita Philip, *Reflections on the Intersections of Environment,* Globalisation, Federalism and Democracy in India 103.

8. *Development and Human Rights in the Context of Globalisation,* in Mahmood Monsbipouri et al., (eds.) (2004). *Constructing Human Rights in the Age of Globalisation,* New Delhi: Prentice Hall of India: 55.
9. Claude Ake, *Dangerous liasions: the Interface of Globalisation and Democracy* in Axel Hadenius (ed.) (1997). *Democracy's Victory and Crisis,* Cambridge: Cambridge University Press: 286-287.
10. Baldev Raj Nayar, *BJP's Economic Nationalism in Theory and Practice* in Ashuthosh Varshney (ed.) (2004). *India and the Politics of Developing Countries,* New Delhi: Sage Publications: 253.
11. Jagdish Bhagwati, *"Globalisation, Sovereignty and Democracy"* in Axel Hadenius (1997). op. cit: 273.
12. *Ibid,* 278.
13. Peu Ghosh, (2009). *International Relations,* New Delhi: PHI Learning Private Limited: 314-315.
14. *Ibid,* 315.
15. Mahamood Monshipouri et al (Eds) (2004).op.cit.: xiii.
16. Mann uel Castells (1997). *The Power of Identity: The Information Age- Economy, Society, and Culture* Vol. 2 Malden, M.A. Blackwell, cited in Mahamood Monshipouri et al. (eds.) op.cit: xvi.
17. Dolly Arora, Globalisation and Reorganisation of Institutional Space: Meaning for Democracy and People's Rights in Kameshwar Choudhary (ed.) 2007 op.cit.: 91.
18. *Ibid,* p: 93.
19. V.P. Menon, (1955). *Integration of Indian States,* Hyderabad: Orient Longman Publishers: 3.
20. See for details in Rajani Kothari (1964), *The Congress System in India, Asian Survey,* December.
21. Arie M.M. Kacowicz, *Regionalisation, Globalisation and Nationalism: Divergent or Overlapping? Alternatives,* Vol. 24, No. 4, October-December 1999: 5-7 cited in M.P Singh and Rekha Saxena (2010). *Indian Politics: Contemporary Issues and Concerns,* New Delhi: PHI Learning Private Limited: 71.
22. M P Singh and Rekha Saxena, op.cit: 73.

23. Lawrence Saez (2002). Federalism without a Centre: The Impact of Political and Economic Reform on India's Federal System, New Delhi: Sage Publications:135.
24. *Ibid:* 139-158.
25. Anand Kumar (2007). op.cit: 531.
26. *Ibid.*
27. Baldev Raj Nayar (2004). op.cit: 228.
28. *Ibid,* 241-250.
29. *Ibid,* 254.
30. Nirrikar Singh and TN Srinivasan, *Indian Federalism, Economic Reform and Globalisation (2002).http://en.wikipedia.org/vviki/United States public debt,* accessed on 9.2.2011, 2 pm.
31. *Ibid.*

4

West Bengal against the Centre: Continuity in Anti-Centrism in Indian Federal Politics

Harihar Bhattacharyya

Introduction

The established global scholarship on federalism (Elazar, 1987; Watts, 2008) have tended to define federalism as a political principle that advocates for two types of rule, national and regional, or shared rule and self-rule, (Elazar, 1987) within the same, compound polity. Federation is seen there as a descriptive institutional arrangement for actualising the above principle. The underlying benefit of federalism, particularly in diverse societies, is political equilibrium and a political union. The former is dynamic and amenable to upsetting challenges, and the latter critically achieved. The third benefit is achievement of federal or national loyalty, along with regional loyalty, the latter being sustained by the method of regional self-rule. All in all, federalism as a mode of governance is difficult but then it is unavoidable in diverse societies. Even in the founding of the US federation, as Watts (2008: 29-30) points out, there was an element of regional political diversity to be protected. But, for post-colonial countries, such as India, where a federation building followed the method of disaggregating of a once centralised colonial state in order to accommodate diversity of sorts and the continuous ethno-regional/linguistic pressures from below, political equilibrium, political union and national loyalty or federal loyalty are easier pronounced than realised. Adapting somewhat a recent theoretical argument in federalism (Erk, 2008), Indian federalism's adaptability to achieve coherence to social and cultural factors, or social and cultural heterogeneity, had gradually decentralised a once high centralised federation creating in its wake more problems of developing a federal/national loyalty. However, that is not be seen as apart from the high doses of centralisation and even personalisation of power in the heydays of late Indira Gandhi, then Prime Minister of India which culminated in the nationally imposed emergency rule for 18-months (June 1975-March 1977). The prime ministership of Mr Narendra Modi since 2014 has exhibited even greater height in this respect. Thus, as Erk (2008) would have us believe, India's was not a case of federalism having been decentralised in order to achieve coherence to diversity alone. The rival process of centralisation was also quite obvious despite diversity. In actual practices, often, both worked in a dialectical manner. If we take a long term view since the early 1990s, there is reason to believe despite all calls for decentralisation, in matters of macro level economic decisions, and deciding priorities of various Centrally Sponsored Schemes, the Centre's great hand is evident. Many State governments complain not without reasons that their economic sovereignty is circumscribed by imposing priorities on the States which have to share significant financial burden that constrain their limited budget.

Argument

The basic argument of this chapter is much of state politics in India (Weiner, 1968; Wood, 1984; Kohli, 1991; Yadav and Palshikar, 2008; Tillin et al eds, 2015; Manor, 2015) took since the late 1960s an anti-Centre political approach in the background of political opportunity created by the decline of the one party dominant system. (Kothari, 1964: 1161-73) This was evident in the rise to state level power many anti-Congress regional and state-based parties which curbed significantly the power of the Congress party in 1967 fourth general elections. While the Emergency (26 June-30 March 1975-77) provided further political opportunity to articulate more strongly what I would term *anti-Centrism*. What remained central to the political formulation of this *anti-Centrism* was the cultivation of regional, or ethno-regional moorings, which were and still are rampant across Indian States. In India's peripheries, most notably in the North East, this anti-Centrism is deeply rooted. The ethno-regional identity acquired political legitimacy since the days of the Congress anti-colonial liberation movements, more particularly with the emergence of Mahatma Gandhi in the 1920s. What was being practiced since 1917 in the actual reorganisation of the Congress party (Bhattacharyya, 2008) was given a formal recognition at the Nagpur Congress of the Congress party in 1920 when the party committed itself to a reorganised federal India on the basis of linguistic units. (Bhattacharyya, 2001; 2008; 2010; Sarangi and Pai 2011?) Oddly enough to recall now, in the famous Rajendra Prasad Report (1938) on Bihar the so-called sons of the soil principle for the Biharis was upheld by Dr Prasad against the Bengalis! (Das Gupta, 2001: 49-78). The various state units of the Congress were in actual practice the political manifestation of the distinct ethno-regional identity in the States concerned. That was in the natural fitness of things because each of the regions/provinces was the homes of such old and powerful *ethnie* as the Tamils, the Bengalis, Biharis, Marathis, Gujaratis, and Punjabis. Even the regions where the communists became more successful are also the distinct ethno-regions, and the communist success was due to successful identification of the communists with the ethno-regional causes. (Sen Gupta, 1972; Nossiter, 1980 and 1988; Bhattacharyya and Nossiter, 1988; Overstreet and Windmiller, 1959; Singh, 1994; Bhattacharyya, 1999). Thus, ethnic identity and ethno-regional identity in India has never been a political taboo. In much of the North East, for instance, ethnicity so far has provided as the basis of public policy intervention by the Centre though not always with success. (Bhaumik, 2007) Pau R Brass (1989: 233-63) argued that, interestingly, this *anti-Centrism* was at its height during the hay days of late Indira Gandhi when in actual practice there was no dearth of funds flow to the States and little reason to raise the bogey of political discrimination. Thus, this *anti-Centrism* has provided the state based leaders with the political weapon in federal politics of bargaining, and as a means of achieving regional political legitimacy. Any student of Indian politics is aware of the deep-seated Tamil ethno-regionalism in Tamil Nadu. This has provided proof to the hypothesis that regional and nation in India are not necessarily antithetical. (Wallace ed, 1985; Mitra, 1999; Bhattacharyya, 2005)

However, in India since independence ethno-regional sentiments and emotions have been utilised almost routinely by most parties except perhaps the BJP and Congress—latter nationally does not do so but does not mind its regional units to do it. In the case of the AIDMK or the DMK in Tamil Nadu, for example, the Tamil ethno-nationalism, rather than a simple regionalism, has been deeply-rooted, which has provided for an effective bargaining tool in anti-Centre federal politics. In West Bengal, the Left, as far as its cultivation of Bengali ethno-nationalism is concerned, is a spent force, and the space has been taken over rather fully by the TMC which has blatantly espoused the cause of the interests of the most Bengalis against the Centre—the state' suffering due to the Centre's policy and deprivation.

This chapter highlights the behavioural aspects of federal politics in India, that is, how federal politics is conducted, operated, its language, terms used to engage in 'federal bargain', the social and cultural repertoire used to buttress a political argument in favour of either the federation or the States' rights. It would be surprising to know that at the time of the making of the Indian Constitution at Constituent Assembly, the so-called provincialists were in most cases in favour of leaving the task of tax collection to the Centre and then dividing the proceeds among the federation and the Units. (Austin, 1999). Austin said that this could hardly be called a traditional defence of States' rights, as one witnessed in the Philadelphia Convention in 1787. Any discerning student of Indian federalism post-1950 will be familiar with a common refrain in the existing writings of Indian feudalism and the Centre-State relations, (Bhattacharyya, 2001; Bhattacharyya, 2009; 2010; Kurian and Verugheese eds, 1980; Sathyamurthi ed., 1985) reflecting on an *anti-Centrism* stance that took shape among the States who began to defend a case of revision of Centre-State relations in favour of more powers to the States. There are two aspects to be considered here. First, ethno-regional loyalties have been mobilised almost routinely across the States in Indian federation. Second, there are States where, due to a peculiar constellation of historical, cultural and political factors, the anti-Centre angst is deeply-rooted and pervades nearly all political parties across the ideological boards, and the *sine quo non* of the mass political culture to be utilised in acquiring political legitimacy and asserting the States' rights.

The case of West Bengal, a post-Partition (1947) creation, is discussed here as a major illustration.

Path Dependency: Making of Political Angst

Bengal's *anti-Centrism* is deeply rooted in her history and culture, the experiences of successive state contraction as a result of administrative fiats, and Partitions; its perception of acute neglect despite being over-burdened with millions of post-Partition (1947) refugees (some 6 millions during 1947-67) (Chatterjee, 2007: 2; also 2007); the restlessness of a highly educated and socially and politically conscious elite known as the *bhadralok* (Broomfield, 1968) to define and defend a homeland space in a land which was constantly subject to changing borders, and the resultant loss of ethno-linguistic brethren.

Within less than a century, Bengal incurred a great loss of territory so that at the turn of India's independence (1947) her territory was found to have shrank from 248,321 sq miles in 1872 (first census) to only 33,524 sq miles in 1951 (Franda, 1968: 10), which was one-seventh of 'Greater Bengal' a century ago. As a result, Bengal had to suffer anomalies in her linguistic and cultural identity since the latter hardly ever coincided with the former.

Franda (1968) reported the mood of the Bengalis:

> In Bengal, feelings of linguistic and cultural identity were heightened by partition (which split the Bengali-speaking areas into two and divided it by an international boundary), by the influx of refugees, and by the communal riots that resulted from partition. While the leaders of Bengal had themselves been a party to partition, the censure of Bengali middle class was directed primarily at central leaders (especially at Gandhi and Nehru), and the changers of 'Hindi imperialism' were rampant. (Franda, 1968: 11)

The fact that the leaders of Bengal, to be precise Hindu Bengali Congress leaders, in most cases, themselves were party to Partition calls for some explanation. While the Congress High Command (Central leadership) was finally ready to accept the price of Partition, the Hindu dominated Bengal Congress also campaigned successfully for the same 'on communal lines' (Chatterjee, 1994: 266). The underlying reason was a homeland for the Hindu Bengalis. Jaya Chatterjee

(2007)'s findings on *The Spoils of Partition 1947-67* are worth-quoting here:

> ....the founding father of West Bengal designed partition in the hope of restoring their privileges and reasserting their dominance in a new homeland. Under their enlightened leadership they expected Hindu West Bengal to restore its long history of decline, survive the disruptions of Partition and win back its rightful place in the all-India arena. These hopes were spectacularly disappointed....(Chatterjee, 2007: 4)

Bengal was perhaps the most ethno-linguistically advanced region in India before independence. This was hardly surprising given the distinctive social, cultural and political leadership of the *bhadralok* since the nineteenth century. And yet, Bengal had faced the most anomalous situation in matters of correspondence between its ethno-linguistic identity, on the one hand, and the administrative size and boundary, on the other. Joya Chatterjee (2007) reported that in 1947 as a result of the Partition of India, about two-third of the territory of Bengal went to form East Pakistan (now Bangladesh). Although about 90 per cent of the Hindu members of the Bengal Legislative Assembly were Congressmen who accepted Partition (Chatterjee, 2007: 264), that was not the entire story because there were resistance and the alternative proposal presented. Sarat Chandra Bose, Subhas Bose's elder brother, for example, thought that in the above, 'Bengal's voice had to be stifled and she [was] to continue to be a pawn in the all-India game'. (Quoted in Chaterjee, 1997: 266)

That the Partition did not assuage the Bengali sentiments was evident in various attempts made by the senior Bengali Ministers (in the Nehru's Cabinet) and politicians who made representations to the Constituent Assembly (CA) (1946-49) as well as to the State Reorganisation Committee (SRC) (1953) claiming more areas adjoining Bengal with Bengali speaking people. Franda (1968: 19) said that Bengal's demands were voiced time and again even in the first Lok Sabha. Consider the following speech with scathing criticism of Nehru delivered in the Lok Sabha by Prafulla Chandra Ghosh, the Chief Minister of Bengal and the Bengal Congress party chief:

The Honourable Prime Minister says: "we won't bother about what happens about Bengal or Bihar". I say with due humility that he is going to bother about the condition of Bengal. If 20,000 people come every month to a State, if two and a half lakh people come every year to a State, the Prime Minister of India will have to bother his head to solve the problem. Our question is not a Bengali question. If one question is not solved, the unity of India will be hampered....

> 'I want to make it clear that I have not come here with a begging bowl. I do not want to evoke the pity and draw the merciful attention of other States...' (Franda, 1968: 29)

It was no wonder that the injury inflicted upon the Bengali sentiments did not remain confined to the Bengal Congress or the top elites. Consider the following statement published in a Calcutta daily in 1948:

> ...'the Biharis have organised squads on the lines of Hitler's storm troopers and Muslims National Guards of pre-partitioned India....They are inciting the Santals...to be fully mobilised for immediate action (against Bengalis).
>
> Has that class which gladly accepted the gallows to assert their claims become extinct? Why are not all the sons of Bengal combining to push on their cause?...To assert the claim of Bengal, we must raise a great agitation. Let the successors of Khudi Ram and Surya Sen rise up.... (Quoted in Franda, 1968: 11)
>
> Sadly, none of the demands of Bengal could be accommodated by the CA, SRC and the Centre.

> All the new federal unit had to be content with was a measure of freedom to pursue its own plans 'on the basis of regional considerations, and to reject or negate unacceptable plans, programmes or policies' (Franda, 1968: 6). Even the SRC which rejected all demands put forward by Bengal admitted 'the partition had aroused in West Bengal the feeling that the state had been 'treated unjustly' (Franda, 1968: 24).

Left's anti-Centrism

While the West Bengal Congress post-independence (1947-67) was largely a divided house of brewing and warring factions, much mellowed in its relationship with the Centre (the same party ruled over both), and still further dissipated in handling the insoluble problems of unending influx of refugees from across the border, the anti-Centre cudgel was taken up by the left, especially the CPI, and then later the CPI-M since the late 1960s in order to bank on Bengal regional moorings by pointing out the failures of the Congress government in the State and also at the Centre to redress Bengal's problems, and thus to build the much needed bases of support. (Bhattacharyya, 1998: 325-47) The available studies of regional communism in India (Franda, 1972; Nossiter, 1982 and 1988; Singh, 1994; Bhattacharyya, 1999; Ram, 1973; Bhattacharyya, 1990) have strongly established the case of regional bases of communism in India. For the communist parties who otherwise, theoretically and ideologically, are opposed to federalism and non-class identity and in favour of centralisation, India's federalism provided nonetheless for a space within which to define a place for them by nursing and nurturing ethno-regional identity. (Bhattacharyya and Nossiter, 1988; Bhattacharyya, 1990; Bhattacharyya, 1999; Bhattacharyya, 2001 and 2003).

To take the example of the CPI-M, the dominant communist party in West Bengal since the late 1960s[1], the *anti-Centrism* has been presented in Marxist jargons as well as in terms of India's national identity and unity, and the related problems of nationalities and secession. The available inner party sources of the CPI-M as well as those published are a testimony to the above. An inner-party document of 1971 was found to be very critical of the Congress led Central government since 1947, which was considered as heavily dependent upon US capitalism. It said:

> In the wake of the Pak army attack on the people of East Pakistan, some 1.5 million refugees have crossed border to take shelter in West Bengal, which is a huge burden. But the Centre has done little to offer as a relief. Some 500 industries in the State remain closed. The Central government has let loose a semi-fascist terror instead in the State.[2]

In the 12th party Conference report (1977-78) the party conjoined its critique of the Emergency Rule in India (1975-77) to attack on West Bengal as the bastion of left politics in the country.[3]

In the 1980s the party's anti-Centre tirade reached a new nadir when the CPI-M led Left Front government in West Bengal (1977-2011) under the leadership of late Jyoti Basu (1977-2000) provided a leadership to many other States such as Jammu and Kashmir, Karnataka, Kerala, Tripura and others (State governments run by anti-Congress parties/ coalitions) in fighting against the Centre for revision of Centre-State relations and for more powers to the States. (Bhattacharyya, 2009: 99-119) The terms in which such postures were expressed were nationality question, secessionism and the States' rights, the latter being not so much known in India's federal debate. The party's 13th Congress (Dec 1988 to 01 January 1989 at Trivandram) resented in its *Political Resolution* under a section appropriately titled 'Centre-State Relations: Aggravation of Nationality Question' (pp. 32-34):

> The aggravation of Centre-State relations in recent years is the expression of the acuteness of the nationality question in the country. The problem of nationality in India can be practically solved if the various nationality constituents of the country are accorded equal opportunities for development and equal status in running the country....
>
> The administration has resorted to growing encroachment of the rights of the States and their economic powers and resources. The process of concentration of powers in the hands of the Centre extending over many years in resulting in secessionist movements in the border States and rousing powerful regional feeling in many others.

The rest of the section dwelt on issues affecting States' rights; their heavy financial burden with lower financial resource; asking for relief on loan repayment etc.

Those not familiar with the CPI-M's political jargons will not be able to decipher from the above the exact meanings. The party's equation of the states' rights with the nationality question in the above is to be understood as the party's defence of regional/local capitalism as against India's big and monopoly capitalism to which the party is opposed. The Centre/central government run by the Congress then was considered to be the representative of India's monopoly capitalism. In this sense the party's defence of ethno-regionalism vis-à-vis the Centre is part of the class perspective of the party rather than an unqualified defence of regionalism per se. But then in a competitive multi-party democracy this class perspective gets diluted with the involvement of the people at large in the political process. And this is where a popular regionalism *a la* Ms Mamata Banerjee and her party TMC is more likely to prevail over a class oriented regionalism.

Late E M S Nambudripad, long time party's general secretary, in a long essay titled 'Centre-State Relations over the Years', published in the theoretical quarterly of the party[4] harped on States rights and autonomy; centralisation of powers; bourgeois-landlord government; linked it to national unit etc emphasising the need for a 'balance between national unity and state autonomy' and not to indulge in centralisation at the expense of state autonomy because that would weaken national unity. In the 1990s, the party harped on or more or less on the same themes, as above:

> 'The last four decades have seen the twin trends of capitalist development heightening regional imbalances and uneven development and the growth of a centre with authoritarian tendencies and concentration of powers which have aggravated the nationalities question. The prolonged and adamant refusal of successive Congress (I) government to reform centre-state relations has aggravated the problem of separatism.....A broad-based movement to demand changes in centre-state relation and for a federals structure must be mounted. Without this the solution to the problem of national unity—the problem in Punjab, Assam and Kashmir—cannot be found.[5]

Nambudripad's critique of growing centralisation and his defence of state autonomy is similarly suggestive of the same understanding, as explained above. His concerns of unity in the wake of the problems in Punjab, Assam and Kashmir are to be understood in the coded defence of the party of regional nationality, or ethno-regional causes.

Even though the CPI-M led Left Front/Democratic Front lost power at the state level in West Bengal and Kerala in 2011, the party has asserted still its *anti-Centrism* on issues, as we shall presently below, which are not at variance with those of the TMC, its arch rival in West Bengal:

> 'The trend of centralising powers in the hands of the Centre and encroaching on the powers of the states has continued without respite. While political

interventions like the use of Article 356 against state governments have declined given the fact that there are coalition governments at the Centre and the ruling alliance often does not have a majority in both houses of Parliament, the assault on the states' rights has gone ahead both in the financial and legislative spheres.....The Centre refuses to devolve 50 per cent of the share of taxes to the states......The setting up of a National Counter Terrorism Centre encroaches on the police powers of the states.. ...The CPI-M has consistently stood for restructuring of Centre-State relations and the party should be in the forefront in taking up the issues of protecting the rights of the states...'[6]

Theoretically opposed to federalism and believer in centralisation in capitalism, the party's defence of states' rights or autonomy is part of the party's political strategy of nursing and nurturing its ethno-regional units in the country.

Table 1: Key Indicators: States and all-India

States	*PPP (2008 $)*	*Life expectancy at birth*	*Mean years of schooling*	*School life expectancy*
Andhra Pradesh	3398.76	64.4	3.06	9.66
Gujarat	3782.87	64.1	4.54	8.79
Karnataka	3269.76	65.3	3.95	9.75
Kerala	5262.89	74.00	6.19	11.33
Maharashtra	3913.14	67.2	5.12	9.86
Tamil Nadu	3835.05	66.2	4.79	10.57
West Bengal	3414.08	64.69	4.36	8.87
All-India	3337.33	63.5	4.10	9.62

Source: hdr.undp.org/content/inequality-adjusted-human development-index-ihdi (accessed on 31/5/16)

From Table 1 it is seen that West Bengal was above Andhra Pradesh, Karnataka and all-India in PPP; for life expectancy rate at birth was better than Andhra Pradesh, Gujarat and All-India; in terms of mean years of schooling, West Bengal was above all-India, Andhra Pradesh and Karnataka; for school life expectancy, West Bengal was only above Gujarat.

Table 2: HDI and IHDI estimate across the Indian States

States	HDI	IHDI
Andhra Pradesh	0.485	0.332
Gujarat	0.514	0.291
Karnataka	0.508	0.308
Kerala	0.625	0.520
Maharashtra	0.549	0.397
Tamil Nadu	0.544	0.396
West Bengal	**0.509**	**0.360**
All-India	**0.504**	**0.343**

Source: hdr.undp.org/content/inequality-adjusted-human development-index-ihdi (accessed on 31/5/16)

In IHDI, inequalities are adjusted to HDI to accommodate redistributional concerns (adopted in 2010 by the Human Development Report in 2010) because HDI conceal inequalities in human development attainment. Table 2 shows that West Bengal's position is better than all-India, Gujarat, Karnataka and Andhra Pradesh.

TMC's anti-Centrism

The so-called 'centrality of the States' in Indian politics hypothesis advanced by some scholars (Manor, 2010; Shastri, 2012) does not seem to cut much ice in respect of West Bengal and the TMC. The TMC (a breakway faction from Congress in West Bengal formed on 1 January 1998 under the leadership of Ms Mamata Banerjee) in India's federal politics within the UPA-II and later on outside of it is of considerable significance not only for ousting the 34 years long Left Front government in West Bengal in 2011 by a coalition of many parties, big and small, but also for being returned with a very big majority in 2016 winning 211 seat out of 294. (Table 3)

Table 3: Party Performance in West Bengal Assembly (2011 and 2016)

Party	Seats in 2016	Votes share Per cent	Seat 2011	Vote share Per cent
AITC	211	44.9	184	38.93
CPI-M	26	19.7	40	30.08
CPI	1	1.4	2	1.8
Congress	44	9.09	42	9.09
AIFB	2	2.28	11	4.80
RSP	3	1.7	7	2.96
BJP	3	10.2	1*	
GJM	3	0.5	3	0.72
SP	---	----	1	0.74
DSP	---	---	1	0.35
SUCI	---	----	1	0.44
Independent	1	2.2	1	3.13

Source: *The Frontline*, Vol. 33, No. 11 (May June), June 10, 2010, 32.

Although it is called All India Trina mool Congress (AITC), it is a regional party confined to West Bengal. It cultivates the Bengali regional identity with a strong populist appeal cutting across classes; its main support bases though are those in the lower down the social scale; the socially and economically marginalised sections in rural and urban areas. The pages of its mouthpiece 'Jago Bangla'[7] ('Rise Bengal') are evocative of the rhetoric of Bengal's past glory, alleged ruination under the Left Front government, and the promise of a bright future. The party manifesto for 2016 Assembly elections is very long and filled up with self-congratulatory and self-complacent stellar 'achievements' on all fronts. The records of achievements are mentioned *ad infinitum* without any authentic sources.

After pulling out of the UPA-II in 2012, the party became virulently anti-Centre on issues which it could not have raised as part of the UPA-II government. It is true that the TMC-run West Bengal government became one of the few States (others were Tamil Nadu, Odisha, Bihar, and Gujarat) which began to voice their opposition to the proposed (23 November 2009) setting up of a National Counter Terrorism Centres (NCTC) by the end of 2012 in order to meet the challenge of terrorism which seemed an all-India issue. Some Congress Chief Ministers of smaller States such as Kerala, Manipur, Assam and Mizoram also voiced their resentment. All the States which openly opposed the move were non-Congress governments. The other issues on which the TMC opposed the Centre were FDI in retail trade and the removal of the cap on FDI in (public) pension and insurance sectors. The TMC's withdrawal of its Ministers from the UPA-II (decided on 18 September 2012) and its failed attempt to move a no-confidence motion in Parliament (21 November 2012) to topple the UPA-II government at the Centre added further feathers to its anti-Centre 'crusade'. Those apart, the TMC government's opposition to acquire agricultural land by the government for industrial purposes even moved it farther to the Left than to the Right—a political culture nurtured and fed on for long by the LFG in West Bengal. Ironically enough, the central to the victory for the TMC-Congress alliance in West Bengal on May 13, 2011 was the charge of Bengal's ruination and underdevelopment under the Left for more than three decades. The statistical evidences (Table 1 and 2) though would suggest otherwise.

The TMC central slogan of 'MA, Mati and Manush' (Mother, Earth and Humanity) appeals constantly to the Bengali common folk, their plight and their improvement. The TMC's exit from the UPA-II cleared the deck to pursue its anti-Centre tirade on a daily basis along with its anti-Left speeches and slogans as well.

Since the TMC hovers around its supreme Mamata Banerjee, the Chief Minister, her public speeches at official and party political meetings and rallies provide evidences for our argument above. Within the space available, we will only refer to some of them.

The following is the statement made by Mamata Banerjee at a TMC rally in Purulia on December 3, 2012[8]:

> The Centre has done nothing to help West Bengal financially in the last eight months. They have made tall promises before the assembly polls (in 2011), but those words never translated into action. We may be poor but not beggars. The Centre wants that we die of hunger. But as long we are in power in the state, we will not let that happen. We may be poor, but not beggars. We know how to get back our rights.[9]

Mamata Banerjee said at Netaji Indoor Stadium to Youth TMC on 21 January 2013:

I have met PM ten times. I cannot do more than this. Shall I go and beat (him up)? Then you will say I have become a goonda.

We cannot allow FDI in retail and other anti-people decisions like repeated hike in diesel and LPG cylinders.[10]

Quoting her speech at the TMC youth rally in Kolkata on 31 January 2013, *The Statesman*, Kolkata dated 5 February 2013 reported under the heading 'Mamataism for TMC Folks':

> I think the Centre should allow the states to collect taxes and govern the states on the basis of that. The Centre collects ₹ 40,000 crore as taxes from the State [West Bengal] annually and gives back only ₹ 19,000 crore which is just 2.5 per cent.[11]

Her speeches and statements have remained a matter of ongoing debates and discussion in the daily media, print and electronic, and antagonised her political rivals, especially the Congress in the state which left the alliance government in West Bengal after the TMC had quit from the UPA-II in 2012.

The TMC *anti-Centrism* went on. On 23 November 2014 with reference to the arrest of a TMC Member. Mr Srinjoy Bose in connection with the Sarada scam by the CBI, Ms Mamata Banerjee burst out: 'I will not be silenced'. 'If we are hit, we will hit back. We are not dependent on you' (Centre/Mr Nardendra Modi). (*The Hindu* 23 November 2014) Ms Mamata Banerjee's strong *anti-Centrism*, at least on the face of it, does not stop even after her astounding electoral victory in 2016 Assembly elections. After becoming the Chief Minister for the second time, she lambasted the Centre on the issue of *Adhar Card* being mandatory for getting benefits of (Central) governmental schemes. NDTV reported (03 June 2016): 'Mamata Banerjee hits out at Centre for 'increasing tax burden on people'.

Conclusion

The foregoing analysis suggests that in India, the operational dynamics of federalism has meant that the space for federal/national loyalty is critically achieved, and the latter occupies the critical interface between national loyalty, on the one hand, and the skillful use and utilisation of strongly embedded regional moorings by the political agencies, on the other. Federal loyalty is never taken for granted in India. If we take the support bases of both the CPI-M and the TMC in 2011 State Assembly elections together, the regional space that is also somewhat anti-Centre, is quite great indeed. The situation is changed differently in 2016. The marginalised electoral position of Congress so far, and the BJP which lost further ground since 2014 in 2016 are indicative of the fact that they represent the Centre. The Left in West Bengal until 2011 managed to keep Congress to the losing side by campaigning against Centrism. In West Bengal, for a long time during the entire period of Left rule, if not before, the Centre was held responsible even for local municipal problems!

In West Bengal since independence anti-Congressism has defined more or less the ideological élan vitae for the Communist parties and other left groups in their daily conduct of politics within India's federal political space. They have been joined later by the TMC in utilising and nurturing an anti-Centre posture. For both, India's reforms (post-1991) have provided further fuel. While the Communist parties, especially the CPI-M have since the late 1970s been demanding major revision of Centre-State relations in favour of both a strong Centre and Strong States, highlighting the need for protection of states' rights (read autonomy), the TMC is yet to make such systematic efforts—the latter's are so far only public utterances and points in the political agitation.

To take up Erk (2010)'s theoretical hypothesis of federal decentralisation as a result of achieving coherence to surrounding societal context (read diversity/heterogeneity): our analysis suggests that Indian federalising process/federation-building has been the result of ethno-regional/linguistic pressures from below but accompanied by further decentralisation of an otherwise centralised federation, structurally speaking. No wonder, Watts (2008), an acknowledged global authority on federalism, says that Indian federation is structurally centralised but functionally decentralised. We have argued that it is not only functionally decentralised; it is also structurally so built because administratively speaking, the Central/Union government is what Paul Appleby said long time back (1953) 'all staff but no line'. The available evidences also show that even in the heyday of late Indira Gandhi, known for her authoritarianism and the Emergency rule, there was no case of discrimination against any particular State.

The final question: why does the TMC triumph in West Bengal over shadowing the long established Left led by the CPI-M? The answer lies first of all in the TMC's ability to successfully take away Left's agenda (pro-poor policies; dole politics; badly run economy; and higher level of public debt of the government). Left's nursing of the regional agenda was more *Bhadralok* centric (urban and rural educated elites) (Franda 1971[12]) and always in controlled measure. The TMC is openly regionalist (with 'populism' being its one goal) and reaches out more easily to the common folk who are benefitted by the governments' (including Central government's) very many welfare schemes plus more. If the girl student under the so-called 'Kanyashree' project (among many others) gets INR 25,000.00 directly into her bank account plus a bi-cycle; if the poorer people including the girl's parents get rice @ INR 2.00, and so on, she/her family will not bother even to elect a dictator! This in no ways underestimates the charisma value of Ms Mamata Banerjee who declared in nearly all election meetings 2016 that she was the candidate in all 294 constituencies. All in all, this anti-Centrism in a complex multi-ethnic federation is not particularly a desirable political practice and precedent for a federation to succeed and hold the vast country together. The great value of federal/national loyalty can hardly be neglected.

NOTES

1. It lost ground, surprisingly, to the Trinamul Congress (TMC) led by Ms Mamata Banerjee, in 2011 and again in 2016.
2. CPI-M 11th Burdwan District Conference Report, 29 Nov-01 Dec 1971: 1-2.
3. CPI-M 12th Burdwan District Conference Report, 30 Dec 1977 to 01 January 1978.
4. *The Marxist*, Vol. 5, Nos. 2-3, April-September 1987, 36-51.
5. CPI-M 14th Party Congress at Madras January 3-9, 1992 (Draft Political Resolution adopted by the CC in its meeting on 19-22 October 1991: 25.

6. CPI-M 2012 20th Party Congress at Kozhikode, Kerala April 4-9, 2012) (*Political Resolution*: 40).

7. *Bande Mataram* remains the slogan of the TMC as well as of the BJP and Congress. In the local context in West Bengal, it salutes mother Bengal. In the all India context, it used to salute mother India. It is the title and first two words of the famous nationalist song composed by Bankim Chandra Chattapadhyay, the administrator-write/novelist of Bengal. In the official website of the party, 'populism' is mentioned as one of the goals of the party.

8. That is, after the defeat of the no-confidence motion against the UPA-II government at the Centre moved by TMC in Lok Sabha which sealed off all relations with the Congress and also after the Congress in West Bengal had left the TMC-Congress coalition in West Bengal.

9. Mamata Banerjee to Centre, NDTV Dec 3, 1012. (http://www.ndtv.com/article/india/we-may-be-poor-but-not-beggaars-mamata-baenrjee-to-ce... (sighted on 4.213) See also http://www.dailymail.co.uk/indiahome/indianews/article-2093974/Mamata-baenrjee-blame... (sighted on 4.2.13)

10. Internet sources: http://news.in.msn.com.national/article.aspx?cp-documentid=252029643 (sighted on 30.1.13)

11. It is difficult to verify such statements; she at least does not care too good about the real basis of what she says in public.

12. Franda (1971) has argued that there is a causal correlation between the regional aspect of communism in Bengal and its regional bhadralok/elite leadership. For details, see 'Regional Moorings of Bengali Communism', 244-52.

BIBLIOGRAPHY

Austin, G. 1999, *The Indian Constitution: The Cornerstone of a Nation* (DelhI: Oxford University Press).

Bhattacharyya, H. and Nossiter, T. N. 1988, "Communism in a Micro State: Tripura and the Nationalities Question" in Nossiter, T. J. *Marxist State Governments in India* (London and New York: Pinters), 144-70.

________1990, "Communism, Nationalism and Tribal Question in Tripura", *Economic and Political Weekly*, Vol. 25, No. 39, 29 September 1990.

________1999, *Communism in Tripura* (Delhi: Ajanta Books International).

________1998, "The Communist Party of India and the Post-Partition refugees: A Comparative study of West Bengal and Tripura" in Talbot, I. and Singh, G eds *Region and Partition* (Karachi: Oxford University Press), 325-47.

2001, *India as a Multicultural Federation: Asian Values, Democracy and Decentralisation (In Comparison with Swiss Federalism)* (Fribourg: Institute of Federalism).

________2009, "Globalisation and Indian Federalism: Re-Assertions of States Rights" in Lofgren H. and Sarangi, P eds. *The Politics and Culture of Globalisation in Australia and India* (New Delhi: Social Science Press), 99-119.

________2010, *Federalism in Asia India, Pakistan and Malaysia* (London and New York: Routledge).

Bhaumik, S. 2007, "Insurgencies in India's Northeast: Conflict, Cooption and Change" (Working Paper No. 10, July 2007) (Washington: East-West Center).

Brass, P R. 1989, "Pluralism, Regionalism and Decentralizing Tendencies in Contemporary Indian Politics" in Wilson, J A and Dalton, D eds. *The States of South Asia Problem of National Integration* (London: Hurst and Co), 223-65.

Brass, P R and Franda, M. M eds, *Radical Politics in South Asia* (Cambridge, Mass.: MIT Press), 281-325.

Broomfield, J H. 1968, *Elite Conflict in a Plural Society: Twentieth Century Bengal* (Berkeley: University of California Press).

Chatterjee, Joya 1994, *Bengal Divided* (Cambridge: Cambridge University Press).

________2007, *The Spoils of Partition (1947-67)* (Cambridge: Cambridge University Press).

Das Gupta, J. 2001, "India's Federal Design and multicultural national construction" in Kohli, A ed. *The Success of India's Democracy* (Cambridge: Cambridge University Press), 49-78).

Elazar, D. 1987, *Exploring Federalism* (Nevada: The University of Nevada Press).

Erk, Jan 2010, *Exploring Federalism: State, Society and Congruence in Austria, Belgium, Canada, Germany and Switzerland* (London: Routledge).

Franda, M. M 1968, *West Bengal and the Federalizing Process in India* (Princeton: Princeton University Press).

________1971, *Radical Politics in West Bengal* (Cambridge, Mass. : MIT Press).

Kohli, A. 1990, *Democracy and Discontent: India's Growing Crisis of Governability* (Cambridge: Cambridge University Press).

Kothari, R. 1964, "The Congress System in India", *Asian Survey* Vol. 4, No. 12, 1661-73.

Kurian, K M. Varugheese, P N 1980 eds, *Centre-State Relations* (Delhi: Macmillan).

Nossiter, T. J. 1982, *Communism in Kerala: A Study in Political Adaptation* (Delhi: Oxford University Press).

________1988, *Marxist State Governments in India* (London and New York: Pinters).

Overstree, G and Windmiller, M. 1959, *Communism in India* (Berkeley: University of California Press).

Ram, M. 1973, "The Communist Movement in Andhra Pradesh" in Brass, P R. and Franda, F M. eds. *Radical Politics in South Asia* (Camb. Mass: The MIT Press).

Sarangi, A. and Pai, S eds. 2011, *Interrogating Reorganisation of States: Culture, Identity and Politics in India* (New Delhi: Routledge).

Sathyamurthy, T. V. ed 1985, *Centre-State Relations in India: The Case of Kerala* (Delhi: Ajanta Books).

Sen Gupta, B. 1973, Communism in Indian Politics (New York: Columbia University Press) .

Shastri, D. 2012, "The Emergence of the States as the New Centres of Indian Politics" (unpub. Paper presented in an international conference in Hyderabad Central University on 'Governance, Democracy and Political parties'; on 1-3 December 2012).

Singh, G. 1994, *Communism in Punjab* (Delhi: Ajanta Books International).

Wallace, P ed. 1985, *Region and Nation in India* (Delhi: Oxford University Press).

Watts, R. L 2008, *Comparing Federal Systems* 3rd edn. (Ontario: Queens McGill University Press).

Weiner, M. 1968, *State Politics in India* (Princeton: Princeton University Press).

Wood, J. ed. 1984, *State Politics in India: Crisis or Continuity?* (Colorodo: West View, Boulder).

Yadav, J. and Palshikar, S. 2008, "Ten Theses on State Politics in India", (www.india-seminar.com/2008/59/591_y_yadav_&s_palshikar.html (accessed on 4/6/2016)

5

Skewed Nature of Indian Federalism: Issues and problems before the smaller states with special reference to North-Eastern States

H. John Sema

Introduction

A federal system, according to Daniel J. Elazara provides a mechanism which "unites separate politics with an overarching political system so as to allow each to maintain its fundamental political integrity. This mechanism is constituted by the distribution of powers between two governments, centre and unit in a way designed to the existence and area of authority of both which according to the traditional norms are considered to be coordinate governments. Obviously, a federal system is a dual set of government while the central or federal government is charged with administration of affairs of national importance, matters of regional or local importance are given to the government of the units variously known as states in USA and India and provinces as in Canada Cantons as in Switzerland. Both the government are coordinate in relation to each other.

A federal system has some important features:

(a) There should be a written constitution as the supreme law of the land from which both the central and regional government derive their authority.

(b) There should be distribution of power between centre and the units. All items of national importance should be given to the centre, items of local importance should be entrusted to the government of the units. It however depends upon the wisdom of the constitution-makers on the placement of residuary items not specified in the list of distribution of power, to assign to the units or to the central government.

(c) Finally, there should be independent and impartial judiciary to interpret the provision of the constitution from time to time to act as an umpire to settle constitutional disputes between the central and regional government and of other national importance.

(d) There should be equal representation from all the member states whether big or small.

The following essential conditions are necessary for the successful operation of a federal state.

- A federal state must have a geographical contiguous area. The size of the state may be vary large or small, but the state must be geographically contiguous.
- As far as practicable, the units of a federal state should enjoy equality of status in respect of their power, though not in respect of their territorial and demographic composition.

- Another character of federal state is overall socio-economic development of the country. No part of the country should remain socially or economically undeveloped or backward, because the condition of regional imbalance may prove destructive to a federal system.
- Also the people of a federal state should be integrated politically as well as nationally and there should be a happy coordination between central and regional government. If all these conditions are successfully implemented in letter and spirit the federal government will be strong and stable.

Indian Federalism

Ever since the framing of the Indian constitution a controversy has been going on among the scholars as to whether the constitution can be truly described as federal or not. Dr B. R. Ambedkar, the chairman of the drafting committee, while introducing the draft constitution observed that, "the draft constitution is federal constitution in as much as it establishes what may be called dual polity".

Although Indian federalism has some federal character in structure but most of its features are unitary in nature. The dominance of the centre over the states especially policy decision-making and over-riding of the centre over the state legislation on issues of local importance, counter-terrorism and security of the state over and above that, there is inequality of representation in both the houses of parliament.

Usually in other federal type of government, there is provision for equal representation to the federating units in the upper chamber of the state (Rajya Sabha). But this principle has been ignored in Indian constitution. It accords representation to the states in the Upper House (Rajya Sabha) on the basis of their population which is supposed to be the most powerful chamber. This means that the states with larger population have more representatives in the Rajya Sabha in comparison with the states with smaller population. This ignored the principle of equality before law whether big or small states. Thus, it could not be able to represent and satisfy the political aspirations of diverse minority ethnic groups' culture, language, religions and region.

Although the Government of India is propagating population control and small family norms but so far there is no amendment of the constitution in this regard and de-limitation of the constituency has not been done as per government population control policy. Moreover, delimitation of the constituency has not been done on the basis of area or geographical location or other criteria but has been done on the basis of population. As such, delimitation of constituency has not addressed this issue and is not in tune with the government policy, as a result population control policy is not successful.

Over-view of North-East Region

The North-Eastern states consist of eight states including Sikkim which has made part of North-East India recently. Previously it was only seven states namely, Arunachal Pradesh, Assam, Meghalaya, Manipur, Mizoram, Nagaland and Tripura.

The region has 2,55,083 square km, with the population of 4,55,87,982 as per 2011 census and density of the population 173 person per sq.km. The literacy percentage of the region is 75.6 per cent as per 2011 census. The biggest state in terms of area is Arunachal Pradesh. It has 83,743 sq.km with the population of 13,82,611 as per 2011 census. The state also has the lowest density of population, 17 person per sq.km. And literacy percentage of the state is 66.95 per cent which is lowest among the North-Eastern states and also below the national literacy rate. The biggest state in terms of population is Assam i.e. 3,11,69,272 as per 2011 census. The state has 78,438 sq.km. The density of population is 397 person per sq.km. Except Assam, Tripura and Imphal Valley (Manipur), the whole region is thinly populated. The highest literacy rate in North-Eastern state is Mizoram i.e. 91.58 per cent and female literacy rate is 89.40 per cent as per 2011 census. The region has 213 tribes and 325 languages of which 175 languages are Tibeto Burman and Mon Khmar family. Among these states, Nagaland is the only state whose decadel growth of population is negative i.e. as per 2001 census Nagaland population was 19,88,636 against 19,80,602 as per 2011 census. The decadel growth rate of Nagaland population is -47. Perhaps in 2001 census highly inflated growth rate was reflected. The literacy percentage of the state is 80.11 per cent, male- 83.29 per cent and female-76.69 per cent respectively.

The North-Eastern region is strategically located from geographical and security point of view. It has international boundary with China in the North, Burma in the East and Bangladesh and Bhutan in the South-West. The North-East is connected with mainland India by a narrow corridor in North-Bengal popularly known as chicken neck or bottle neck. Except Assam Bhramaputra valley and Imphal valley, most of the area is hilly. The valley's are pre-dominantly inhabited by Hindus and Muslims, Christianity has taken deep-roots in the hill states in Nagaland and Mizoram where 95 per cent of population are Christians and hill districts of Manipur and Meghalaya are also predominantly Christians. Most of the Arunachal people follow Buddhism and Animism and Tripuris are predominantly Hindus.

The Perception of North-Eastern States towards Indian Federalism

When the constitution of India was framed by the founding fathers, there has been anxiety in the minds of the elites of the North-Eastern states and particularly the Assamese elites, that in a federation with strong centre, the big units of the federation have got an advantageous position. As predicted, under the present dispensation of the constitution of India, the Union Parliament is under the domination of representatives from the bigger units of the federation. As a result, the interest of small states are marginally heard or neglected. The Assam Tribune one of the pioneer newspapers in those days clearly expressed, this apprehension in one of its editorial in November 19, 1949 where it stated that "In a federation in which centre is unduly strong, it is the small province like Assam which have to suffer. Their representation in the central legislative is very small and therefore, they can hardly influence the cause of central polity". No doubt, the central authority must be sufficiently strong to hold the subordinate units together, but just strong and it should not be that strong which will go against the interest of the state. In other words, the need for strong centre should not be taken to mean the annihilation of the federal principles.

This apprehension however, proved to be true. Right from 1950 till date the leaders of the North-Eastern states had not been able to make any impact on the central government. The North-East people felt that their interest would go by default due to lack of adequate representation in the central government. This lack of representation could be directly or indirectly responsible for the negligence of the centre towards the North-Eastern states. The huge central establishment at New Delhi is conspicuous by the absence of North-Eastern personnel. The central political field is practically closed to North-East politicians and nobody wants to think of North-Eastern people in central cabinet with the exception of few Assamese that also Minister of State. Despite having 8 (eight) states, altogether the number of member of Parliament from the North-Eastern states are having 25 only in Lok Sabha and 14 in Rajya Sabha which is less than the states of Bihar, West Bengal, Uttar Pradesh etc.

That is why very often unpopular government actions or appointment in these states transpire to have been made at the behest of the influential persons at the centre who have access to the corridors to powers neglecting the aspiration and interest of the region who are too far away to be influenced by the public opinion at the centre. Thus, the North-East people have no access to central leaders at New Delhi.

Sl.No	*Name of the State*	*No. of Seats in Lok Sabha*	*No. of Seats in Rajya Sabha*
1	Arunachal Pradesh	2	1
2	Assam	14	7
3	Manipur	2	1
4	Meghalaya	2	1
5	Mizoram	1	1
6	Nagaland	1	1
7	Sikkim	1	1
8	Tripura	2	1
	Total No. of Seats	**25**	**14**

At present in the NDA government there is no single cabinet minister from the North-Eastern region. In the previous UPA regime, there were only few Minister of State, that also DONER (Development of North-East Region) Minister and one junior Minister of State.

In the Parliament, there is hardly any voice for the people of the North-Eastern people. One of the most glaring example is when the North-Eastern States are demanding the revocation of Armed Forces Special Powers Act (AFSPA), the Government of India and armed forces are opposed to its revocation on the pretext of security and territorial integrity of the nation and law and order despite mass protest for withdrawal of AFSPA and hunger strike by Miss Irom Sharmila for more than ten years. The Government of India did not pay any heed to the cry of the people.

But whereas, when the Home Minister wanted to use armed forces to combat Naxalite infested areas in the heartland of India, there was hue and cry from both ruling party as well as opposition party which united against the use of armed forces to crush the Naxalite on the pretext why should the army be used to fight against our own brothers and sisters. This is law and order problem and therefore only the police force should be requisitioned and deployed in this area to maintain law and order. Even the armed forces themselves refused to involve themselves and combat the Naxalites on the pretext that they should not fight against their own brothers and sisters.

In this regard, are the North-Eastern states not our own brothers or are they not Indians? The Government of India, thus maintains double standard/yardsticks on the similar issue. Is not anybody who indulged in terrorist activities are the same whether he/she participate in the insurgent movement, secessionist or naxalism or in any form? Is not it is discriminatory against a particular section of the people? Is that the rule of law should be differently applied against certain sections of the people? This is quite obvious on the issues relating AFPSA and NCTC. On the issue of setting up NCTC (National Counter Terrorism Centre) proposed by the Home Ministry to combat and cleanse all terrorist activities in the states. All states are apprehensive on the ground that centre may in the name of combating terrorism can arrest, search anybody without any warrant and the state will be under the dictate of the centre and especially the smaller states who have no influence at the centre at all will be at the greater risk, so they opposed the move that such act should not be passed like AFSPA. So all the big states opposed the setting up of National Counter Terrorism Centre and hence it could not be passed in the parliament. But had it been opposed by the smaller states alone, the central government would have ignored with deaf ear and would have easily passed the bill overriding the wishes of the smaller states. The North-Eastern states in the name of Disturbed Area Act are under the grip of armed forces where (Armed Force Special Powers Act) AFSPA is covered in some areas of Assam and

Arunachal Pradesh and whole of Manipur and Nagaland in the name of insurgency problems. That is why the people of North-East region feel neglected and isolated from the mainstream Indian politics. Thus, the lack of adequate representation and discriminatory treatment are responsible for discontentment and alienation that breed secessionist and insurgency movement in the region. This lack of emotional integration and territorial disconnectness is directly or indirectly responsible for alienation of people from the North-East to the mainstream Indian political system.

That is why, whenever there is Lok Sabha election, the people hardly participate in the Lok Sabha election in the North-East and particularly in Nagaland, because there is only one seat in the Parliament which they feel will not make any impact in the number game for forming government as well as policy/decision making.

Recently, North-East Parliamentary Forum was formed at New Delhi from the North-East Region in order to have common platform and unitedly raise their voice for the cause of North-Eastern States on all issues relating to security, political, socio-economic and all round development of the region. But so far they could not able to ventilate the issues and problems that has been confronting to the region neither in the parliament nor outside the parliament.

In this regard unless there is equal representation in the Parliament, in both the Houses as in the case of America whether big or small in terms of size of the territory or population, and if there is equal representation from all states in the parliament, the process of alienation would be contained. If India wanted to be united and a powerful country, then she should accommodate the diverse political aspirations and wishes of all sections of the society. She should adopt American federal principle of equal representation of all the states irrespective of the size, population, economic condition of the state (s). Hence, whether the big states in India should bifurcate/trifurcate/split into smaller states or the big states should sacrifice their number of representatives in the parliament on their own volition for the sake of India's unity and integrity that would make India one of the most powerful country in the world.

References

1. Johari, J.C. *Principles of Modern Political Science,* Pub. by Sterling Pub. New Delhi 1992.
2. Singh, Mahendra Prasad, *Indian Federalism: An Introduction,* Pub. by National Book Trust India, New Delhi, 2011.
3. Constituent Assembly Debate.
4. Phukon, Girin, *Politics of Regionalism in Northeast India,* Spectrum Pub. New Delhi, 1996.
5. Saez Lawrence, *Federalism without a centre,* Sage Publication, New Delhi, 2002.
6. The author is grateful to Prof A.K. Singh, Department of Political Science for his input in the paper.

6

Indian Federalism, Sikh Identity and Akali Demand for State Autonomy

Sukhjit Singh

The Indian federation experienced serious tension between the Centre and the states over the issue of greater autonomy to the states in the period following 1967 general election. In the earlier phase, due to accommodative policy of the Prime Minister Jawahar Lal Nehru, the relations between the two remained largely smooth. The giving up of the accommodative model, the deinstitutionalisation process of Congress party by Prime Minister Indira Gandhi, the persistence of economic backwardness of the states coupled with socio-cultural awareness, led to the demand for greater autonomy for the states resulting in strained Centre-states relations. The demand for more autonomy to the states became loud as dominant position of the Congress Party getting eroded in new political forces in the form of regional political parties like DMK, Telgu Desam, Akali Dal,

Assam Gana Parishad, and National Conference which raised the issue of greater autonomy to the states.

In the legal-political vocabulary, the term autonomy denotes self-government.[1] It differs from the term independence as the latter implies the right of separation from another political entity, while the former implies that "for important political and economic matters, a particular area will remain within the territorial jurisdiction of another political entity and possess political freedom in its own sphere without any interference by that entity."[2] It refers to the capacity of a unit in federal system to function independently of the central government in certain matters which belong exclusively to its domain.[3] It also implies an arrangement of power sharing between the Centre and state governments and an attempt on the part of the states to solve their problems with their own resources within the framework of the Constitution. The term identity refers to the self-perception of a group of people who consider themselves as different from others. Such a group tends to define itself not only with reference to their own characteristics but also referring the others as strangers.[4] Common history, common language, common culture, common religion, sense of belongingness and attachment to a particular area are the important source of the formation of identity.[5] Sikhs as a community, having all such characteristics are fully aware about their distinct identity. Their leadership has always been in search of a political setup in which their national aspirations can be fully realised.

Indian society is heterogeneous in which different groups and nationalities differ from each other on the basis of language, culture, history and in some cases religion too. Each nationality possesses its own distinct identity based on one or more than one factors. A feeling has set in that centralised political system of India may threaten, dilute or destroy their distinct identity. This is the reason that regional political parties, directly or indirectly attached to the distinct groups and nationalities, have been in search of a mechanism which might protect their distinct identity by preserving the separate religion, language, traditions and culture. The working of the Indian Political system shows that the demand for greater autonomy to the states has been raised by the regional forces to protect the distinct identity of the people of the respective regions.

It has been noted that the basis for the demand of state autonomy is not the product of a single determinant but a product of the manifold factors-social, religious, cultural, political and economic.[6] It is only because of the heterogeneous character of the Indian society. In the case of Punjab, it is religion, language and culture; in the case of Jammu and Kashmir, it is religion, language, culture and history; in the case of Tamil Nadu and Andhra Pradesh, it is language and culture; in the case of Nagaland, it is again language, religion and culture.[7] Apart from this, economic and political factors have played equally important role in this regard. Economic deprivation of a particular region has also been used by the regional political forces in favour of greater autonomy to the states.

The year 1967 proved watershed in the history of Centre-state relations in India, because in eight states*, non-Congress governments came to power for the first time. The step-motherly treatment given to the non-Congress governments by the centre, excessive centralisation and the tendency of the Centre to further encroach upon the state jurisdiction, discrimination in matters of allocation of financial resources, financial stress of the states, partisan and dominant role of the Planning Commission of India in the planning process, misuse of Article 356 of the Constitution to dethrone the popularly elected governments with the help of the Governors, deployment of the paramilitary forces without the consent of the affected states, desire of the people of a particular region or a state to preserve its distinct language, culture and religion, made states and regions to raise the issue of greater autonomy to the states.[8]

The DMK government in Tamil Nadu raised the issue of greater autonomy to the states in 1969. It appointed a three member Committee with P.V. Rajamannar as its chairman to inquire into the possibility of restructuring the Centre-State relations on federal lines. The committee submitted its report in 1971 favouring greater autonomy to the states. The CPM government of West Bengal in 1977 submitted a 'Memorandum on Union-State Relations' to the central government asking for more powers to the states. Thereafter, the issue of greater autonomy to the states became a frequently discussed question in the Indian polity. A meeting of the four Southern Chief Ministers in March 1983 and Srinagar Conclave held from 9 to 11 October 1983, unanimously passed revolution to restrict the jurisdiction of the Centre on the four subjects namely, Defence, Foreign Affairs, General Communications and Currency[9]. In the wake of growing dissatisfaction among the states, the Government of India appointed a Commission in 1983 with Ranjit Singh Sarkaria as its chairman to examine and review the Centre-state relations and suggest measures for its smooth functioning. The Commission ignored the just claims of the states on the ground that in the wake of threat to the unity and integrity of the country, powerful Centre was inevitable.[10]

The failure of the Sarkaria Commission in addressing the key demands, kept the issue of greater autonomy alive. In May 2000, Chief Ministers of all the states at the Inter-State Council meeting urged the Centre to consult the states before imposing arbitrary economic decisions on them. After a month in June 2000, a Conclave of the Chief Ministers and Finance Ministers of nine state governments was held at New Delhi in which unanimous decision was taken that share of the states in the divisible pool should be increased from 29 per cent to 33.3 per cent. They also urged the Centre to lower the interest rate on central loan from 12.5 percent to 10 per cent.[11]

The National Conference government of Jammu and Kashmir appointed 'State Autonomy Committee' on

29 November 1996. It submitted its report on 13 April 1999. Accepting the report as it is, the Jammu and Kashmir State Legislative Assembly passed *Autonomy Resolution* on 26 June 2000. The recommendations of the Committee[12] sought to make wholesale changes in the relations between the Centre and the State of Jammu and Kashmir which were in operation after 1953. According to the report, the Centre's jurisdiction over the state will be confined only to defense, foreign affairs and communication. Article 356 would not be applicable to the state. There would be no room for Election Commission of India, Supreme Court and All India Services to exercise their powers in relation to Jammu and Kashmir. There would be separate charter of Fundamental Rights in the State Constitution and no special provision for SCs, OBCs and STs would be applied to the state. The State will have its own Governor entitled as Sadar-i-Riyasat and Chief Minister known as Wazir-e-Azam or Prime Minister. The recommendations met severe criticism from the Centre. Even the Union Government of whose National Conference was a ruling partner did not consider it fit to discuss the report in Parliament. With the emergence of the coalition era since 1996, the regional political parties asserted their rights more forcefully. Their resistance to the imposition of President's rule in Bihar and West Bengal by the Vajpayee Government in 1998, stern opposition to the creation of the National Centre to Counter Terrorism (NCTC) in 2012 by the UPA Government and rejection of the Modi Government's idea of linking the river waters testifies the growing assertiveness of the regional political parties. Now in the age of coalition politics, regional forces are not willing to play secondary role in the Indian political setup.

Akali Demand for State Autonomy

Like other regional political parties of India, the Shiromani Akali Dal has also remained consistently in the forefront to ask for greater autonomy to the states. The party believes that in autonomous regions, various communities and regions may have full avenues and opportunities of self-development and growth. The growth and development of various regions, in turn, would ensure a stronger and united India. The Akali Dal, the oldest regional political party is the first to raise the issue of greater autonomy to the states. The party believes that instead of weakening the Centre, it would strengthen the national unity and integrity. Akali Dal argues that body can be strong only if the parts are strong. If any part of the body is weak, the whole body gets affected and cannot work effectively. Same principle applies to the body politic of Indian sub-continent. The Dal has shown dissatisfaction over the working of the Indian political system which has crippled states' sphere of action. Although, like other regional political parties, party seeks autonomy for the states due to excessive centralisation, misuse of Article 356, partisan role of the Governor, discriminatory treatment by the Planning Commission, financial dependence of the states over the Centre and pre-partition promises of the Congress to the Sikh leadership, yet the dominant motive behind the autonomy move is to preserve the distinct religious, cultural and linguistic identity of the Sikhs. Akali Dal is of the view that minorities can feel safe and secure only in a true federal setup. As the Sikhs are a minority in India (1.7 per cent as per 2011 census), therefore, assimilative designs of the Hindu majority community, backed by the powerful centralised state, might absorb them within the parent fold of Hinduism. It is the dominant urge of self-preservation which stirred the Akali leadership to seek an area which might provide them a sense of security. To attain this objective, Akali Dal even made certain changes in its Constitution in 1974. The new provision sought "the preservation among the Sikhs of a consciousness of an Independent Panthic identity and carving out a territory, wherein the national sentiments and nationhood of the Sikh Panth may find the fullest embodiment and expression."[13]

Paul Wallace, a Punjab watcher has written that, "minority attitudes underline the Sikh political behaviour despite the community's apparent numerical, economical and political dominance in the state, and it is not without cause."[14] K.R. Bombwall is also of the view that "it would be injustice if we analyse the Akali concept of autonomy without taking into consideration its commitment to the preservation of an independent political status for the community."[15] To press the autonomy demand, Akali Dal passed several resolutions and submitted memorandums to the various commissions, which were set up to review the working of centre-state relations. No attention has been paid so far by the Centre to the Akali demand; rather the communal elements described the demand as 'separatist', threatening the very unity and integrity of the country by. A noted scholar of Sikh history J.S. Grewal rightly observes that "a type of political set up was conceived as paramount by the Sikhs to check the grave threat to their identity and existence from the aggressive communalism of Hindus and Muslims".[16]

The cardinal notion of the Sikh system is that religion cannot survive without the attainment of political power. The Sikhs were able to rule certain parts of Punjab in the eighteenth century during the times of Banda Bahadur and Misal period. Maharaja Ranjit Singh (1799 1839) further consolidated political power of the Sikhs and ruled the state from 1799 to 1839. Due to internal bickering, his successors failed to retain power and lost to the Britishers in 1849. The loss of power created crisis of identity for the Sikhs. The consistent efforts by the radical Hindu body Arya Samaj, in the last quarter of the nineteenth century to undermine the philosophical and ideological roots of Sikhism stirred the Sikh leadership. The Chief Khalsa Diwan was set up in 1902 to protect the social, cultural, and political interests of the Sikhs. In 1909, the British government provided separate electorates to the Muslims under the Minto Morley Reforms Act. The Chief Khalsa Diwan also appealed to the government to make similar provision for the Sikhs which was rejected due to complex and communal character of the Punjabi society. The Diwan continued its efforts, as a result of which, the British government recognised the perceived sense of insecurity among the Sikhs and provided separate electorates to the Sikhs and reserved 18.3 per cent seats in the Punjab Legislative Council under the Montague-Chelmsford Act of 1919.[17]

The formation of Shiromani Akali Dal on 14 December 1920 proved vital to protect the Sikh interests at socio-religious and political level. During the two parallel movements- Gurdwara Reform Movement and Non Cooperation Movement (1920), both Congress and Akalis came close to each other. However, in the name of secularism, the Nehru Report* in 1928 recommended the abolition of separate electorates in Punjab.[18] The recommendation raised apprehensions in the minds of Akali leadership about the sincerity of the Congress' designs. Akali leader Baba Kharak Singh appealed the Sikhs to "throw the report into the dustbin".[19] Congress Party was caught in a tricky situation as the next annual session of the Congress was to be held in Lahore. It was difficult for the party to make the session a success without the support of the Sikhs. Realising growing dissatisfaction among the Akalis, the Congress party rectified its decision to abolish the separate electorates. The Congress leadership at the Lahore session (December 1929) assured the Sikhs that "no future Constitution of India shall be acceptable to the Congress that does not give the Sikhs full satisfaction."[20] The same pledge was reiterated by Mahatma Gandhi on 15 July 1934 when Khalsa Darbar deputation met him at Lahore. Gandhi assured the deputation that "no Constitution would be acceptable to the Congress which did not satisfy the Sikhs."[21]

In 1940, the Muslim League passed a resolution at its Lahore session for the creation of a separate state for the Indian Muslims called Pakistan. League President Mohammad Ali Jinnah raised the point that being separate nation, Muslims should have their own homeland in which they could preserve their heritage and traditions. The demand created fears among the Sikh circles because the areas of proposed Pakistan included the whole of Punjab- the homeland of the Sikhs. In the wake of past hostility of the Muslims towards the Sikhs, the Sikh leadership after a careful thought concluded that Sikh interests would not be safe in such a proposed Islamic state. By this time, the Congress Party had changed its stand over the issue of the creation of Pakistan. Mahatma Gandhi supported the C. Raja Gopalachari Formula (1944) which provided that if Muslim League supports the Congress in the attainment of independence, plebiscite would be held in the Muslim majority areas regarding as to whether the Muslims want the creation of Pakistan or to remain with Hindustan. The Sikh leadership got upset over this sudden development as Mahatma Gandhi used to boast of that Pakistan could be created only over his dead body. On 22 March 1946, the Executive Committee of the Akali Dal passed a resolution in favour of a Sikh state. The establishment of such a state was considered vital for the promotion, preservation and protection of the religious, cultural, economic and political rights of the Sikh nation.[22]

However, the top Congress leadership assured the Sikhs that a favourable environment would be provided for their unhindered growth by devising a mechanism on federal lines. Speaking at Calcutta on 7 July 1946, Nehru assured that "the brave Sikhs of Punjab are entitled to special consideration. I see nothing wrong in an area and a set up in the North, wherein the Sikhs can also experience the glow of freedom."[23] Again speaking in the opening session of the Constituent Assembly on 9 December 1946, Nehru promised, "Adequate safeguards would be provided for the minorities in India. It was a declaration, a pledge and an undertaking before the world, a contract with the millions of ... Indians and therefore in the nature of an oath which we must keep."[24] He promised a federal setup in which "states shall posses and retain the status of autonomous units together with residuary powers.[25]

The political system on federal lines is considered a better mechanism to protect the social, cultural and political interests of the minorities, especially their distinct identity. In the wake of the promises and assurances of the Congress Party, the Akali leader Master Tara Singh took the decision to tag Sikh destiny with India. Contrary to the pledges and insurances, in the post-independence period, the Congress leadership totally ignored what it had promised to the Sikhs in the pre- partition days. In the immediate post-partition phase, Hinduism resurged in a strong manner, creating doubts about the secular credentials of the Indian State. In Punjab, Arya Samaj committed attacks on the distinct identity of the Sikhs and ridiculed Sikh symbols. It led a virulent campaign that Sikhism is merely a branch of Hinduism which came into being to protect the Hindus from the Muslim atrocities. As the Muslims have gone to Pakistan, therefore, the Sikhs should come back to the parent fold.[26] The Akali leadership reacted sharply to such attempts of Hinduising the Sikhs. Master Tara Singh in February 1948 put forth the demand to give the Sikhs the right to self-determination within the Indian union so that Sikhs could maintain and preserve their cultural, linguistic and religious identity. He retorted:

> "We have a culture different from the Hindus. Our culture is Gurmukhi culture and our literature is also in Gurmukhi script. We want to have a province where we can safeguard our culture and tradition. We want the right of self-determination for Panth in religions, social and political matters."[27]

To create a sense of security among the Sikhs in the newly emerged hostile environment, Sikh members of the Punjab Legislative Assembly submitted a memorandum to the Constituent Assembly in November 1948. The memorandum sought fifty per cent reserved seats for the Sikhs in the Punjab legislature, five per cent in the central legislature and forty per cent reservation in the government services. More importantly, the memorandum held that if this demand was not acceptable, then the Sikhs should be allowed to form a separate province comprising seven districts* of Punjab in which they form numerical majority.[28] The Congress leadership refused to entertain the demand on the ground that religion based demands cannot be accepted in a secular state. Instead of assuaging the injured feelings of the Sikhs, the government clubbed the Sikhs with Hindus under Art 25(2)(b) of the Constitution, thereby, denying separate identity to them. This was a huge setback to the Sikh community because such a provision of the Constitution put their distinct identity in doubt, bringing them within the fold of Hinduism. Two Sikh representatives in the Constitution Assembly - Hukam Singh and Bhupinder Singh Mann felt utterly disappointed over this development. Both the representatives refused to sign the Indian Constitution on 26 November 1949 saying that "the Sikhs do not accept this constitution, the Sikhs reject this constitution."[29]

Sikh leader Master Tara Singh considered the formation of the Punjabi Suba as the only measure to protect and preserve the distinct religion, language and culture of the Sikhs. By this time, the demand to reorganise the states on linguistic basis has been raised by the distinct linguistic and cultural groups in other regions of the country. The formation of Telgu speaking Andhra Pradesh and Tamil speaking Tamil Nadu as a result of bifurcation of the Madras Presidency in 1953 compelled the Indian government to rethink about the solution of the growing problem of linguistic and cultural nationalism. The Government of India appointed the States Reorganisation Commission in 1953 under the chairmanship of Fazal Ali with H.N. Kunzru and K.M. Pannikar as the two other members to explore the possibility of reorganisation of the states on linguistic basis. Akali Dal submitted a memorandum to the Commission seeking the creation of language based Punjabi Suba by detaching Hindi speaking areas (present Haryana) from Punjab.[30] Hindu bodies like Hindu Maha Sabha, Jan Sangh, RSS and Arya Samaj joined hands to oppose the Akali demand in a strong manner. The opposition to the demand followed from their fear of Sikh domination in the reorganised Punjab. These bodies formed Maha Punjab Samiti to give a united fight to the Akalis. The Samiti submitted a joint memorandum to the Commission for the creation of 'Maha Punjab' by merging the existing state of Punjab, PEPSU*, Himachal Pradesh, Delhi and few districts of Western Uttar Pradesh.[31]

The State Reorganisation Commission submitted its report in the end of 1955. It rejected the Akali claim for Punjabi Suba. Contrary to the Akali demand, it recommended the formation of Maha Punjab by merging the areas of Himachal Pradesh and PEPSU into Punjab. The Commission even put the question mark on the distinct character of the Punjabi language, declaring it akin to Hindi language.[32] The Akalis dubbed the report as "a conspiracy to destroy the Sikh nation." Akali leader Master Tara Singh described it as "a decree of Sikh annihilation."[33] To mollify the Akalis, Prime Minister Nehru entered into an agreement (Regional Formula)[34] with the Akalis in March 1956. The formula envisaged the merger of PEPSU in Punjab, the creation of two Regional Committees* for the Punjabi speaking and Hindi speaking areas to discuss the developmental policies and programmes for the respective regions before their enactment into a law by the state legislature and continuance of the Sachar Formula. As per the provisions of the Sachar Formula[35] (1 October 1949), Punjabi in Gurmukhi script was declared as the compulsory language to be taught in the Punjabi speaking region right from the very first class in the school. To sabotage the Regional Formula, the Arya Samaji Hindus of the Jalandhar division refused to learn Punjabi. The Hindu bodies led by Arya Samaj raised the bogey of 'Hindi in danger'.[36] The communal minded

Hindus used most abusing, insulting, provocative and offensive language against the Punjabi language and raised derogatory slogans such as 'ura aira nahi parhenge, gandi bhasha nahi parhenge' (we shall not read the alphabet of the filthy language).[37] Such acts of the Hindu organisations provided necessary excuse to the Chief Minister Partap Singh Kairon to linger on the implementation of the Regional Formula. The Akali leadership reacted sharply to such developments. Akali Dal (Master) passed a resolution at the Hari Singh Nalwa conference, held at Ludhiana on 4 July 1965. The resolution said:

"This conference recalls that the Sikh people had agreed to merge in a common Indian nationality, on the explicit understanding of being accorded a constitutional status of co-sharers in the Indian sovereignty along with majority community... The Sikh people have been systematically reduced to a sub-political status in their homeland, Punjab. This conference, therefore resolves after careful thought that there is left no alternative for the Sikhs in the interest of self-preservation but to frame their political demand for securing a self-determined political status within the Union of India".[38]

The reorganisation of Punjab on 1 November 1966 failed to satisfy the aspirations of the Sikh leadership because many Punjabi speaking areas* were left out despite the stiff opposition from the Akalis. The reorganisation further heightened the already growing sense of alienation and discrimination among the Sikhs. Akali leader Master Tara Singh accused the central government of creating a lifeless Punjabi Suba and declared that "Sikhs would not accept this lifeless state."[39] The provisions made in Sections 78 to 80 of the Punjab Reorganisation Act 1966 were detrimental to the economic interests of the state and its people. Under these sections, the control, maintenance and distribution of the rivers waters and hydel power of Punjab were vested in the central government, depriving the state of its legitimate control over the river waters.[40] The provision was conceived as an effort on the part of the Union government to destroy the agriculture of the state, the only means of livelihood of the majority of the Sikh farmers of Punjab. Article 3 of the Indian Constitution, whereby the Parliament is entitled to change the boundaries of the states, was deliberately misused by the Central Government to place the Punjab at a disadvantageous position. Akali leadership accused the highly centralised Indian political system responsible for such a pathetic situation of Punjab and the Sikhs.

Akali Dal (Master), a radical faction of Akalis, passed a resolution in December 1966 in favour of self-determination for the Sikhs within the Indian union as provided to the state of Jammu & Kashmir under the Indian Constitution.[41] The moderate faction Akali Dal (Sant) followed the suit but in less radical terms. In the election manifesto, issued during the assembly elections of 1967, its President Sant Fateh Singh sought more powers for the state to secure more powers to the provinces in order to maintain the territorial integrity of the country and also to secure more smooth and friendly Centre-State relations."[42]

The assembly elections of 1967 proved watershed in the political history of Punjab as Congress hegemony was seriously undermined. No political party could secure the required majority in the assembly to form the government. As a result of leading role of Akali Dal (Sant) president Sant Fateh Singh, a coalition government of United Front[*] was formed in the beginning of March 1967 under the Chief Ministership of Justice Gurnam Singh. The Congress Party which had ruled the state since 1947 tried to dethrone the United Front Ministry but failed to achieve the desired objective. However, the opportunity came when dissident Akali leader Lachhman Singh Gill came out of the government with his 16 supporters in November 1967. The Chief Minister Gurnam Singh advised the Governor D.C. Pavate to dissolve the assembly.[43] At the instance of the central government, the Governor turned down the advice. Rather he facilitated the establishment of Lachhman Singh Gill government with the outside support of the Congress party. In this whole episode, the role of the Governor Pavate became controversial. He refused to accept the advice of the Chief Minister Gurnam Singh regarding the dissolution of the assembly. The Governor was bound to accept the advice of the Chief Minister as the latter was not defeated at the floor of the house. The fall of the Akali government within nine months of its formation and working experience while running the government, convinced the Akalis that the political and economic salvation of the state lies only in greater autonomy to the state. A sense of deprivation engulfed the Akali mind that Congress is not willing to allow the Sikhs to enjoy political power in the state which is considered vital for protecting the socio-religious and cultural rights of the Sikhs. In September 1968, Akali Dal passed a Resolution at Batala which favoured greater autonomy to the states. The resolution said:

"In the last 20 years in the political life of the country, great changes have taken place which necessitate reconsideration of the Centre-State relations. The Congress Party in power has abused the constitutional provisions to the determent of the non-Congress governments. Akali Dal demands that in the light of the changed circumstances, Constitution of India should be given a correct federal shape and the states should have greater autonomy."[44]

It is believed that resolution was largely based on the philosophy of Sardar Kapur Singh (a dismissed ICS officer turned politician) who used to say that "the Sikhs are sui-genesis, a free and sovereign people and this right is inalienable and cannot be compromised. The concrete realisation of this status of the Sikh people is possible within the sovereign and territorial integrity of the country".[45] And that "a member of the Khalsa is sovereign citizen by his birth right, and subjugation and slavery is antagonistic to his status as a member of the order of the Khalsa."[46] A noted Sikh historian Khushwant Singh is also of the view that being a chosen people (Raj Jati), Sikhs are predestined to rule.[47] To pursue the demand for state autonomy more vociferously, Akali Dal reshaped its policy programmes. On the basis of such policies, Akali Dal passed Anandpur Sahib Resolution in October 1973. The resolution, known as Magna Carta of the Sikhs, reopened the issue of state autonomy and also sought to redress the grievances of the Punjab in general and Sikhs in particular.

The preamble of the resolution states that "the Shiromani Akali Dal is the very embodiment of the hopes and aspirations of the Sikh nation and as such is fully entitled to represent them."[48] The purpose of the Akali Dal as mentioned in this resolution is "to preserve and keep alive the concept of distinct identity of the Panth and to create an environment in which national sentiments and aspirations of the Sikh Panth will find full expression, satisfaction and growth."[49] The resolution further adds, "the Panthic political aim is definitely based on the directives of the Tenth Lord which is engraved on the pages of Sikh history and in the mind of the Khalsa Panth, the ultimate objective of which is the pre-eminence of the Khalsa".[50] The Political demands in the resolution called for the incorporation of Punjabi-speaking areas, which were left out at the time of reorganisation of Punjab, restricting the centre's jurisdiction to defence, foreign affairs, currency and general communications and safeguards for the Sikh community living outside the Punjab.[51] The resolution denounced the foreign policy of India as useless and detrimental to the interests of the country.[52] It appealed to the central government to cultivate good relations with the neighbour countries. Akali Dal clarified that the demand was made to improve relationships with Pakistan because Sikhs face difficulties in obtaining visa to visit their religious shrines in the wake of strained relations between the two countries.

The use of theological language in the resolution made it a subject of controversy. According to K.R. Bombwall, "the Akali claim of pre-emptive right to exercise political power cannot be entertained especially keeping in view the basic postulates of a secular and liberal democratic state".[53] The Jan Sangh and CPI leadership was more critical. Both the parties argued that acceptance of such a resolution would lead to the balkanisation of the country. These parties charged the Akalis of a design for creating a Sikh dominated theocratic state. Balraj Madhok, leader of the Jana Sangh dubbed the resolution as 'disruptive' which seeks special status for a minority community "throwing to the winds all democratic norms and basic postulates of humanism and secularism."[54] The Jana Sangh also raised objections over the Akali claim that Sikhs are a separate nation. The party described the Sikh religion as merely a branch of Hinduism. Even the CPM leader Harkishan Singh Surjit, a staunch supporter of state autonomy, described the resolution as a serious challenge to the secular character of our state and laid the basis of separation, endangering the unity and integrity of the country.[55] Commenting on the Akali demand to establish friendly relationships with the neighbouring states, the opposition blamed that Akalis wanted to make Pakistan a safe haven for the Sikh extremists to run the anti-national activities. In support of their argument, they quoted the appeal of the Sikh hardliner Jagjit Singh Chauhan on Pakistan radio during war in 1971. Chauhan had exhorted the Sikhs of Punjab to revolt against the coercive authority of India and only two years later, the Akalis passed the Anandpur Sahib Resolution.[56] Instead of addressing the genuine grievances of the Punjab in general and Sikhs in particular, the central government took certain decisions which were perceived by the Akalis as highly detrimental to the economic interests of the Sikhs and Punjab. In 1974, Defence Ministry of India issued a circular that henceforth, the recruitment in the army would be made on the proportional basis rather than merit.[57] This provision was certainly bound to reduce the Sikh strength in the army from twenty per cent to just two per cent. The decision was dubbed by the Akalis as 'anti-Sikh' because the community was to suffer the most as it constitutes merely two percent of the total population of the country. The centralised political system and Unitarian tendencies in the Indian polity reached its zenith in 1975 with the imposition of national emergency.

Akali Dal launched Save Democracy Morcha to oppose the emergency. Revengefully, Prime Minister Indira Gandhi, violating the provisions of the Punjab Reorganisation Act 1966, ruled in 1976 that Punjab and Haryana would use the waters of Sutlej, Ravi and Beas in equal proportion.[58] The award was a grave violation of the Act as the Act had provided that movable and immovable property between Punjab and Haryana would be shared in the 60:40 ratios. Already, certain institutions were established by the central government which started working against the interests of the farmers. The Food Corporation of India procures food grains in an arbitrary manner and many times impose quality cuts. The Agricultural Costs and Price Commission was set up in 1965 to advise the central government in fixing the prices of food grains. The farmers have no role in the fixation of price of their food grains. There is also Central Water Commission and Central Electricity Authority, whose prior sanction is necessary for a state to set up new irrigation and electricity projects.[59] The Thein Dam project, considered vital for the agricultural economy of Punjab, was submitted to the centre in 1964 but was not cleared for two decades.[60] The Former Prime Minister Inder Kumar Gujral revealed that Punjab was often discriminated by the central government while allocating big industries to the states. He shared that during his brief tenure as Minister in the Ministry of Planning in 1976, five additional Sugar Mills were sanctioned to Punjab which after his departure to Moscow, were reallocated to some adjoining states.[61]

The central government passed 42nd amendment in 1976 whereby the subject of education was transferred from State List to the Concurrent List. The amendment was conceived by the Sikh leadership as the most dangerous and detrimental to the interests of the minorities and various nationalities.[62] Anti-Sikh stance of the central government of the Congress Party in the Sikh-Nirankari clash (13 April 1978) assured the Akalis that Congress is out to push the Sikhs to the wall and reduce their homeland Punjab to a marginal position.

The Akali Dal reverted to the demand for greater autonomy to the states in 1978 as the party believed that it is the highly centralised political system which is responsible for all the miseries of the states and the minority communities. The Anandpur Sahib Resolution, as passed in 1973, was adopted by the General House of the Akali Dal at Ludhiana conference on 28-29 October 1978. Moving a political resolution in this conference, SGPC President and Akali leader Gurcharan Singh Tohra held that the federalisation of the Indian polity is essential "for preserving and safeguarding the being and self-identity of the nations and nationalities that collectively make the Indian people."[63] He said that "India is a country characterised by religious, cultural, ethnic and linguistic diversity. This diversity is reflected in the variety of nations, nationalities and minorities living in India.... But the majoritarian approach has unleashed centrifugal tendencies as a sanction against it. If we really seek a genuine national integration, conditions must be created wherein our nations, minorities and nationalities would get woven into the national fabric while keeping intact their identity. The requisite conditions can be created only in the form of a pluralistic society which is by its very nature demands a federal framework. It is only in such a federal set up that the Sikh community which is a nation, sui-generis, as well as a national minority and other nations, nationalities and minorities can hope to keep their identity intact."[64] Clarifying the meaning of autonomy, Tohra said:

"The question of autonomy is not at all that of merely placing additional resources at the disposal of the states, giving the units some more say at the decision-making levels and in the planning process. The crux of the matter is that political sovereignty is not the prerogative, predicate, attribute or quality of the Centre alone; both the Centre and states must share the political sovereignty in a coordinate manner. Seen from this angle, the case for autonomy to the states is essentially a question of creating and realising a true federal polity".[65]

To give a true federal shape to the Indian polity, Tohra suggested certain measures which sought the inclusion of the term 'federal' in the Preamble of the Indian Constitution, redistribution of subjects between the centre and states, assigning residuary powers to the states, ensuring impartial role of the governor, establishment of a democratic government when constitutional machinery breaks down in the states, decentralisation of financial powers and reactivation of the Finance Commission.[66] Another Akali faction, Akali dal (Talwandi) put forth another version of the Anandpur Sahib Resolution at a World Sikh Convention, held at Anandpur Sahib in April 1981. The resolution said, "an autonomous region in the north of India should be set up wherein the Sikh interests are constitutionally recognised as of primary and special importance."[67] The demand was based on the assurance of the Prime Minister Nehru, as made to the Sikhs in July 1946. The resolution further added, "The Sikh autonomous region may be conceded and allowed to frame its own constitution."[68]

The provisions regarding the federalisation of the Indian polity as included in the Anandpur Sahib Resolution had nothing to do with separation or disintegration. But due to its theo-political ideology, it became a potent weapon in the hands of the anti-Akali forces to beat the drum that Akalis are separatists. To setlle down the dust, Akali Dal (Longowal) President Sant Harchand Singh Longowal released an authenticated version of Anandpur Sahib Resolution in November 1982. Justifying the resolution in the Indian Parliament, Longowal said that "resolution was nothing more than a device to guard against the danger of further encroachments through repeated and ill-conceived amendments of the Constitution by which provincial powers have been curtailed by the central government against the spirit of a truly federal Constitution. He categorically denied that the resolution envisaged a separate or even an autonomous Sikh state and was only meant for better readjustment of centre-state relations."[69]

The Akali demand for state autonomy at this stage was not without sound reasons. In the beginning of 1980, the central government dismissed the Akali government of Parkash Singh Badal without any substantial ground. The motive behind dismissal was to clear the path for the establishment of the Congress government in the state. The Congress government of Darbara Singh proved merely an agent of the central government so far as the protection of the interests of Punjab were concerned. In 1981, Prime Minister Indira Gandhi persuaded Punjab Chief Minister Darbara Singh to sign an agreement with the Haryana and Rajasthan states. The River Water Agreement (1981)* allowed the non-riparian states to exploit the river waters of Punjab. The agreement was taken as a huge setback to the economic interests of the farming community of the state. The economic and political issues soon got coloured with the religion. In 1981, the central government banned the wearing of Kirpan (sword) by the Sikhs during flights. The decision was taken as an attack on the religious freedom of the Sikhs. Under Article 25 of the Indian Constitution, Sikhs have been allowed to carry Kirpan as it is an integral part of the external five Sikh symbols. The grievances of the Sikhs became manifold with the passage of the time as the central government paid no heed to remove such real or perceived grievances. To get the Sikh grievances redressed, Akali Dal submitted a charter of demands to the central government in September-October 1981. The acceptance of such demands was considered vital for the survival of the distinct and corporate identity of the Sikhs. The important demands included - to grant Holy City status to Amritsar, Installation of Radio station at Harmandir Sahib for the relay of Kirtan, permission to carry Kirpan during flights, the enactment of the All India Gurudwara Act, Amendment to Art 25(2) (b), recognition to the personal law of the Sikhs and acceptance of the Anandpur Sahib Resolution.[70]

Several rounds of conversations took place between the Akalis and the central government in 1981 and 1982 but concrete solution could not come out. Akalis launched Dharam Yudh Morcha (Religious war) in August 1982 to pressurize the government to accept the Akali demands. During the morcha, Akali Dal (Logowal) President Harchand Singh Longowal submitted a memorandum called 'you Owe Justice to Us', to the members of the Indian Parliament. The memorandum stated that "India is a multi-national, multi-lingual and multi-religious land. In such a land, a microscopic minority like the Sikhs have genuine forebodings that they may lose their identity in the vast ocean of the overwhelming Hindu majority. Their misgivings are heightened by arbitrary manner in which they are defined as Hindus under Art 25 of the Constitution."[71] Longowal argued that the only safeguard against such a threat is the implementation of the Anandpur Sahib Resolution which seeks to establish true federal polity in India.

During the Year of 1983, the situation in Punjab deteriorated day by day. The growing cult of violence among the Sikh militants and killings of innocent people led to Operation Blue Star in the first week of June 1984. The supreme Sikh temporal seat Akal Takhat in Amritsar was completely destroyed by the Indian army. To take revenge of this sacrilege, Prime Minister Indira Gandhi was killed by her two Sikh bodyguards on 31 October 1984. The death followed well organised riots against the Sikhs at Delhi and other places resulting in the killing of almost 3000 innocent Sikhs. The persecution consolidated the feelings of insecurity among the Sikhs and alienated them from the mainstream.[72] The new Prime Minister Rajiv Gandhi, emotionally charged over the death of her mother Indira Gandhi, dubbed the Anandpur Sahib Resolution as separatist charter. He compared the Anandpur Sahib Resolution with Lahore Resolution of the Muslim League (1940) which ultimately had led to the partition of the country.[73] In the wake of such criticism, Sant Harchand Singh Longowal had to clarify the content and nature of the Anandpur Sahib Resolution. He said, "let us make it clear once and for all that the Sikhs have no design to get away from India in any manner. What they simply want is that they should be allowed to live within India as Sikhs, free from all direct and indirect interference and tampering with their religious way of life.[74] Prime Minister Rajiv Gandhi realised that growing militancy in Punjab might endanger the unity and integrity of the country. Sensing the gravity of the situation, he signed 'Punjab Accord' with Harchand Singh Longowal in July 1985 to solve the Punjab problem. Under this accord, it was agreed that the Anandpur Sahib Resolution would be referred to the Sarkaria Commission, the stance which was denied earlier.

The Anandpur Sahib Resolution as submitted to the Sarkaria Commission in 1985, sought restructuring of the Centre-State relations on true federal lines. The resolution also reminded the Commission of promises, Nehru had made to the Sikhs and the minorities that they would be co-sharers in the political sovereignty of free India and that they would have full opportunity for preserving their identity as well as all avenues for autonomous self development.[75]

The resolution also suggested certain measures for the realisation of the genuine federal setup in India. For this, it sought the incorporation of the word 'Federation' in the Preamble of the Indian Constitution, Centre's inability to destroy or dilute the ethnic and cultural identity of the federating units, redistribution of subjects between the Centre and states, residuary powers with the states, equal representation to the states in the upper house irrespective of their size and population, impartial role of the Governor, immediate provision of elections in the states if constitutional machinery breaks down, federalisation of financial powers to lessen the financial dependence of the states over the Centre, reactivation of the constitutional duties of the Finance Commission, deletion of the directive powers of the centre and decentralisation of the planning process.[76] The memorandum also urged the Commission that all Punjabi speaking areas which were left out during the reorganisation of Punjab (1966), should be included in the Punjab. The Memorandum further said that "in this new Punjab and in other states, the Centre's jurisdiction should be restricted to defence, foreign affairs, currency and general communications. All other subjects should be transferred to Punjab and other states which would be fully entitled to frame their own laws on such transferred subjects.[77]

While making recommendations in 1987, Sarkaria Commission toed the line of the nationalist forces, putting the unity and integrity above all other considerations. It recommended nothing which could go against the idea of a strong Centre. The Commission noted that history of this vast sub-continent proves that centralisation has triggered a chain reaction of divisive forces, while a strong Centre with paramount powers, was the essential condition for protecting the unity and integrity of the country."[78] However, the Commission issued certain guidelines to regulate the partisan behaviour of the governor, to check the misuse of Article 356, to decentralise the planning process and lessen the financial dependence of the states over the Centre. The question of growing alienation and subsequent assertions of the minority communities in India remained untouched by the Commission. The Commission should have addressed the question of minorities and suggest how the feelings of alienation among them can be removed. The Commission thought otherwise and concluded that "While the union-state relations were intended to be worked on the basis of cooperative federalism and consensus in all areas of common interest, they have not been so worked and the forums envisaged by the Constitution for that purpose have been established.[79] The constitution is basically sound and has all flexibility to meet the variety of exigencies but it has not worked on the principles of cooperative federalism and consensus.

The recommendations of the Commission were not at par with the expectations of Akali Dal. Above all, it recommended nothing which could provide a needful security to the minorities like Sikhs who had genuine fears about the continuity and survival of their distinct identity in the vast ocean of Hinduism. The state oppression on innocent Sikh youth during militancy phase (1978-1993), further heightened the fear-psychosis among the community members. The inability of the central government to ward off such apprehensions had resulted in the popularity of the radical elements within the Akalis. The protagonists of the separate Sikh state in the form of Khalistan gained currency during the militancy phase. In the 1989 Lok Sabha elections, Simranjit Singh Mann, a staunch supporter of the Khalistan, along with other radical bodies like AISSF, won 9 Lok Sabha seats out of the total 13 seats in Punjab. Mann expressed doubts about the survival of the Sikhs in Hindu dominated India. In a memorandum to the Prime Minister Chander Shekhar during latter's visit to Punjab on 28 December 1990, he justified the demand of the Sikhs for the right to self-determination, describing Sikhs as 'colonial subjects' under the government of India.[80] In 1994, Akali Dal of Simranjit Singh Mann held a convention at Amritsar to discuss the Sikh problems and find out the ways to secure their religious and cultural rights in the future. At the conclusion of the convention, a declaration was issued which sought to make India a confederation. The Amritsar Declaration envisaged that "there is a great importance of separate region for the Sikhs because their aspirations can be realised only with the creation of such an area. The Akali Dal feels that India is a sub-continent, consisting of various nations and cultures, each one with distinct heritage. This sub-continent needs restructuring of its polity into a confederation of various cultures. If the Indian government fails to establish such a confederation, then Akali Dal would be left with no other alternative, but to wage a struggle for a sovereign Sikh state."[81]

With the return of normalcy in the state, the idea of sovereign Sikh state holds no ground among the Sikhs. But, the Akali demand for state autonomy is still alive. In 2000, the Government of India constituted a National Constitutional Commission to Review the Working of the Indian Constitution. Akali Dal (Badal) reiterated the demand for the establishment of a true federal system. It also sought the deletion of the word Sikh from Art 25(2) (b) of the Indian Constitution which clubs Sikhs with Hindus. The provision gives the wrong impression about the independent identity of the Sikhs. The sovereign doctrinal identity of Sikhs, which distinguish it from Hinduism, has been affected by this provision and a question mark has been put on its independent status as a religion in the comity of religions of the world. Akali Dal argued that Sikhs have separate identity from Hindus and hence should not be clubbed with Hindus.[82] Akali Dal has reiterated its demand for state autonomy during the Lok Sabha Elections of 2009. In its election Manifesto, Akali Dal promised the setting up of truly federal structure which is the only guarantor of national unity and prosperity on the one hand and strong, prosperous and confident minorities on the other. Centre-State relations would be recast in a manner that the states shall have full opportunities for the cultural growth and development of their respective regions.[83]

Thus, the Akali demand for state autonomy has its roots in the early fifties. Since partition, they have always been in search of a political set-up which could be helpful in maintaining and preserving the distinct culture and religion of the Sikhs. Whenever the ideological and physical attacks on Sikhs and their religion took place, the Akalis always raised the issue of state autonomy and sought the establishment of an autonomous area within the Indian Union where the Sikh religion and culture could be protected. Akali Dal firmly believes that only a true federal setup can produce conducive environment for the preservation and full development of the minorities. The Akali demand for state autonomy has met with severe criticism at the hands of the nationalist forces which dubbed the demand as a step forward towards separate Sikh state. However, the Akali Dal thinks otherwise and argues that full avenues for the growth of the minorities would certainly strengthen the country. The past experience has shown that whenever the dominant majority or the Indian state tried to reabsorb the minorities like Sikhs in the name of promoting nationalism, the move proved counterproductive. The solution of the socio-religious, cultural, economic and political problems of the minorities like Sikhs lies only in the establishment of the genuine federal polity.

NOTES

1. Roger Scruton, *A Dictionary of Political Thought,* London : Macmillan,1984, p. 33.
2. Yog Raj Sharma, "Anatomy of the Autonomy" paper presented in a Seminar on "Autonomy" organised by the Department of Political Science, University of Jammu, 18-20 February 2000, p.1.
3. Prabha Dutta, *Regionalisation and Indian Politics,* New Delhi: Sterling Publishers, 1993, p. 95.
4. As cited in John Armstrong, "Nations before Nationalism" in John Hutchinson and Anthony D. Smith, ed., *Nationalism,* New York: Oxford University Press, p. 141.

5. Anthony D. Smith, *The Ethnic Origins of Nations,* New York: Basil Blackwell Limited, 1986, pp. 14-30.

6. Chandra Pal, *State Autonomy in Indian Federation: Emerging Trends,* New Delhi: Deep and Deep, 1984 p. 47.

7 *Ibid,* p. 49.

* The Eight States were Bihar, West Bengal, Kerala, Tamil Nadu, Orissa, Punjab, Rajasthan and U.P.

8. Dalip Singh, "Restructuring our Federal Polity: Need for Fresh Perspective on Autonomy", *The Tribune,* 6 August 2000.

9. S.S. Tiwana, "Centre-State Relations in India: A Plea for State Autonomy", *Punjab Journal of Politics,* Vol. XXVI, No. 1, 2002, p. 12.

10. *Ibid,* p. 17.

11. *Ibid,* p. 19.

12. *The Report of the State Autonomy Committee,* Jammu, April 1999, pp. 89-105.

13. As Cited in Gopal Singh, "Complexities of the Question of Sikh Nationality", *Punjab Journal of Politics,* Vol. XVIII, No. 2, 1993, p. 66.

14. Paul Wallace, "Sikh Minority Attitudes in India's Federal System" in Joseph T.O. Connell, ed., *Sikh History and Religion in the Twentieth Century,* New Delhi: Manohar Publishers, 1990, p. 271.

15. K.R. Bombwall, "Akali Demand for State Autonomy: Nature, Rationale and Motivation", *Political Science Review,* Vol. 20, Nos. 1-2, 1981, p. 152.

16. J.S. Grewal, "Sikh Identity, The Akalis and Khalistan" in J.S. Grewal and Indu Banga, ed., *Punjab in Prosperity and Violence: Administration, Politics and Social Change 1947-1997,* Chandigarh: K.K. Publishers, 1998, p. 69.

17. Gurdarshan Singh Dhillon, "Evolution of the Demand for Sikh Homeland", *Indian Journal of Political Science,* Vol. XXXV, No. 4, October-December 1974, p. 363.

* Nehru Report refers to the report of the Committee which was set up by the Congress Party in 1928 with Moti Lal Nehru as its chairman to consider and determine the principles of the future Constitution of India.

18. Kailash Chander Gulati, *The Akalis : Past and Present,* New Delhi: Atlantic Publishers, 1974, p. 38.

19. *Ibid.,* p. 42.

20. Devender Singh Duggal, *The Truth About the Sikhs,* Amritsar: SGPC, n.d., p. 18.

21. Sangat Singh, *The Sikhs in History,* New Delhi : Uncommon Books, 2001, p. 202.

22. Rajinder Kaur, *Sikh Identity and National Integration,* New Delhi: Intellectual Publishing House, 1992, p. 47.

23. "Great Betrayal of the Sikhs", a speech in Parliament by Sardar Kapur Singh on 6 September 1966 rejecting the Punjab Reorganisation Bill Chandigarh: Shankar Printing Press, n.d., pp. 3-4.

24. Gurmit Singh, *History of Sikh Struggles,* Vol. II, New Delhi: Atlantic Publishers, 1991, p. 284.

25. *Jawaharlal Nehru's Speeches,* Vol. I, September 1946 to May 1949, Government of India: Ministry of Information and Broadcasting, 1949, p. 6.

26. A.S. Narang, Storm over the Sutlej, New Delhi : Geetanjali Publishing House, 1983, p. 96.

27. As quoted in, Satya M. Rai, *Partition of the Punjab,* Bombay: Asia Publishing House, 1965, p. 225.

* The Seven Districts included Hoshiarpur, Jalandhar, Ludhiana, Amritsar, Ferozepur, Gurdaspur and Ambala.

28. Ajit Singh Sarhadi, *Punjabi Sube Di Gatha* (Punjabi), (Punjabi Suba- A Story), Sarhind: Lok Geet Parkashan, p. 166, 1992, p. 166. Also see Rajiv A. Kapur, *Sikh Separatism: The Politics of Faith,* London: Allen and Unwin, 1986, p. 210.

29. Harchand Singh Longowal, "Why the Sikhs Seek Amendment in Article 25 of the Constitution of India", Published by Gurcharan Singh, Secretary, Shiromani Akali Dal, n.d., p. 4.

30. Sarhadi, n. 28, pp. 236-238.

* PEPSU was formed in 1948 by merging the Sikh princely states like Nabha, Patiala, Jind, Kapurthala and Malerkotla.

31. Rai, n. 27, pp. 236-237.

32. Baldev Raj Nayar, *Minority Politics in the Punjab,* New Jersey: Princeton University Press, 1966, p. 53.

33. M.J. Akbar, *India: The Seize Within,* New Delhi: UBSPD, 1996, p. 151.

34. Nayar, n. 32, p. 232.

* The members of the Regional Committees consisted of MLAs from the respective regions. The committees were assigned 14 subjects on which they could initiate legislative proposals dealing with social and economic development of the concerned areas.

35. Gulati, n. 18, p. 150.

36. Rai, n. 27, p. 246.

37. Gurmit Singh, *History of Sikh Struggles,* Vol. 1, New Delhi: Atlantic Publishers, 1989, p. 123.

38. Jaswant Singh Mann, *Some Documents on the Demand for Sikh Homeland,* Chandigarh: Manjit Printing and Publishing Company, n.d., p. 97.

* These areas included Dalhousie, Chandigarh, Pinjore, Kalka, Ambala City, Una, Shahbad block of District Karnal, Sub Tehsils of Guhla and Tohana, Rattia block of District Hissar, Sirsa and Ganganagar.

39. Kaur, n. 22, p. 62.

40. Gurdarshan Singh Dhillon, *India Commits Suicide,* Chandigarh: Singh and Singh Publishers, 1992, p. 28.

41. Bombwall, n. 15, p. 155.

42. As quoted in Ajit Singh, *Shiromani Akali Dal: Religio-Political Study,* Kapurthala: Arman Publications, 2005, p. 106.

* United Front was the Conglomeration of Akali Dal (Sant), Akali Dal (Master), Jana Sangh, CPI, CPM, SSP and PSP.

43. Dalip Singh, *Punjab Diyan Millian Jullian Sarkaraan* (Coalition Governments of Punjab), in Punjabi, Patiala: Publication Bureau, 1996, p. 118.
44. Devender Singh, *Akali Politics in Punjab (1964-1985),* New Delhi: National Book Organisation, 1993, p. 137.
45. Mann, n. 38, p. 78.
46. *Ibid*, p. 59.
47. Khushwant Singh, *A History of the Sikhs: 1839-1988,* Vol. 2, New Delhi: Oxford University Press, 1999, p. 343.
48. *The Draft of the New Policy Programme of the Shiromani Akali Dal,* Amritsar: Jaspal Printing Press, 1977, p. 16.
49. *Ibid.*
50. *Ibid*, p. 20.
51. *Ibid*, p. 21.
52. *Ibid.*
53. K.R. Bombwal, "Sikh Identity and Federal Polity: A Critique of Akali Position" in Gopal Singh, ed., *Punjab Today,* New Delhi: Intellectual Publishing House, 1987, p. 160.
54. As cited in Singh, n. 42, p. 114.
55. Harkishan Singh, Surjit, *Deepening Punjab Crisis: A Democratic Solution,* New Delhi, Patriot Publishers, 1992, p. 123.
56. A.C. Kapoor, *The Punjab Crisis,* New Delhi: S. Chand and Company, 1985, p. 197.
57. Singh, n. 24, p. 33.
58. Dhillon, n. 40, p. 50.
59. "Punjab Government Memorandum" in Report of the *Commission on Centre-State Relations,* Government of India Press, Part II, Nasik, 1987, pp. 901-904.
60. Dhillon, n. 40, p. 97.
61. *Ibid*, p. 71.
62. M.S. Dhami, "Political Parties and State Autonomy Issue: A Case Study of Akali Party", in K.R. Bombwal, ed., *National*

Power and State Autonomy, Meerut: Meenakshi Parkashan, 1977, p. 157.

63. *Federal Polity,* Speech of S. Gurcharan Singh Tohra, delivered on 29th October 1978 at the All India Akali Conference held at Ludhiana, Amritsar, 1978, p. 3.

64. *Ibid,* p. 6.

65. *Ibid,* p. 12.

66. *Ibid,* pp. 13-15.

67. Government of India, *White Paper on the Punjab Agitation,* New Delhi, 1984, p. 6.

68. *Ibid.*

69. Singh, n. 47, p. 345.

* The agreement was signed in November 1981 between Punjab, Haryana and Rajasthan on the insistence of the Prime Minister Indira Gandhi. Under this agreement, 1.32 m.a.f. surplus water was recorded in the rivers of Punjab, was shared between the Punjab and Rajasthan. Punjab was given 0.72 m.a.f. whereas Rajasthan was given 0.60. It was also agreed that Satluj Yamuna Link Canal would be constructed within two years to divert the river waters of Punjab to Haryana.

70. White Paper, n. 67, pp. 31-35.

71. As cited in Mark Tully and Satish Jacob, *Amritsar: Mrs. Gandhi's Last Battle,* Calcutta: Rupa and Company, 1985, p. 51.

72. Satya M. Rai, "The Structure of Regional Politics in Punjab", in Paul Wallace and Surendera Chopra, ed., *Political Dynamics and Crisis in Punjab,* Amritsar: Guru Nanak Dev University, 1988, p. 353.

73. Singh, n. 24, p. 28.

74. Harnik Deol, *Religion and Nationalism in India: The Case of the Punjab,* London: Routledge, 2000, p. 102.

75. "Anandpur Sahib Resolution" as submitted by Akali Dal to *Commission on Centre-State Relations,* n.59, p. 859.

76. *Ibid.*

77. *Ibid.*

78. Report of the *Commission on Centre-State Relations,* Government of India Press, Part 1, Nasik, 1987, p. 5.

79. *Ibid,* p. 18.

80. Singh, n. 42, p. 126.

81. As cited in Kuldip Kaur, *Akali Dal in Punjab Politics: Splits and Mergers,* New Delhi: Deep & Deep Publications, 1999, pp. 195-196.

82. *Proposals of the Shiromani Akali Dal Submitted to the National Commission to Review the Working of the Constitution,* pp. 19-21.

83. Election Manifesto of Shiromani Akali Dal, issued during Lok Sabha Elections of 2009, pp. 22-26.

7

Self-Rule and Autonomy: Politics of Contestation in Jammu and Kashmir

Gull Wani

India and Pakistan have traditionally pursued policies on Kashmir around their concerns regarding territoriality and sovereignty. In recent years more so during General Musharraf's tenure as Pakistan president dialogue and peace process helped the stakeholders to make an incremental shift towards people-centric approach. The people to people contact, trade and flow of new ideas have made it possible to evolve new and innovative approaches to conflict resolution. In December 2006, General Musharraf offered out of box options to Kashmir conflict and specified that Kashmir will have same borders and regions their self-governance. In Jammu and Kashmir state it generated renewed debate on autonomy or Self-rule within and between parties particularly two regional parties which forms the subject matter of this paper. The two main regional political parties i.e., National Conference (NC) and People's Democratic Party (PDP) have come out with documents to build up the public opinion and also offer solution to the vexed issue.

In the above context two issues that crop up and need to be examined are: (a) the National Conference's formulation of greater autonomy in the backdrop of its critical scrutiny by PDP, (b) the PDP's Self-rule formulation and see as to what extent it is different from the greater autonomy. My objective is limited to the extent of examining the two questions at an academic level and see how autonomy and self-rule can be applied as formulations for conflict resolution in Jammu and Kashmir.

Conceptual Frame: Both self-rule and autonomy are most sought after and resisted devices for conflict resolution in many parts of the world where conflicts have become intractable for internal and external reasons. Despite their popularity, both formulations are controversial and many conflicts are themselves about the demand for and resistance to them. Both formulations seem to offer a way out of the conflict and secure some breathing space as an interim or even ambiguous expedient while long term solutions are explored and negotiated. The fact that states which already have some form of autonomy or where autonomy has failed are still engaged in new forms of autonomy shows the dynamic nature of autonomy and self-rule formulations. The assertion by PDP that autonomy is no constitutional word and is a political slogan amounts to imposing unnecessary political limitation on it. In the Political Science lexicon self-rule and autonomy are very often used inter-changeably. The difference lies only in context, emphasis and extension of these formulations at a specific time and location. The word autonomy means living under ones own laws. Hence, it refers to self-rule. Autonomy is a means of distribution of power in order to preserve the unity of a state and its population. Pervez Musharraf himself treated the two concepts synonymously. Eminent Jurist Thomas D Musgrave also holds that, "Autonomy involves self-governance for a specific part of the population of a state within which it may be established on either a territorial or personal basis." He further argued, "....it should be considered as an alternative form of self-determination in international law".[1] A Finnish Jurist Professor Suksi Markku considers "autonomy as self-governance" because "autonomy culminates in the question of self governance".[2] Many experts including A.G. Noorani regard the autonomous province of South Tyrol as a model of self-governance. In contemporary times the right to self-determination has increasingly been re-interpreted in terms of internal constitutional orders for political and autonomy rights of minorities. Such a view of self-determination has some support in certain national constitutions as well. A number of constitutions now recognise an entitlement to self-governance, such as the Philippines in relation to its indigenous people and the Muslim minority. Spain also guarantees autonomy to certain regions and invites others to negotiate with the centre for autonomy. The constitution of Ethiopia gives its nations, nationalities and people the right to seek wide ranging powers as states within a federation. The fact that the self-rule formulation has come from general Musharraf and had larger impact and coverage has evoked interest even in the separatist camp. The chairman of Hurriyat Conference (M), Mirwaiz Farooq believes that self-rule cannot be the final solution of the Kashmir issue but a step forward towards a solution. He said, "Self-governance can never be a final solution. It can be a confidence-building measure like the demilitarisation, towards a solution" (*Kashmir Times*, Jan 1, 2006).

PDP's Self-Rule Framework: It was in October 2008 that PDP came out with a document on self-rule entitled as *"Jammu and Kashmir: The Self-Rule Framework for Resolution"*. The party recognises that we are living through a period in which definitions of cultures, societies, sovereignty and nationality are changing very rapidly and radically. In fact, the party factors its self-rule formulation in the shifting notions of politics and economics in contemporary world order. This position of the party has also intellectual support at the global level. It was possible through this vision that in Europe, the Basque in Spain, the Italian Catalan, and the Irish IRA militants have been reduced to non-entities under the secular umbrella of the European Union. In the unique context of shifting economic landscape through globalisation, Strobe Talbott (former US Deputy Secretary of State) also called for resolving conflicts based on a yearning for self-determination by combining "the promotion of democracy on the part of the central government with an effort to help would be break-away areas benefit from cross-border economic development and political co-operation". The PDP's comprehensive formulation of self-rule has three sub-components:[3]

(i) A new political super-structure that integrates the region and empowers sub-regions. The centrepiece of the governance structure under self-rule is the cross-border institution of Regional Council of Greater Jammu and Kashmir.

(ii) A phased economic integration that transcends borders. A critical element of self-rule is the economic integration across the line of control.

(iii) Constitutional restructuring that ensures sharing of sovereignty without compromising political sovereignty of either nation state. For self-rule to operate effectively, Articles 356, 249 of the Indian constitution, the Sixth amendment to the state constitution and All India Services Act, 1951 are to be rolled back. Further, it is a part of the design of self-rule that Head of the State be elected from the regions of Jammu and Kashmir by rotation.

In the PDP Executive Committee meeting on 23rd January, 2006 Vice-president, Mr. Muzaffar Beigh claimed that self-rule is not autonomy as is being projected by certain quarters. To him autonomy is no constitutional phrase and is only a political slogan. From PDP standpoint, autonomy has nothing to empower people and is merely an arrangement between the National Conference and the Centre. It has no economic content. Contrary to it, self-rule, PDP claims could re-define the political and economic relationship of the state with India and Pakistan without compromising on the sovereignty of both the countries. In fact, in the self-rule document, the party claims that self-rule refers to autonomy from the nation-state of India, whereas autonomy connotes relative autonomy from the Government of India. The party further claims that autonomy refers to empowerment of the Government of Jammu and Kashmir vis-à-vis the Government of India whereas self-rule refers to empowerment of the people of Jammu and Kashmir.

There are certain compulsions for PDP to appear different and also to project its formulation differently as it has cast itself as an alternative regional party to National Conference. Since the social and electoral base of the National Conference and the PDP are almost same, the obvious battle lines are being drawn along the lines of self-rule and greater autonomy. The People's Democratic Party has taken the cue from General Musharraf's "out of box solution syndrome". He stressed innovative ideas and on many occasions ruled out accession of Kashmir to Pakistan and independent Kashmir as solutions to the Kashmir tangle. Second, PDP's linking of self-rule and self-reliance is broadly connected with assertion of newly emerging socio-economic groups making their presence felt on the chessboard of political landscape. These groups and marginalised categories are challenging the old and entrenched politico-economic formations that came into prominence in the aftermath of power transition of 1947. Third, PDP's look different approach is also to occupy the space of separatist political formations particularly of the moderate type which too have been supportive of General Musharraf's flexible approach on Jammu and Kashmir.

But, all these/this should not distract our attention from a certain ambiguity which PDP is making use of in the messy and changing political scenario of the state. Let it be clear as claimed by eminent jurist A.G. Noorani, "Self-rule or autonomy is defined according to the situation, whether of a people or tribe or a people within a territory". The ambiguity in PDP formulation is obvious if we may consider the following points. First, the political superstructure outlined by PDP suggests a Regional Council of Greater Jammu and Kashmir with 50 members. The respective state assembles of J and K and Pakistan-Administered Kashmir (PAK) shall elect 40 members. The remaining 10 members will be nominated, five each by the governments of India and Pakistan. Such a politico-constitutional engineering required that the document of self-rule should have been equally debated and discussed in the PAK with political parties and other groups. The party as such does not make any reference to that anywhere in the document. It is probably because of this neglect that there has been no clear response to it in the other part at the level of political leadership or at the level of civil society. Second, the PDP has erected its formula of self-rule on a high pedestal by talking about issues like sharing of sovereignty and trans-border arrangements. The party probably pins its hope on the growing India-Pakistan cordiality and does not recognise the need for an India-Pakistan agreement on such a formulation. Many experts dealing with South Asia have realised the need for such an agreement. A.G. Noorani in this regard states, "Experience has amply demonstrated the futility of a New Delhi-Srinagar accord without a prior India-Pakistan accord. The intra-Kashmir talks will get nowhere without such a roadmap agreed between India and Pakistan". The fact is that autonomy has been a cause of great contention because it is associated with assertions or qualifications on the state sovereignty. Autonomy becomes less problematic, if it can be disassociated from sovereignty. China's official position is that it would be prepared to discuss autonomy for Tibet if the Dalai Lama acknowledged that Tibet was an inalienable part of China. The success of autonomy negotiations may therefore, depend on diffusing, fragmenting or fudging sovereignty. It is here that the PDP document is silent and does not suggest as to how self-rule formulation can be worked out in its external domain without India and Pakistan adhering to certain ground rules to be outlined in a bilateral agreement. Third, the PDP on several occasions has come out squarely for the protection of autonomy as guaranteed under Article 370. On one occasion its vice-president Muzaffar Beigh claimed that autonomy and self-rule are same. Mehbooba Mufti has on several occasions' castigated leaders who, in her view, were responsible for making erosions in Article 370. She and her party took a stand on 'Jammu and Kashmir Resettlement Bill' which party found perfectly in the domain of special constitutional position of the state. The PDP in its document has also taken a strong position on Article 370 and its temporary nature. The party considers the Article as a permanent feature of the constitution of India and believes that its abrogation will have serious consequences even on the accession of the state to the Indian Union. Lately, the Justice Saghir Committee on Centre-State relations submitted its report to the state Chief Minister. Interestingly, the report presents greater autonomy and self-rule as almost synonymous.

National Conference and its Autonomy Framework: In order to traverse the odyssey of the National Conference on autonomy issue, one comes across four phases through which it has gone: (a) autonomy up to the time Article 370 was adopted, (b) from 1949-1953, (c) autonomy from 1953-75 and (d) the struggle for autonomy from 1996 to the present. During all these phases, both autonomy and economic self-reliance remained central to the party's ideology and politics. Though there was politico-ideological affinity between the NC and the Indian National Congress even before independence; the leadership of the former never wanted a constitutional arrangement that would either obliterate the autonomous legacy of the freedom struggle of Kashmir or tamper with their vision of 'Naya Kashmir' as envisaged in 1944 plan of the party. Thus, the National Conference favoured accession with autonomy. Sheikh Abdullah stated, "Central leadership wanted our complete merger but our special circumstances and objectives of our movement did not allow it". Again National Conference leaders did not want an instrument of accession that would exceed the items which had been transferred to the Centre under the Instrument of Accession. The state was accorded a special status under Article 370 of the Indian constitution and on 26th January 1950, the first (Application to J and K) order was made by the President of India strictly in accordance with the Instrument of Accession. The remaining powers were left for the state to take care of in its own constitution. The National Conference under Abdullah and Jawaharlal Nehru were instrumental in hastening the process for a variety of internal and external reasons. The PDP criticism against National Conference is valid to the extent that the autonomy arrangement was largely premised on the understanding reached between the National Conference and the Centre and probably not based on wider consensus. The point to be noted is that those were the times of one dominant party system both at Centre and in the State. In fact, experience globally suggests that autonomy arrangements which have been negotiated in a democratic and participatory way have a better chance of success than those which are imposed. Many systems of autonomy that were established in the dying days of colonialism were arbitrary than negotiated in an inclusive fashion. In most instances, members of groups for whose benefit autonomies were established had little understanding of the mechanisms to operate it. At best, the arrangements were inter-elite bargains. The PDP has a point when it refers to the Kashmir's autonomy debates as one in which regions were not sufficiently involved. But then the fault does not lie with the National Conference or its leader. The state was externally drawn into a larger conflict between India and Pakistan and there were strong voices for abrogation of Article 370 in different regions of the state internally. Jammu and Ladakh saw movements for application of the Constitution of India to the state in its entirety rather than positive movements for regional autonomy. All this should not make the PDP to conclude that internal autonomy addresses only Kashmiri sentiments. It needs to be reiterated that years latter in the State People's Convention convened in 1968 by Sheikh Abdullah the question of regional autonomy for regions was accepted, in principle, by the National Conference.

In the second phase of the autonomy movement (1948 to 1953) Sheikh Abdullah headed the government as Prime Minister and was dismissed in 1953. A closer scrutiny of events suggests that the National Conference during this period fought singlehandedly both for the retention of autonomy and economic self-reliance of the state. Any serious student of political economy of the state will agree that the early edifice for a self-reliant state was erected by the National Conference through two of its revolutionary measures: the Big Landed Estates Abolition Act of 1950, through which land was transferred to the tiller and free education from primary to university levels. Sheikh Abdullah presided over a benevolent state acting in an optimal way to benefit the society as a whole. It was because of autonomy that land reforms in Jammu and Kashmir became possible without compensation. This was exactly the period when the Supreme Court of India struck down many land reforms related legislations in many states of India. Over and above, the hereditary rule was abolished and replaced by a constitutional head of the state. The first university was established and the government set up planning system modelled on the Soviet Union's five-year plans. However, from the point of view of democratic protestations, the government under the NC did not welcome organised opposition. It retained the powers of detention and suppression of hostile press comments. In retrospect, it needs to be emphasised that one of the important requirements for autonomy to be desirable and successful is that it needs a culture of democracy and accountability which was in deficit in the state at that point of time for obvious political reasons. Autonomy arrangements are most likely to succeed in states with established traditions of democracy and the rule of law. Autonomy arrangements require give and take; they depend on frequent negotiations for the adjustment of relationships or in the implementation of law. It is because of this that autonomy to be successful needs a certain political culture of democratic contestation and participation. Unfortunately, the transfer of power in 1947 never translated in the process of de-tribalisation and de-feudalisation of politics; so essential for autonomy arrangements to be successful in the state.

The third phase of autonomy (1953-75) saw its massive erosion and subversion of democracy and Kashmir Accord emerging out of long parleys. The accord was signed between same political parties and political dynasties which were active on state's political scene right from 1947. Indira Gandhi projected the 1975 Accord as a device to bring Sheikh Abdullah back to power. On the other hand, Sheikh described the Accord of 1975 as a change of strategy. From the constitutional point of view, the most important feature of the Accord was the Prime Minister's statement that the Article 370 has become a permanent feature of the constitution of India. Though Sheikh referred to the broken promises from time to time but his government mainly concentrated on building up of institutions and infrastructure in the state. Democracy was revived as became clear after 1977 elections, more so because there was hardly any section of political opinion not represented in the electoral process. Further, a Single Line Administration system too was introduced where district became the unit of planning and development. However, differences in the interpretation of events that took place in 1953 and thereafter became a source of constant irritation between Centre and the State. Even after the 1975 Accord, Sheikh Abdullah described the post-August 1953 period as a "dark patch of 23 years". Speaking in the border town of Mendhar in Jammu region of the state, Sheikh Abdullah said, "His whole being, body and spirit was lacerated with wounds". Further, looking from point of self-reliance, Sheikh Abdullah not only tried to do away with the 'subsidy culture' which he considered as a bribe but also tried to do away with the culture of economic populism which had taken roots as a part of New Delhi's policy of building up of a 'parasitic capitalism' whereby economic policies were determined by political motivations, causing unbalanced growth. Moreover, outside the politics of political parties either at state or central level, institutions like Supreme Court of India too recognised that internal autonomy as provided under Article 370 is no longer a political gimmick. In the 1984 case of Khazan Chand vs. the State of Jammu and Kashmir, the Supreme Court unambiguously held that the State holds "a special status in the constitutional set-up of the country". Keeping in view the unique position of the Jammu and Kashmir state, the Sarkaria Commission refrained from discussing J & K's distinct constitutional status because the question "bristles with political complexities and is not a mere legal issue".

The fourth phase of autonomy (since 1996) under the NC started in altogether different internal and external context. The years since 1990 had seen death and destruction in Kashmir and all that was achieved through the Kashmir Accord of 1975 was rolled back. The Burkina Faso declaration was the first public effort by an Indian Prime Minister after the onset of insurgency to review the Centre-State relations.

The declaration was followed by elections and restoration of the democratic process in the State. The 1996 elections in the state were contested by the NC and won 59 seats out of 87 on the plank of autonomy. This phase was also marked by a hot debate on Centre-State financial relations. Serious economic issues impinging on autonomy of the state came up for a lot of debate. Unlike in the first three phases, the fourth phase saw a change even in the configuration of power at the central level. With the growth of regional parties, India was increasingly moving towards political federalisation. Further, power at Delhi had started shifting towards the South. It was now a Prime Minister outside the Nehru Dynasty-Narasimha Rao who in 1995 announced that the Union government would be prepared to consider autonomy "short of Independence" for Jammu and Kashmir. Welcoming this on behalf of the National Conference, Dr Farooq Abdullah asked the Union Government to issue an order under Article 370 to restore the state's autonomy in terms of the Delhi agreement of 1952. The National Conference boycotted the parliamentary elections of 1996 when it found that the Government of India is no longer serious on the issue of autonomy. Finally, after forming the Government in the aftermath of 1996 assembly elections, the National Conference formed two committees on state and regional autonomy and passed a resolution on autonomy in the state legislature on June 26, 2000 which was rejected by the BJP led National Democratic Alliance at the Centre. The National Conference, however, continued to project autonomy formulation as a way to conflict resolution in Jammu and Kashmir and equated it with the self-rule formula of General Musharraf. Though the National Conference (NC) Autonomy Report says nothing about how the state can move towards financial autonomy, nevertheless, issues central to it were taken up by the Farooq Abdullah Government at several levels with the Government of India. Some of these issues like the status of the Indus Water Treaty transfer of Salal and Uri Power Projects to the state, security related expenditure, arrears accruing out of reversal of special category state status from the 1990s were very important. Further, it was during this phase that the state government undertook a mega-power project at Baglihar in the state sector.

However, there are three issues which sharply distinguish this phase from the earlier three phases. One, that there is a growing regional and sub-regional resentment in the state and political innocence of the earlier phases is over and hence the need for more accommodation and cooperation. Second, though NC's claim that it contested the 1996 elections on the plank of greater autonomy and won by a massive majority, there was a lack of consensus on this formulation amongst major players on Kashmir's political chess-board. Third, Jammu and Kashmir conflict has entered into that phase where parties and stakeholders have to move from competitive bargaining to distributive bargaining. All the three factors have added new dimensions to the whole problem. The NC may have to fine-tune its formulations keeping in view imperatives of globalisation on one hand and compulsions of borderless economy on the other. However, on internal dimension the NC report on greater autonomy is more radical and revolutionary compared to what PDP provides in its self-rule document.

There are different denunciations against the NC's autonomy formulation that it is a political gimmick and the party has certain has often trivialised the issue and not inculcated a political culture of accommodating dissent and inner party democracy. There was no point for the party to stay in alliance with the BJP-led NDA after the autonomy resolution was rejected by it. But certain mode and method of politics perpetuated by successive central governments in the aftermath of 1953 was quite harsh not only to Sheikh Abdullah but also to his party as well. To Sumantra Bose, "the prime reason for radicalisation of political dissent in

Indian Kashmir, culminating in insurrection in 1989-90, was the purposeful stifling of opposition within institutional politics by the Indian state, operating in collusion with local client elites, since 1950". In this connection, three things need to be underlined. First, in the post-1947 period successive central governments continued with the border state policy of erstwhile Britishers with regard to the Jammu and Kashmir state. The state was focused only from the national security angle. It was in this context that grant of the autonomous status was considered as serving "thin end of the secessionist wedge". Second, leaving aside greater autonomy for the state, even minimum political dissent and representative governments were not accommodated by the central governments. The National Conference-led governments bore all the brunt. After the 1983 elections, the National Conference won and its legislature party elected Farooq Abdullah as the leader and B.K. Nehru swore him as Chief Minister. But the governor learnt later from the Intelligence Bureau of India (IB) that M. L. Fotedar, an unconstitutional authority handling Kashmir affairs on behalf of Indira Gandhi, had rung up to say that B.K. Nehru had shown haste in accepting National Conference's letter electing Farooq as their leader. It is a huge political tragedy of the state that in spite of autonomy, state governments have been arbitrarily dismissed and political dissent obliterated from time to time. The principal reason for a refusal to restore autonomy is the fear that it will lead to secession. It, however, needs to be reiterated that autonomy brings secessionist claims to an end and strengthens the moderate element in all political formations. The breakup of the former Soviet Union and the federation of former Yugoslavia was the result of the failure to put in place a genuine federation. It is important that confidence between India and Pakistan grows and both states advance the cause of a non-territorial solution to the Kashmir problem. It is only then that self-rule or greater autonomy can be operated, otherwise, as Robert Wirsing claims, "Autonomy cannot be relied upon as the principal catalyst to usher in a new future for Jammu and Kashmir".[4]

NOTES

1. Thomas D. Musgrave; *Self-determination and National Minorities;* OUP; pp. 207-8.
2. Quoted by A. G. Noorani in "A Working Paper on Kashmir", *Frontline,* March 24, 2006, p. 51.
3. Jammu and Kashmir People's Democratic Party's *Jammu and Kashmir: The Self-Rule Framework For Resolution,* Srinagar October, 2008, pp. 57-60.
4. Robert Wirsing; *Kashmir in the Shadow of War,* p. 218.

8

Statehood Demands in Globalising India: Retrospect and Prospect

Guljit K. Arora

This chapter examines the issue of rising statehood demands in India while considering the historical context, factors that matter in the formation of states, and globalisation induced and the other socioeconomic-politico changes taking place in an interconnected manner in India's multicultural and democratic federal political economy.

The paper concludes that the simmering pressures for smaller administrative units viz. Bodoland, Bundelkhand, Coorg, Gorkhaland, Harit Pradesh, Koshalanchal, Mithilanchal, Saurastra, Telangana, Vidharbha etc. have to be studied carefully given that many states have been created in the past and some of these have performed well keeping in view the other developments. The country may consider making districts as politico-economic and administrative units while redrawing the administrative boundaries of the existing states to be further monitored by and placed under Regional Councils. But the everlasting solution lies in improving political culture at all levels, and early we do better it is.

The Context

After Independence on 15th August 1947, India - a union of States and a parliamentary system of government, adopted Constitution on 26th November 1949, which came into force on 26th January 1950 (Basu, 1983). Keeping in view the different goals enshrined in the Constitution in the background of colonial past and need to build up the nation, India moved ahead to structure its system of government based on principles of mixed economy.

The most immediate and the key task before Indian leaders was to consolidate, strengthen and preserve the unity and security of India, and project the nation state as an institution of social and economic transformation while fully recognising India's wide regional diversities with respect to cultural and socio-economic development variables. Retrospectively, in the post-independence period, from consolidating and strengthening Indian union to build up the nation state as an instrument of transformation, India has travelled a long way with the market preserving federal political economy system having inbuilt necessary capabilities to move further.

During the 60s and 70s, India followed the system of economic governance in the framework of centralised federalism, which produced positive results and also improved growth rates through macroeconomic situation deteriorated (Bagchi, 2008). However, the framework of centralised economic planning could not adequately provide a solution to the deep-rooted problems for the people of India. The social and political problems relating to caste, religion, regionalism, language etc constantly haunt the nation and in fact, has taken over the economic issues.[1]

By the end of 1980s, India witnessed severe economic imbalances both on internal and external fronts and had to adopt the process of liberalisation, privatisation and globalisation (hereafter LPG). This process has got deep historical roots and requires conscious human decisions to be taken in order to create more space for the private economy, and further integrate with the world (Arora: 2002). It works to ultimately influence each and every sector of the economy, and sets in motion all-round changes at all levels with far reaching implications for the people (Arora: 2009). At the receiving end, it is only the people who constitute those very entities and structures, and ultimately are the gainers or losers.

The three-tier federal structure validated by the written Constitution of India offers a great deal of administrative, economic and political freedom to the constituent units including redrawing the domestic political map. But the way political economy of the federation in India has worked over the period shows, states at times take unreasonable positions for economic and social gains and political accommodation.[2] This has become a common feature in the arena of coalition politics (Arora: 2004).

Pressures for new smaller political units and more regional autonomy fueled by inter-regional inequalities with respect to economic and social variables have always been present and at times got intensified. These inequalities are not only of very high order, but have become much more complex over the period. Some of the regions continue to stagnate, in spite of the more than five decades of economic planning and development, and the significant proportion of the Central public sector investment in these regions (Kurian, 2000). Globalisation has further compounded the inequity problem in the backward regions. It has also been argued that most of the secular institutions which can and have the potential to play a very conducive role in the growth of a civil society have come under stress. The people have lost faith in the institutions of "state" because the "state" which can help in creating conditions and provide enabling environment have not come up to those expectations (Mahajan: 1999).

It is feared that during the period of ongoing globalisation induced transition, the poor are likely to get further marginalised and their frustrations will rise. Given that the population is non-homogeneous, and geographic regions are socially differentiated, the level of general economic frustrations of the people is likely to be exploited by political elites and allied population groups. The growing politicisation and multiparty system and aggressive rule flouting mechanism continue to be used to hold on to power. Political arguments based on strong regional identities for having smaller administrative units are likely to be widespread and people may launch agitations under political leaders at the regional level for new jurisdictions. It is a different matter if politicians place a discount on the future with a feeling that they may not be in power long enough to see benefits of state creation, electoral or otherwise (Tillin: 2011). Even the economic arguments in favour of smaller states may be put forward strongly on grounds of improved allocation and efficiency including cost efficiency, enhanced accountability, and increased resource mobilisation (Tanzi: 1995). Formations of Chhattisgarh, Jharkhand and Uttarakhand in November 2000 are clear examples of what Tillin calls politics of intent, but not without agitation by the people led by politicians. It is in this backdrop, this paper is conceived in five sections as follows.

States Reorganisation: The Historical Perspective

Any discussion dealing with statehood demands and/or for smaller administrative units would be incomplete without reviewing briefly the historical background of states' reorganisation in India. During the period of British India, the purpose of reorganising provinces was to uphold the direct authority of the supreme power in areas of vital economic and strategic importance and fill the political vacuum arising from the destruction and collapse of the former principalities (SRC: 1955). Since the need for the rationalisation of administrative units was not seriously felt during the early phases of the rise of the British power in India, the accretion of territories was gradual and not based on the actual needs or affinities of the people.

In the nineteenth century, there emerged an emotional integration of different language groups with the phenomenal development of regional languages which further generated consciousness of being a distinct cultural unit. The linguistic principle for the first time figured in December 1903, when the proposal for the partition of Bengal was mooted, which later on assumed the form of Partition Resolution. The linguistic principle was pressed into service only as a measure of political exigency, dispersing revolutionary elements and for administrative convenience. The Bengal State, which included Bihar and Odisha, partitioned, but it was treated as "a flagrant violation of linguistic affinities"[3].

O'Donnell Committee (also known as Orissa Committee) while taking into account different factors attached a primary importance to "the wishes of the inhabitants where they can be clearly ascertained"[4]. Consequently, the State of Orissa was created by joining together the Oriya speaking areas of the provinces of Bihar, Orissa, the Central Provinces and Madras. However, Sind also came into existence along with Orissa.

The political parties did not approach this problem of reorganising provinces in an aggressive manner in the early years. The linguistic principle, for instance, was strongly opposed by the group led by Dr Annie Besant at the session of 1917. In the subsequent years, the Congress became more defined on redistribution of provinces on a linguistic basis. Andhra, Utkal, Sind and Kamataka became separate provinces'. In All Parties Conference held in the year 1928, the Nehru Committee though extended full support to the linguistic, geographical, and financial principles also gave an overriding consideration to the wishes of the people and the linguistic unity of the area concemed". The British Empire reorganised provincial territories as early as 1903 with the partition of Bengal. India Statutory Commission (1930) recommended a readjustment of provincial boundaries, which ultimately led to the creation of Sind and Orissa in 1936. The period between 1936 and 1947 was relatively a quiet.

Post-Independence Period

Immediately after achieving Independence, the country had three main problems. First, how to keep the Provinces together under the Central authority as the provinces can become Independent and enter into negotiations with any foreign power (Shukla (Singh): 2001). It was further confirmed by M. A. Jinnah (Chandra, 2000). Second was how to reorganise provinces into administratively viable units; and the third, how to put States into the constitutional structure of the independent India.

The Government of India followed a three-fold process of merger and integration in a framework known as Patel Scheme. About 562 former Indian states, known as Princely States were constituted into a federation. The Indian Constitution recognised four categories of States and each category was given a pattern and status of its own. The Indian States thus lost their identity and became the constituent part of one uniform political organisation.

The Congress leaders changed their outlook on the subject of provincial redistribution after the partition. Speaking before the Constituent Assembly (Legislative) on 27th November 1947, the Prime Minister, while conceding the linguistic principle, remarked: "First thing must come first and the first thing is the security and stability of India"[7]. The Drafting Committee of the Constituent Assembly recommended the appointment of a Linguistic Provinces Commission (known as the Dar Commission). The Dar Commission reported against any reorganisation given the prevailing circumstances and emphasised, "... everything which helped the growth of nationalism had to go forward and everything which impeded it had to be rejected or should stand over"[8].

The issue of States' reorganisation remained a high priority issue for the Congress. The Congress appointed another Committee (December 1948, laipur Session) known as the l.Y.P. Committee, consisting Shri Jawaharlal Nehru, Sardar Vallabhbhai Patel and Dr Pattabhi Sitaramayya. This Committee after having considered the question of linguistic provinces, the Dar Commission Report and problems that had arisen since Independence sounded a note of warning against the linguistic principle and stressed on the unity, security, and economic prosperity of the country. These Commissions no doubt gave utmost importance to national unity, security and the emotional and physical integration of the country, and preferred to postpone the formation of new states. However, it agreed to the formation of the Andhra State, under the influence of and as agreed by Andhra Provincial Congress, the Tamilnadu Congress and the Madras Government; but it did not agree to the formation of the Karnataka State for lack of unanimity among the great majority of the people of Mysore State (SRC, 1955).

Some Factors that Matter in the Formation of States

The process of reorganising the constituent administrative units and their altering, merging, changing boundaries or integrating with other States though vital, is a complex process and requires a thorough examination of the historically varied considerations as consequences thereafter may turn out to be far reaching. Historical factors vary from region to region and time to time as peoples' requirements keep on changing, and historical backgrounds across regions are a complex interplay of linguistic, administrative, geographical, economic and other factors operating since the time immemorial.

The analysis, thus, becomes difficult and explanations turnout to be contradictory. For instance, linguistic basis justifying the creation of a region may not be financially viable, and even this region may culturally be heterogeneous.

The process related to reorganisation of boundaries gets further compounded if political pressures for decentralisation are serious, socio-economic development policies are not in line with economic realities, and the people become skeptical about the socio-economic consequences and their dynamics of exogenous pressures for globalisation. This is best explained by Sri Krishna Committee Report on Talangana which was constituted in 2010. Even after the elaborate work, the Committee could not give any resolution to Telangana problem. It laid out six options for different configurations of the three constituent regions of coastal Andhra, Rayalaseema and Telangana.

Since pressures for smaller states and political decentralisation continue to be present and have grown persistently over the period, it would be useful to review factors and their dynamic interrelationships in the decision making process linked to states' reorganisation and alternation of their boundaries. Some of the most important factors are language, culture, administrative and economic viability, unity, strength and national security, geographic size, historical traditions and constitutional structure and its provisions.

Globalisation and Changing Socio-Economic Realities: Impending Dangers

In the era of globalisation, the twin process of redesigning macro economic policies and increasing international exchange and market interdependence takes place simultaneously. With further advances in information and communication technologies (ICT) such changes are likely to affect the entire socio-economic structure of the economy by generating pressures for reform in political organisations and thereby in intergovernmental relations which challenges the plurality of identity of human beings [Bagchi: 2008]. Over the period, the emergence of multilateral agencies such as World Trade Organisation (WTO) and Free Trade Agreements while enlarging the scope of multinational agencies further weaken the independent nation-states and their traditional controls in domestic economic and political spheres.

The market driven international economic integration also requires administrative decentralisation, federal restructuring, ancl fiscal devolution on the one hand and international systems of public finances and an environment, in which tax induced distortion of trade and production factors in interregional conflicts the other. The Central government has 'to vacate a number of areas of taxation resulting into reduced revenue resources, Thus, poor regions and their capacity to undertake basic socio-economic services would further suffer. Discretionary powers of the Centre and its capacity to reach tax bases (Reddy, 1999) also get reduced with the traditional sources like profits of "state" owned enterprises (SOEs) cease to be available with them. Eleventh Financial Commission made even parts of grants in aid under Article 275 of the constitution conditional on fulfilling fiscal reform targets. Thus, fiscal restructuring at the state level emerged as the foremost task in the reform agenda (Howes *et al*, 2003, ed.)

Simultaneously, states have to compete more intensely ever more than before for human, physical and financial resources. The relatively poor States given their meager resources, lack of competitiveness to attract new investments and the declining fiscal transfers from the Centre are likely to further suffer on account of compression of expenditure on health, education and essential public services (Rao and Chakraborty: 2006). They also witness distortions in social investments patterns. With the nation-state becoming relatively a less significant player and TNCs more powerful, the weak regions lag far behind and also loose grip over conflict management instruments at the political level with a reduction in the absolute power of those in power (OECD, 2001).

The reduced role of the "state" as a producer, promoter and regulator, pressures for federal restructuring, and changes in tools and systems of public finances are expected to further weaken the poor regions and bring a change in rules and culture that shape the system of governance. Not only that religious identity and coalition politics are advancing in the direction of cultural nationalism, the existing economic disparities across the States have reached to intolerable order, and are further rising in spite of various governmental measures [Kurian, 2000, Montek, 2000; Dasgupta, 2000]. Within the relatively high income states, some of the regions are known to be deplorably poor. Vidarbha and Marathwada in Maharashtra, Rayalaseema and Telangana in Andhra Pradesh, Eastern part of Uttar Pradesh, North Karnataka in Karnataka and so on shows a dual structure and the topsidedness of the state's development process [Kurian, 2000].

Liberalisation has added fuel to the fire by further accentuating the inter-state income inequalities and bringing a qualitative deterioration in many ways. With reduced involvement of the Central Government in the economic management, the "disparity between the northern and southern halves of the country has become more entrenched during the nineties". It argues that interstate disparities have gone "beyond the margin of tolerance" and cannot be justified by differences in tax structures and tax rates of the States [Bhattacharya, 1999]. Such inequalities generate unequal development of economic resources and opportunities in different regions of the country.

The voice about 'sons of the soil' policy followed by sub-regional movements for separate states or greater autonomy become common to be further appropriated by political bosses. The general hostility and conflict between the local people and the so-called outsiders encourage unintended migration of productive resources and also create fear in the minds of migrants. This has happened in the case of Maharashtra in 2007, when local politicians started taking postures, against Bihari and Punjabi migrants in Maharashtra and forces of communalism, casteism also become active to raise the level of peoples' frustrations and social disenchantment.

India's experience with centralised economic planning, "market oriented federalism" and federal finance practices has not been that satisfactory if seen in term of levels and trends of Inter-state inequalities, poverty, unemployment, social consumption, and illiteracy. Different federal institutions like NDC, Inter-State Council, Rajya Sabha and even Supreme Court lack regular coordination and have failed to address the different federal problems efficiently (Arora: 2004).

The emerging fiscal disorder in term of states' continued dependence on the Centre and their revenues continuously falling short of expenditure and the way this gap is being financed including through the design of central transfers to states, the institutions of Planning and Finance Commissions is fraught with serious implications for long-term growth performance, and the financial plans of the States and their fiscal autonomy (Chakraborty: 2010; Rao: 2010). With the reduced size of the plans and cut in fiscal transfers, the expenditure on productive investments and building capital formation declines. Investments in education, public health, and water supply and sanitation have externalities, elements of public good and affect regional growth [Lall, S: 1999]. Therefore, the Central assistance in the Eleventh Plan for infrastructure development which constitutes less than one per cent of the total Eleventh Plan outlay for states may undermine the inclusive growth (Rao: 2011).

The 73rd and 74th amendments introduced in 1992 empowering the local people to plan from below validated by the Constitution, continue to be illusory for the general masses. Issues related to the actual transfer of powers to local levels, exploitation of local resources, political and operational problems related to transfers and financial controls, representation for disadvantaged groups still remain unresolved besides informational problems and lack of necessary finances and functionaries at the local levels if there is collusion between Panchayats and private taxpayers. The track record of political parties shows a general non-seriousness about decentralisation as observed by many Finance Commissions. The Thirteenth Finance Commission has seriously and rightly so viewed this problem. The classic cases are that of Member of Parliament Local Area Development Scheme and of Legislative Assembly Local Area Development Scheme. Nobody has imagined the distortions if all the three million local government representatives ask for local area development shares which appears to be more legitimate than that of MLAs and MPs (Oommen: 2010).

India's multilingual, multicultural and post-colonial democratic federal setting shows serious weakening. Regional aspirations as reflected in too many regional parties to run the government at the Centre are rising. Local interests, aspirations and even prejudices have found strong expressions over the period with the further rise of regional consciousness and deeper penetration of coalition politics in India. The growth of local patriotism and loyalty to a region and its language and culture has grown into feelings of hostility and a basis for regional conflicts. This is clear from instances of rising hatred against migrants in some states as cited above.

Social differentiation in India is prominently reflected in 22 constitutionally recognised national languages (besides 93 classified languages corresponding to 1652 mother languages (minor and dialects) and more than three thousand indigenous caste groups [Frankel, 1978:20] further supplemented with six major religions. The tribal population constituting over six per cent of total population is dispersed all over India into four hundred tribal communities [Chandra, 2000]. An open expression of such a social diversity finds place in political and social life creating hurdles in cohesiveness and consensus required for sound political governance, particularly with more than 170 regional and unrecognised, 36 states and six national political parties existing in the country and coalition politics assuming an important place in political governance and administration of the country. The vision and perspectives have been missing in policies related to language, culture, and national integration; and as a result, the national goals related to secularism, unity in diversity etc. have become much more complex".[11]

The forces of globalisation go much beyond the free trade of the material products or services. It includes trade of images and information, media and culture and all these can mold young minds, influence tastes and impose values. The TV and media programmes of the advanced countries can invade and crowd out the local cultures by virtue of financial backing, government subsidies, and techniques used to design the programme to look fascinated. With the rising threats of cultural invasion from outside over the period, local frustrations combines with corruption, work loss due to increase in disputes and crime rate (Panchmukhi, 2000) given the right for political expression are likely to emerge stronger over the period. Such frustrations can be exploited as Dunn rightly highlights; "In politics, human beings act to achieve immediate purposes and, less steadily, to serve or secure their enduring interests .... "[12].

Electoral system based on adult suffrage, and territorial constituencies have given rise to vote-bank based political cultures and leaders. Even the political parties are arbitrary, autocratic, lack inner democracy and unaccountable. In the Congress with 208 Lok Sabha members, more than one-third owe their status to their families. The excessive use of money, muscle power, and moneyed interests have encouraged political violence and political corruption, and the upcoming of the politicians with criminal charges (about 30 per cent) in the current parliament and non-serious political parties leading to declining political values and cultures. It is a sad commentary of the Lok Sabha that Parliament proceedings in December 2009 had to be abandoned with as many as 34 members with questions listed against their names not turning up during question hours. And one hour costs around ₹ 14 lakh[13]. There are also "signs of widespread election fatigue leading to popular disinterest in and cynicism towards politics"[14].

With the emergence of coalition politics and its increased penetration, power is getting shifted to the smaller parties and aspirations of the various ethnic, religious and linguistic groups have been rising. Consequently, there is a change in the distribution and the balance of power between the urban and rural; national and regional political parties and also between the executive and the legislative. This redistribution of power is often used for meeting the petty goals based on narrow considerations [Chelliah, 1998]. Pressures emerging out of regionalisation of politics, political aspirations and pluralities enable people to be more vocal of their economic frustrations and social choice. Such rising frustrations of the people seen in the regional context if not adequately accommodated may ultimately get exploited as demands for smaller administrative units by the local political bosses. The process of globalisation and its implications seen in the emerging socio-economic and political realities given the multilingual, multiethnic, and multicultural structure of India highlights that globalisation induced transition once completed will have serious socio-economic and political implications for the society[15].

The character of the conflict in the three layers of government, the Centre, States, and the local governments witnesses a sea change, but conflict management tools continue to be "appease-now" policy. Regional groups highlighting their cultural and historical roots have become much more assertive (Kothari, 2001); and the conflict management has become increasingly complex (Sanghavi and Thakkar, 2000). The globalisation accompanying the economic frustrations of the marginalised people residing in poor areas at large and the rising regional income inequalities across the country requires a people friendly inclusive growth and can not be left alone to market forces (Nayyar, 1998). But unchecked globalisation induced socio-economic inequalities in a fragmented society in which people owe strong allegiances to religion, language, region, caste, their economic frustrations and compulsions can easily be molded into regional identities and movements. People as excluded and marginalised regions fraught with distrust and regional frustrations become more vulnerable for exploitation.

In the long run, there may not appear any real consensus without accommodating the demand for smaller administrative units. The case of Telangana[1] deserves mention. This is more than half a century old well articulated demand for which mass protests with serious political backing have been observed. The submission of the recent Sri Krishna Committee (2010) has given its preferred choice of united state with the establishment of a constitutionally empowered body, a Telangana Regional Council (TRC) to safeguard the interests of this region. But political tensions continue and people remain disenchanted.[2]

Thus, in a situation of deprivation politicised on ethnic, class, caste or regional grounds, people can be mobilised to fight for separate states for cheap political gains. How long such demands remain managed, depends on historical the socio-cultural complexity and heterogeneity of the people and margin of fluidity offered by the society in adopting different identities. The political history of India shows that "administrative efficiency and faster economic development were essentially the by-products, but not the causative factors...and were never the reasons for the Centre in first place to initiate such reorganisation"[3].

Conclusion, Challenges and Future Prospects

Historically, the division of India during the British period into British provinces and Indian States was in itself fortuitous and had no historical basis[4] The present India comprising 28 States and 7 UTs including National Capital Territory of Delhi emerged out of 20 enactments relatable to Article 3 of the Constitution. Indian Constitution clearly empowers Parliament to admit, establish or form new states; and alter areas, boundaries or names of the existing states; and further provide for of the First and the Fourth schedules etc.

Trends of lop-sided development, mass poverty, massive unemployment, rising income inequalities have led to political disenchantment and economic frustrations of the people. The vernacular media led information resolution at the local level poses serious challenges to the dominance of national political c1aims[5] Hindi media has played a vital role in creating an alternative public discourse which has brought regional issues on par with national issues and creating more space for marginalised population groups. For details see (Neyazi, 2011).

Given the socio-economic and political background of the country, economic frustrations may change into political formation culminating into regional movements for statehood demands. These are easily exploitable as an instrument of political opportunism simply because people can be identified in terms of small regional identities. Following Rahul Gandhi's poll campaign of favour smaller states, recently in November 2011, the Chief Minister of Uttar Pradesh passes the resolution in state assembly to divide UP into four parts: Awadh Pradesh, Bundelkhand, Paschim Pradesh and Purvanchal. The ball was shifted into centre's court, which is still indecisive about Telangana.

The issue of reorganisation of the boundaries of administrative units constituting the nation is not an easy task. One finds interplay of historical, geographical, linguistic, cultural and economic factors in the existing regions besides area specific local problems and development potentials varying across regions[6]. At the same time, pressures for reorganising states such as Bodoland[7], Coorg, Bundhelkhand, Gorkhaland, Khoshal, Harit Pradesh, Maru Pradesh, Mithilanchal, Saurastra, Telangana and Vidarbha are already existing. In most of the cases, such demands are not superficial given there historical basis, prolonged agitations, economic rationality, and vernacularisation of the public sphere influencing and informing citizen at the local levels. The country is aware of the approaches followed by the British, the Indian National Congress, and factors considered in the post-independence period.

Each case thus deserves to be examined on its own merits as background features and peculiarities would be different. But before arriving at any conclusion, totality of circumstances cannot be ignored in the perspective of the generally recognised factors. There is a need to appreciate that alteration of state boundaries and creation of new states has to be regarded as a means to an end rather than an end in itself to achieve the higher levels of welfare of the people. The creation of Chhatisgarh, Jharkhand and Uttaranchal and the tripartite Agreement with the Government of West Bengal, centre and Gorkhaland Territorial Administration to give more autonomy to the hill region of West Bengal in July 2011 has increased local aspirations for forming a separate state of Gorkhaland along with raising others' aspirations elsewhere.

In the changed scenario, an objective evaluation of the existing administrative boundaries may be undertaken but it should be context specific and should be seen in totality of circumstances, and developments taking place in broader socio-economic-political contexts. India's future as a nation of economic strength, technological and administrative resources and democratic federal polity depends on the growth and the composition and the configuration of the constituent units and their social development in which socio-political factors will continue to play a leading role. In such a situation, India may consider district as an administrative and economic politico units while redrawing state boundaries and the reconstituted states monitored by and placed under Regional Councils of states. But this process of change to a large extent is in the political hands and leaders to create governance mechanism and socio-economic institutional structures, which are people-sensitive, people-friendly, people participatory and people inclusive.

NOTES

1. This situation is best described by Thomas (quoted in Chandra 2000, p. 487).
2. The democratic processes have resulted into recognition of its policies in which assertion of identity based on religion, caste, dialectical and local language, community have assumed importance thereby making state level analysis as an autonomous discipline. Kumar A (2009).
3. SRC 1955, p. 10.
4. SRC 1955, p. 10.
5. SRC 1955, p. 13.
6. Quoted in SRC 1955, p. 14.
7. SRC 1955. p. 14.
8. SRC 1955. p. 15.

9. "Distortions in social investments get adversely influenced by the demonstration effect of the elite on consumption patterns and lifestyles of the poor adding to their frustrations and exclusion of the large majority of the population.

10. Shaw 1999, p. 969.

11. Faust and Nagar 2001, p. 2879.

12. Tillin 2011.

13. The last time it happened in 1991, twice in 1983, five times in 1985, three times in 1988 and twice in 1989 (Economic Times, Ist Dec 2009).

14. Yadav 1999, p. 2393.

15. With regional inequalities, federal distortions; failure of state institutions to meet the intended objectives; the growth of regional consciousness and aspirations along with the caste based, identity and 'coalition politics' getting deeply penetrated, the political climate continues to be working against the poor, the delivery systems are managed by corrupt and unmotivated public servants. The complex interplay of all these developments and corrupt political practices in partnership with bureaucracy and business has failed to check the deteriorating public policy-making environment and the unabated black money transfers (illicit financial blows) and political corruptions. Estimates show that gross trade mispricing constituting about 18 per cent of India's GOP at end-2008 during 1948-08 was shifted out of India (Kar, 2011). Political corruption highlighted in Commonwealth 2010 Games and 2G Spectrum causing ₹ 70,000 crore and ₹ 1.76 lakh crore losses to the national exchequer respectively are of frightening scales. These trends have damaged political climate in the country in which poor are also the stakeholders.

REFERENCES

Arora, G.K. (1991), "Emerging Fiscal Crisis and Centre State Fiscal Relations", *Mainstream,* February 16, Feb. 23, Feb. 30, 1991, pp. 15-20. pp. 17-26, and pp. 26-30).

Arora, G.K. (2002), Globalisation, Federalism and Decentralisation -Implications for India. Bookwell.

Arora, G.K. (2011), Global Governance, Globalisation and Developing Countries, *Ind J of Soc Enquiry.*

Bagchi, Amresh (2008), Globalisation and Federalism: Uneasy Partners, *EPW,* Sep 20: 41-48.

Basu, Durga Das (1982), Introduction to the Constitution of India, 9th Ed, New Delhi.

Bhadury, Amit (2008). "Predatory Growth", *EPW,* 19th April XLII, 16:10-13.

Chakraborty, Pinacki (2010), "Deficit Fundamentalism Vs. Fiscal Federation Implication of 13th Finance Commission's Recommendation", EPW (XLV, 48) Nov:56-63 Participative Development 17.

Chandra, Bipin (2000), India after Independence, Penguin Books.

Chelliah Raja J (1999), Liberalisation, Economic Reforms and Centre State Relations", in (ed) India's Economic Reforms and Development.

Dunn, J (2000), The Cunning of Unreason: Making sense of politics (New York: Basic Books, p. 98).

Frankel, Francise, R (1998), India's Political Economy 1947-77, Delhi, Oxford University Press.

Government of India (2010), Committee for Consultation on the Situation in Andhra Pradesh, December, also known as Shri. Krishna Report.

Harriss, J (1999), "Comparing Political Regions across Indian States: A Preliminary Essay: *EPW.* Nov. 25.

Howes, Stephen, Ashok Lahiri and N. Stem (eds, 2003), State-level Reforms in India, Macmillan, New Delhi.

India, Government of (1955), Report of the States Reorganisation Commission, pp. 1-266.

Kannan, KP and G Raveendran (2009), "Growth sans Employment: A quarter century of Jobless Growth in India's Organised manufacturing", 7 March XLIV, 10:80-89.

Kar, Dev (2011), An Empirical study on the Transfers of Black money for India 1948-2008, *EPW* (XLVI, 15), April 9: 45-54.

Sabyasachi and S Sakhtiivel (2007), "Reforms and Regional Inequality in India', *EPW,* 24th Nov, XLII, 47:69.

Kothari, Rajni (2001), "People should control the rules", Deccan Herald, September 2.

Kumar, Pradeep (2000), "Demand for new States", *EPW,* August 26-September 2, (XXXV, 35 and 36) 21. Kumar, Ashotosh (2009):"Rethinking State Politics in India: Regions within Regions *EPW* (XLIV, 19), May.

Madhab, Jayanta (1999), "North-east" Crises of Identity, Security and Underdevelopment", *EPW,* February 6-12 (XXXIV, 6): 320-322.

Nayyar, Gaurav (2008), "Economic Growth and Regional Inequality", *EPW,* 9th Feb (XLIII), 6:58-67.

Neyazi, Tabrez Ahmed (2011), "Politics after Vernacularisation: Hindi Media and Indian Democracy, *EPW* (XLVI, 10) March 5: 75-82.

Oommen, M.A (2010), "The 13th Finance Commission and the Third Tier", *EPW* (XLV, 48), 27 Nov: 92-8.

Ramaswamy, KV (2007), "Regional Dimension of Growth and Development", *EPW,* 8th Dec, XLII, 49.

Rao, C.H. Hanumantha (2011), India and China: A Comparison of the Role of Social Political factors in Inclusive growth, *EPW* (XLVI, 16), April 16: 24-28.

Rao, M.G. and Pinaki Chakraborty (2006), Multilateral Adjustment lending to states Hastening to Fiscal Correction of softening of Budget Constraints; *Journal of International Trade and Econ Deve* 15(3), 335-57.

Rao, M.G. (2010), "The 13th Finance Commission's Report Conundrum in Conditionalities" *EPW* (XLV, 48) 27th November 46-55.

Sarangi, Asha (2006), "Ambedkar and the Linguistic States-A Case of Maharashtra", *EPW,* Jan 14: 151-6.

Srinivastu, K et al (2011), "Shri Krishna Committee, Though But Unavailable" *EPW* (XLVI, 10) March, p. 16.

State Reorganisation Commission (1956) was also popularly Known as Fazal Ali Commission.

Tanzi Vito (1995), "Fiscal Federalism and Decentralisation-A Review of some Efficiency and Macro Economic Aspects, in Michael

Bruno and Boros Pleskovic, Annual World Bank Conference on Development Economics, pp. 295-329.

Thirteenth Finance Commission 2010-2015, Vol. II and earlier Reports also.

Tillin, Louise (2011), "Statehood and the Politics of Intent", *EPW*, May (XLVI, 20): 34-38.

9

Centre-State Fiscal Relations in the New Era of Niti Aayog and the Bygones Era of Planning Commission

B.K. Pandey and M. Saravanan

India is the largest democracy following federal form of governance. This paper makes an attempt to examine the then existing arrangements of fiscal relation between the Union and States governments in the context of the presence of the Planning Commission and how the relations have changed post the Fourteenth Finance Commission and the setting up of Niti Aayog. It also briefly delineates the fiscal imbalances between the Central Government and State governments and also the inter-state and intra-state imbalances.

Taxation Powers and Expenditure Responsibilities

It will be essential to look at the Constitutional provisions regarding fiscal federal structure, which has an important bearing on the inter-government transfers of resources.

The Constitution clearly demarcates the taxation powers of the Union and the States. Under Article 246 of the Constitution, there are three Lists, namely, the Union List, the State List and the Concurrent List. While the Central Govt. has exclusive powers to make laws for subjects listed in the Union List, the State Governments has exclusive powers to make laws for subjects listed in the State List. Union List has thirteen taxes; State List, nineteen taxes. There are no taxes listed in the Concurrent List.

The important taxes listed in the Union List or those assigned to the Centre are taxes on income other than agricultural land, duties of custom, duties of excise except those on alcoholic liquor for human consumption, corporation tax, estate duty in respect of property other than agricultural land, terminal taxes on goods and passengers carried by railways, sea or air, taxes other than stamp duty on transactions in stock exchanges and futures markets and taxes on sale and purchase of goods other than newspapers, when such sale takes place in the course of inter-State trade or commerce.

The important taxes listed in the State List are land revenue, taxes on agricultural income, taxes on land and buildings, taxes on mineral rights subject to restrictions imposed by Parliament, duties of excise on alcoholic liquor for human consumption, taxes on sale and purchase of goods other than newspapers, taxes on goods and passengers carried by road, taxes on vehicles, taxation on professions, taxes on luxuries including on entertainments, taxes on entry of goods into a local area and taxes on advertisements other than those published in newspapers and broadcast by radio or television.

Under Article 246, the Constitution also provides for subjects in respect of which the Union and the States have exclusive jurisdiction to make laws. In addition, a few subjects are listed in the Concurrent List in respect which both the Union and the States have concurrent powers to make laws.

As in other major federations, subjects of national importance, such as, defence, foreign affairs, money and banking, communications, national highways, shipping, ports, airways and macroeconomic management have been assigned to the Centre. Subjects of regional concern, such as, public order, agriculture, irrigation, public health and sanitation, roads and bridges not specified in the Union List and industries other than those declared by Parliament to be of strategic importance are assigned to States. The important subjects specified in the Concurrent List are criminal law, administration of justice, contracts, forests, economic and social planning, population control and family planning, education and newspapers.

The subjects listed in the Union and the State Lists broadly define the expenditure responsibilities of the Centre and the States, respectively. From the division of subjects between the Union and the States, it is evident that there is a considerable gap between the taxation powers of the States and their expenditure responsibilities. Unlike the States, the Centre enjoys taxation powers with higher revenue potential, while States revenue potentials are modest, in relation to their functional responsibilities.

Fiscal Deficit of Centre and State Governments

As per the Indian Public Finance Statistics 2014-2015, Ministry of Finance, the fiscal deficit at Centre has increased 14 times from Rs 37,606 crore in 1990 to Rs 5,31,177 crore in 2014-15. Correspondingly the fiscal deficit of States rose by close to 16 times from Rs 18,558 crore to Rs 2,93,978 crore. The combined fiscal deficit increased by almost 15.5 times.

As percentage of the GDP, the fiscal deficit of the Centre and the States have decreased, though the dip in the former is relatively sharper. The fiscal deficit as a ratio of GDP peaked around six per cent for almost six times, post-1990-91. Though the Central and State deficit rates follow a similar pattern, there is no corresponding periods of peaks or troughs. The deficit rates of States have not coincided with increases in the deficits and vice versa. The table and chart below reflect the fiscal deficit of the Centre and States for the period 1990-91 to 2014-15.

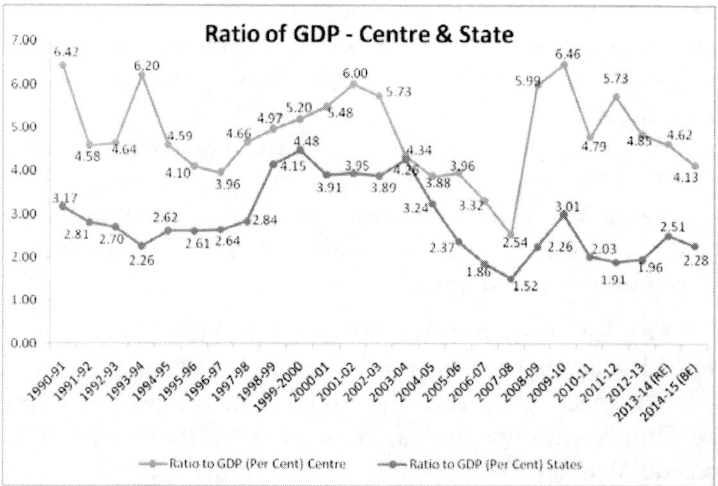

Source: *Indian Public Finance Statistics 2014-2015, Ministry of Finance.*

Fiscal Deficit of Centre and State Governments

The Fourteenth Finance Commission Report observes the following about the first decade ending 2010: "The fiscal deficit of the Union Government relative to GDP declined steadily from 6.1 per cent in 2001-02 to 4.5 per cent in 2003-04. The FRBM Act mandated reducing the fiscal deficit to three per cent by 2008-09. The Union Government achieved this target in 2007-08, with the fiscal deficit declining to 2.5 per cent of GDP. However, in 2008-09 the Union Government undertook several fiscal expansionary measures such as revision of pay scales based on the recommendations of the Sixth Pay Commission, waiver of farm loans and the expansion of the Mahatma Gandhi National Rural Employment Guarantee Act (MGNREGA) to all districts from the 200 districts it was originally slated to cover. In addition,

Year	*Fiscal Deficit (₹ in Crore)*		*Ratio to GDP (Per Cent)*		*Combined Fiscal deficit of Centre and State Govts*	
	Centre	*States*	*Centre*	*States*	*Rs in crore*	*Per cent*
1990-91	37606	18558	6.42	3.17	53320	9.10
1991-92	30844	18942	4.58	2.81	45849	6.80
1992-93	35909	20917	4.64	2.70	51643	6.67
1993-94	55257	20126	6.20	2.26	70310	7.89
1994-95	48030	27350	4.59	2.62	70739	6.77
1995-96	50253	31993	4.10	2.61	77400	6.31
1996-97	56242	37490	3.96	2.64	86650	6.11
1997-98	73204	44688	4.66	2.84	110289	7.01
1998-99	89560	74810	4.97	4.15	157910	8.76
1999-2000	104717	91555	5.20	4.48	184596	9.17
2000-01	118816	84898	5.48	3.91	194915	8.99
2001-02	140955	92736	6.00	3.95	223165	9.50
2002-03	145072	98387	5.73	3.89	231763	9.16
2003-04	123272	120990	4.34	4.26	233452	8.26
2004-05	125794	105130	3.88	3.24	233051	7.19
2005-06	146435	87608	3.96	2.37	237187	6.42
2006-07	142573	79979	3.32	1.86	220617	5.14
2007-08	126912	75690	2.54	1.52	199375	4.00
2008-09	336992	127320	5.99	2.26	459908	8.17
2009-10	418482	194962	6.46	3.01	610851	9.43
2010-11	373591	158374	4.79	2.03	529594	6.75
2011-12	515990	171798	5.73	1.91	688434	7.64
2012-13	490190	198076	4.85	1.96	683418	6.76
2013-14 (RE)	524539	284642	4.62	2.51	806383	7.10
2014-15 (BE)	531177	293978	4.13	2.28	821903	6.38

oil prices escalated sharply, leading to a rise in subsidy. As a consequence of all this as well as the global crisis, the fiscal deficit of Union Government increased to six per cent in 2008-09 and 6.5 per cent in 2009-10." (The marginal difference in the figures quoted above table and in the Fourteenth Finance Commission Report is due to different data sources.)

Institutional Mechanism for Intergovernmental Transfers – Planning Commission Era

The then existing transfer system had multiple channels—Finance Commission transfers, Planning Commission transfers and transfers from Union Ministries. A substantial portion of Central transfer to State consists of general revenue sharing of proceeds of certain levied taxes, which is the primary mandate of Finance Commission. Finance Commission is a constitutional body that recommends devolution of proceeds from Central taxes to States and provides grants-in-aids, which are basically transfers designed to cover for the deficit between projected expenditures and revenues after tax devolution. Finance Commissions transfers are meant for non-Plan expenditures of the States.

The Plan transfers were decided by the Planning Commission, which is the second channel for Central transfers to the States. The total Plan Expenditure consisted of Central Plan and Central Assistance for State/UT Plan. Planning Commission provided assistance to States in the form of grants, which were meant for development plans of the States. Out of the total Plan Expenditure, around 25 per cent went as Central Assistance for State/UT Plan and the rest was distributed for Central Sector Schemes (CS) and Centrally Sponsored Schemes (CSS). Central Assistance to State Plan or Additional Central Assistance (ACA) Scheme were part of the State Plan and were broadly divided into two categories (a) Block Assistance – such as Normal Central Assistance (NCA) and Special Central Assistance (untied) and (b) Scheme based ACA such as AIBP, JNNURM, RKVY, BADP, NSAP. The mode of transfer was usually Treasury route (except MPLADS).

The Central Assistance for State/UT Plan included Normal Central Assistance (NCA), Special Plan Assistance (SPA), Additional Central Assistance (ACA) for Externally Aided Projects EAP and other ACA schemes like Accelerated Irrigation Benefits Programmae, NSAP, BRGF, JNNURM, RKVY etc. The Normal Central Assistance, which is about 25 per cent of the total Central Assistance for the State Plan, were distributed among Special Category States and General (Non-Special) Category States in the ratio of 30:70. The 30 per cent of the funds earmarked for Special Category States were distributed pro-rata among the States on the basis of plan projects formulated by them. The balance 70 per cent of the funds were distributed among General Category States on the basis of Gadgil-Mukherjee formula, which gives a 60 per cent weightage to population, 25 per cent weightage to SDP, 7.5 per cent weightage to fiscal management and the remaining 7.5 per cent weightage to special problems of these major States. The Gadgil formula for Normal Central Assistance had undergone three revisions, the last one in 1991 which has been referred to us Gadgil-Mukherjee formula. Following the recommendations of the Twelfth Finance Commission, the practice of giving loans to the State have been done away with from 2005-06 onwards.

Although in absolute terms, the resources transferred through the Planning Commission did not decline, the structure of the transfer underwent a change in the sense that only 25 per cent of the resources were transferred through NCA which were untied and goes directly into the State Budget. Another change which has impacted the decline in absolute resources to States is that NCA consists only of grants and not loans. States are receiving resources indirectly in the form of Central Sector Schemes, Centrally Sponsored Schemes and other ACA schemes like Accelerated Irrigation Benefits

Devolution and Transfer of Resources from the Centre

(₹ in billion)

S. No.	Item	2010-11	2011-12	2012-13	2013-14 (Accounts)	2014-15 (Budget Estimates)	2014-15 (Revised Estimates)	2015-16 (Budget Estimates)
1	States' Share in Central Taxes	2194.90	2555.90	2915.30	3182.70	3857.60	3662.20	4855.20
2	Grants from the Centre (i to v)	1635.00	1864.20	1886.80	2059.50	4751.10	4617.50	4072.80
i)	State Plan Schemes	776.40	876.70	916.20	899.70	2704.40	2644.20	2032.40
ii)	Central Plan Schemes	35.90	27.40	26.70	34.30	174.60	135.50	119.00
iii)	Centrally Sponsored Schemes	328.30	431.20	454.80	450.00	886.40	887.20	878.30
iv)	NEC/Special Plan Schemes	5.40	6.80	5.20	4.20	9.10	7.90	9.10
v)	Non-Plan Grants	489.10	522.00	484.00	671.30	976.60	942.80	1034.10
3	Gross Loans from the Centre	94.80	99.00	112.00	108.70	231.80	222.40	255.40
4	Gross Transfer	3924.60	4519.10	4914.20	5351.00	8840.50	8502.00	9183.40
5	Repayment of Loans and Interest Payments Liabilities	186.60	193.70	192.40	191.30	196.90	197.30	203.80
6	Net Transfer of Resources from the Centre	3738.10	4325.40	4721.80	5159.70	8643.60	8304.80	8979.60

*: Include Ways and Means Advances from the Centre. NEC: North Eastern Council.

Source: Reserve Bank of India/ Budget Documents of Government of India.

Programme, NSAP, BRGF, JNNURM, RKVY etc. The share of State Plan outlays in total Plan outlays witnessed a sharp declined from over 63 per cent in the First Five Year Plan to around 40 per cent in the Eleventh Plan.

Finally, Central Ministries provides assistance to States in the form of grants, under various schemes and programmes, which are grouped broadly under Central Sector Schemes and Centrally Sponsored Schemes. Under Central Sector Scheme (CS), the resources are spent usually on Union Subject by the Central Ministries/ Departments/ Agencies. Centrally Sponsored Scheme (CSS) are those schemes which are funded by Central Ministries / Departments and implemented by States or their agencies irrespective of their pattern of Financing and which do not fall under the Centre's sphere of responsibility. The mode of transfer of resources to the States may either be Treasury route (through Consolidated Fund of the State) or Society route (Direct Transfer).

Vertical Imbalance

In Indian fiscal federalism, decentralisation is seen more in incurring expenditures than in sharing revenues. As pointed out by M. Govinda Rao (Fiscal Decentralisation in Indian Federalism), "the Central Government could exercise control over one-third of the revenues, but its share in raising revenues is two thirds. In contrast, State and local governments raised only about one-third of revenues, but the revenue accrual to them was about two-thirds." This has led to the rightful clamour from the States for an increased resource transfers to them commensurating their growing responsibilities. In fact, States have demanded an increase in their share of Central taxes from 29.5 per cent to 50 per cent. The vertical imbalances are due to the Constitutional arrangements and developments till date. A higher share of revenues to States would reduce the prevalent high degree of imbalance. Even though the division of net proceeds of Central taxes have been rationalised over years, the States demand that a higher percentage of proceed be transferred to the States to bridge the existing imbalance. The fiscal imbalances of the states are structural in nature, constrained by inability to raise additional revenues. The expenditure responsibilities of the states have increased faster than its revenues. As the fiscal situation of the Centre is precarious state, the state governments will have to depend more on its own resources rather than depending on Central transfers.

Horizontal Imbalances

Growing regional imbalances both inter-State and intra-State are matters of serious concern and are counter to the objective of realising the goal of inclusive growth. Out of 28 States, 17 States have been categorised under General Category or Non Special Category States based on their economic characteristics and the remaining 11 States that are relatively economically backward are grouped under Special Category States. The per capita revenues and per capita expenditure differ widely between these two groups and also between each State within these groups. The revenue and tax-GSDP ratio of Special Category States are generally lower than the General Category States. However, even within the General Category States, they vary hugely. For example, the per capita net state domestic product (NSDP) in the richest state (Haryana) in 2007-08 was over 5.4 times that of the poorest state (Bihar) even when only the large states are considered. The impact of Goods and Services Tax (GST) (if passed implemented shortly) would be another interesting aspect to be seen in the near future, as its impact varies between States that generate their manufacturing or services.

Inter-governmental Transfers post-Niti Aayog and Fourteenth Finance Commission

In the year 2014-15, two major events happened: Planning Commission was dismantled and a new institution arrangement was decided to be put in its place. The report of the Fourteenth Finance Commission (FFC) was submitted and later accepted. Following the closure of Planning Commission, there was no requirement for approval of Plan grants to the States. Further, FFC dissolved the need for the distinction between Plan and Non-Plan funds. The main changes that have come into existence following the setting up of Niti Aayog and the acceptance of FFC are given below:

- *Higher devolution to states:* States' share in net proceeds from tax collections to be 42 per cent instead of 32 per cent recommend by the Thirteenth Finance Commission.

- *Resource transfer:* Tax devolution be the primary route resource transfer to states.

- *Grants to local bodies:* Grants to be distributed to states for local bodies on the basis of the 2011 population data; the grants be divided into two broad categories on the basis of rural and urban population — constituting gram panchayats, and constituting municipal bodies.

- *Types of grants:* A basic grant and a performance grant — the ratio of basic to performance grant be 90:10, with respect to panchayats; and 80:20 in the case of municipalities

- *Total grants:* The total grant recommended is ₹ 2,87,436 crore for a five-year period from April 1, 2015, to March 31, 2020. Out of thes, ₹ 2,00,292.20 crore to be given to panchayats and ₹ 87,143.80 crore to municipalities.

- *Disaster relief:* Up to 10 per cent of the funds available under the SDRF can be used by State Governments for natural disasters that they consider to be 'disasters' within the local context in the State and which are not included in the notified list of disasters of the Ministry of Home Affairs.

- *Post-devolution revenue deficit grants:* A total of ₹ 1,94,821 crore on account of expenditure requirements of states, tax devolution and revenue mobilisation capacity of the states. These will be given to 11 states.
- *Delinking of schemes:* Eight centrally sponsored schemes (CSS) will be delinked from support from the Centre and some CSS to have a change in sharing pattern of grants between Centre and States.
- *Cooperative federalism:* There are recommendations considering various options to strengthen the cooperative federalism and its institutional arrangement.

Conclusion

Over the years, especially after the process of liberalisation was started in 1991, the role of Central planning was diminished, so has been the role of Planning Commission. When the private sector income increased sharply and public sector income declined, the States saw an opportunity to regain ground lost to the Planning Commission. However, this did not happen as Plan transfers have become more tied to schemes and projects with substantial allocations going for Centrally Sponsored Schemes. The States have now asked for reduction in the allocations for CSS and for larger untied transfers to State governments. Even in this changed economic situation, planning still has an important role. At this juncture, there was a need to strengthen the cooperative federalism and also understand the nuances of market forces. This resulted in closure of Planning Commission and setting up of Niti Aayog. As GST is likely to be implemented shortly, the fiscal landscape would evolve in a different manner, when juxtaposed with the changes already seen following the implementation of the recommendations of the FFC.

REFERENCES

Budget Document 2016-17, Government of India.

Govinda Rao, M., "Changing Contours in Federal Fiscal Arrangements in India".

Govinda Rao, M., "Fiscal Decentralisation in Indian Federalism", 2000.

Indian Public Finance Statistics, 2011-2012, Ministry of Finance, Government of India.

Report of (Puncchi) Commission on Centre-State Relations, Volume III, March 2010.

Report of the Fourteenth Finance Commission.

Report of the High Level Expert Committee on Efficient Management of Public Expenditure, Planning Commission, Government of India, July, 2011.

State Finances: A Study of Budgets of 2012-13, Reserve Bank of India, January, 2013.

Twelfth Five Year Plan (2012–2017) Document, Volume I, Planning Commission, Government of India.

Union Budget 2013-14, Government of India (indiabudget.nic.in)

10

Regional Business and Federalism in India

Himanshu Roy

Introduction

The chamber of commerce in India was first established in 1834 in Calcutta; after the British East India Company's external trading right was liquidated by the British parliament in 1833. It was followed by the formation of Madras and Bombay chambers of commerce in 1835 and 1836 respectively. These chambers were of European merchants formed to protect their trading interests under the new circumstances of Free Trade. The first Indian merchants' chamber, different from theirs, was formed in 1885 in Coconada. It was named as the Native Merchants Chamber. It was followed by the formation of Bengal National Chamber of Commerce and Industry (BNCCI) in 1887. Its constitution was drafted by A.O. Hume and was revised by W.C. Bannerjee, the founders of the Indian

National Congress. Subsequently, in the decades to come many other chambers were formed, the prominent among them were the South Indian Chambers of Commerce and the Andhra Chamber of Commerce.

Role of Chambers: Pre-Independence Period

Actually, the regional chambers, in need of protective market and other requisite support for their business from their local governments, believed that linguistic provinces will provide them the required support in their business expansion as most of the chambers, in the initial years of their formations, had emerged out of the dominant linguistic regions of the time. It was reflected in their public representations and in mass support to the movements that demanded the creation of linguistic provinces or sought the annulment of partition as in the case of Bengal in the early decade of twentieth century. For the objective of the regional chambers was *"to aid and stimulate the development of commercial enterprise in the regions and to protect the commercial interests of all persons trading there in...For example, the BNCCI had intended from the very outset that... the chamber should all along regard itself as virtually interested in the economic development of Bengal in a manner which would not be possible through unqualified membership, as businessmen with their principal centres outside Bengal could not devote concentrated attention and enthusiasm for the development and economic welfare of this Province. It is this limitation of its scope which imparts a distinctive strength to the chamber from the point of view of this state"*[1] (italics mine). Following this objective, it uncompromisingly opposed the partition of Bengal in 1905. In fact, at the planning stage itself, when the partition was being proposed in 1904, the chamber had opposed the idea. Subsequently, it supported the anti-partition agitation which was guided predominantly by its economic consideration.[2] The agitation and the role of the chamber in it, later on, facilitated two things: (a) a beginning of annual sessions of the Indian Industrial Conferences which were organised along with the annual sessions of the Indian National Congress since 1905 and (b) a change in the industrial policy of the Government of India which began to offer 'help and guidance' through provincial governments to native business in area like handloom weaving and leather processing. The Madras government in particular provided considerable impetus to the application of this new policy. These developments prompted the formation of the Southern Indian Chambers of Commerce in 1909 and subsequently in the formation of other such chambers in the later decades which played catalytic role in the federalisation process premised on the creation of linguistic provinces. These chambers were consulted by the governments to seek their views on business policies that were also granted constitutional right to send their representatives to the legislative councils to represent the collective interests of the business, which, in turn, obviously sought conducive business policies from the government.

Simultaneously, the chambers applied collective pressure on the Congress, particularly after 1905, to influence it to accept the principle of federalisation (in 1916) and of linguistic provinces (in 1920) as the basis of reorganisation of administrative units of the country and of constitutional divisions of powers between the federating units as the mode of governance. Jolted by the 1909 Act, which had fuelled separation of its social constituents, the Congress was afraid to part away with any further social blocks. The prevalent latent current in the legislative councils also prompted it to accept this new arrangement. This can be judged from the fact that immediately after the consent of the Congress the Madras, Bihar and Odisha legislative councils passed the resolutions in 1921 exhorting the governments to reorganise the administrative units on the basis of linguistic provinces. In 1927, when the Simon Commission arrived at in India, the government of India and the India office were flooded with the memorandum to be forwarded to the Simon Commission for 'the amalgamation of the Oriya speaking people' and for 'the formation of separate Andhra,

Tamil and Kannada provinces'. Subsequently, resolutions were "moved in the Central legislature for the formation of separate Andhra, Tamil and Kannada provinces, and a resolution urging the formation of a separate Andhra province was adopted in the Madras Legislative Council"[3].

The chambers' role in the federalisation process further accelerated in 1940s. The Southern Indian Chamber of Commerce strongly recommended to the Industrial Planning Committee of the Madras government that economic planning should be primarily provincial in nature and the government should "do everything to improve the trade and industries and help to retain as big a slice of them as possible for the benefit of the sons of the soil"[4] . The chamber was dismayed to observe that the citizens of Madras province were being outwitted by nationals of other provinces in matter of race for industries and enterprises and demanded in a resolution of industrial and commercial conference that 'regional interests should be safeguarded.'[5] The Bengal National chamber too had put forth its own regional plan for the development of its province. The countervailing force to the regional interests was the presence of the Federation of Indian Chambers of Commerce and Industries (FICCI) representing the collective interests of the big business, which itself had emerged out of the regional chambers of commerce in 1927 and was now against their dominant roles in the regional market. It opposed the principle of regionalisation of industries and urged that private enterprise should be given the full freedom and facilities to establish industries in places most suitable for such development. It regretted that every time a proposal to establish an industry in the Madras presidency is given, it is turned down on the ground that the firm sponsoring the establishment of that industry does not belong to that presidency. It complained that the present policy of regional development would lead to the creation of monopolies for persons of firms born only in a particular district of province.[6] The FICCI was afraid that under the Cabinet Mission Plan, which was premised on the classical concept of federalism envisaging larger powers for federating units and lesser powers for centre, the provinces "will exercise a larger measure of autonomy on all matters pertaining to the province. Almost all the aspects of trade and commerce will thus be exclusively provincial spheres".[7] It urged the central government "to include special provisions in the Constitution Act... to provide that any unit, province or State shall not have power to pass any laws or take any executive action prohibiting or restricting the entry into or export from one unit or province to another of any goods of any class of description. It should similarly be laid down that no unit or province should be entitled to impose any tax, cess, toll or due which, as between goods manufactured or produced in one province or unit and similar goods not so manufactured or produced, discriminate in favour of the former."[8] This demand was urged despite major shift in the central government's economic policy in 1945 that had transferred the control of 20 major industries from the purview of provincial governments to the central government.[9] More, when the Constituent Assembly was formed the big business lobbied through different constitutional committees and sub-committees to put more number of industries/business sectors under the purview of the central government. Yet, despite such acts, it was so afraid of the power of the regional business that it did not let pass any opportunity that struck at their interests. And in its role, it was ably supported by the political leadership which was best expressed by the Nehru themselves. In 1928, for example, while presenting the Swaraj constitution for country Motilal had envisaged a unitary form of government that had nullified all the struggles of the regional business till then for the federalisation process which the Congress in principle had agreed to. Later, in 1948, addressing the Annual meeting of the FICCI, Jawaharlal had observed that "more dangerous than communalism is provincialism. And if every province formulates its own economic policy and adds new obstacles then it is unwanted.[10]

The inter relations of business and politics in quest for monopolistic market and absolute power reached its crescendo in the last months of 1946 and early months of 1947 [11] when an unrelenting Jinnah and Muslim chamber of commerce in quest for their own power and market, not conceded by the Congress and big business, actuated partition of the country. The Congress propelled by the FICCI used this situation for their respective benefits. They agreed to partition the country and then on the pretext of curbing the fissiparous trend appropriated all the major political – economic powers of the provinces and put them under the purview of the central government. The structure of powers of the federating units as envisaged by the Cabinet Mission Plan was radically altered for ever under the new Constitutional scheme after partition. The regional business's dominant role in the provinces, the kind of which existed in the pre-partition years, seized to exist in independent India. Their system of representation in the legislatures, the Constitutional right earned after a tenuous struggle against the colonial state, was dismantled forever.

Post-independence

Fortunately, the regional business did no give up the fight. It propelled the masses to force the central government for the reorganisation of the states on linguistic basis despite strong opposition of the Congress leadership and of big business represented by the Linguistic Provinces Commission of the Constituent Assembly, Linguistic Provinces Committee of the Congress Party and the Citizens' Committee of the J.R.D. Tata, H.P. Mody and Purshotamdas Thakurdas respectively.[12] For, it may be noted here, the big business was never in favour of reorganisation of states premised on the linguistic basis after 1927, neither did the political leadership voluntarily willed itself to the principle of federalism and linguistic provinces. It agreed to the cause only under the duress of regional business and mass pressure that compelled the passage of different resolutions in legislatures and at party's forum in pre-partition years and of the constitution of the State Reorganisation Committee, finally, in 1953.

The formation of the linguistic provinces, however, did not alter the power structure of 1950 constitution. Rather, it only created new states which were in tune with the constitution with elementary powers to be of little use for the regional business. It did not alter the dominant position of the big business and of central government acquired after the partition which had appropriated the residuary and other major powers of the state as envisaged by the Cabinet Mission Plan. The regional business in retaliation began to invest in regional parties which had began to acquire political power since 1967 after the formation of the linguistic provinces commended from 1956-57. In the next 30 years, by 1987, major linguistic regions of the country were reorganised into provinces and their governmental powers gradually came under the control of the regional parties. Or the regional parties began to play major role in the provinces. And in few exceptional cases, the national parties began to play limited role of regional parties. In other words, it may be derived that where regional business was dynamic, the role of the regional parties had been more assertive in the provinces[13] which is best reflected, four decades later, in the dismantling of the One party dominant system and of the emergence of bi-coalitional system at federal level in which the regional parties play an assertive role, and in the emergence of the bi-party, bi-coalitional system existing at the provincial level.[14] In brief, the Congress which was votary of the unitary system as an ideal model of polity and accepted the principle of federalism premised on linguistic basis only under duress was itself thrown from the pedestal by the regional forces in course of development. The dominance of the Congress party was dismantled forever and it was substituted by an alternative national/ regional party systems at the centre and in the provinces. More, in the twist of history the regional business, which was seeking a place under the sun from the Congress, initially, itself became the part of the global business under the growing liberalisation process of capital unleashed by this Party. It transcended its regional character, when the opportunity beconned it, and transformed itself into a pan-Indian, pan-global group. Their entry into top 50 business houses reflects their transformation and is proved by many case studies. Sanjay Baru[15], for example, brings out to the notice that how small business organisations (Nagarjuna, Dr Reddy's Lab., etc.) with the help of their local governments, local financial institutions and in the collaboration with Trans National Corporations developed themselves to be in league with the big business. Their struggle for and success in the termination of the license – permit raj, which was more favourable to the big business, facilitated such development, and in the process of it its organisational structure, its expansion and functioning and its market share and visibility underwent transformation; and its development, simultaneously, propelled the establishment of regional stock exchanges and ensured their vibrancy. The regional business firms became a part of the listed companies on these stock exchanges and then catapulted themselves to the national stock exchange.

Emerging Trend

All these developments had their impact on the regional politics which varied in different regions in different degrees. Under the new social milieu propelled by globalisation a new trend is witnessed that indicates the gradual substitution / marginalisation / cooptation of regional parties in different states which had provided alternative to the Congress system after 1967. The new emerging alternative to the Congress party is Bhartiya Janata Party that has intruded into government formation or has begun to play an important role in it in the provinces from Goa to Arunachal and from

Odisha to Karnataka. Although, it has yet to prove itself as a pan-Indian party on long-term basis, nonetheless it has become a new alternative political mascot of global capital in India that propels standardized / uniformal attributes in different regions while co-opting in itself the sanitised versions of the regional specifics. It simultaneously reflects, in reverse way, that in the course of expansion of market economy, a section of the regional business has grown into to become a part of the big business and a large section gets the opportunity of accessibility to capital, market and technology to become partner in global business. Their elephantine expansion in short duration reflects their success and also gets reflected in the composition of the Confederation of Indian Industries and of the Associated Chambers of Commerce (Assocham)[16] which are different from the old big business of the FICCI.

Conclusion

Apparently, it may seem dichotomous at this political juncture, to note the gradual marginalisation of the regional parties. But a rigorous analysis of the emerging economic trend and of the party systems in the provinces indicates the subterranean changes underway. The universal standardized attributes of the cosmopolitan production bases of the economy under globalisation has impacted on the culture and politics of the day resulting into cooptation of varied regional political elements by the BJP, the alternative political mascot of the global capital which is expanding its wings in the regions. Its refutation is possible if, alternatively, the regional parties themselves act to represent the global capital in the regions. Both the developments, however, are yet to be proved on long term basis.

REFERENCES

1. Bengal National Chamber of Commerce and Industry, *Souveneir Volume* 1887-1962 Calcutta, pp. 39, 49.
2. *Ibid.*, p. 113.

3. Suniti Kumar Ghosh, *India's Nationality Problem and Ruling Classes*, Kolkata, 1996, p. 17.
4. *Ibid.*, p. 20.
5. *Ibid.*, pp. 20-21.
6. *Ibid.*
7. Federation of Indian Chambers of Commerce and Industries, New Delhi, *Proceeding of the* 20th *Annual Meeting*, 1947, Volume 3, p. 86.
8. *Ibid.*
9. *Ibid., Proceeding of the* 20th *Annual Meeting of Federation of Indian Chambers of Commerce and Industries*, Volume 1, 1946, p. 128.
10. *Ibid.*, Volume 3, p. 29.
11. V.P. Menon, *Transfer of Power in India*, Calcutta, 1957, pp. 358-9.
12. Suniti Kumar Ghosh, *opcit.*, pp. 12, 14, 24.
13. Sanjay Baru, 'Economic Policy and Capitalism in India' in *Transforming India* (ed.) F. Frankel *et. al.*, Oxford, 2001, p. 226.
14. Himanshu Roy, 'Party Systems and Coalition Politics in Indian States' in M.P. Singh and Anil Mishra (eds.) *Coalition Politics in India*, Manohar, New Delhi, 2004.
15. For detail, see Sanjay Baru, *opcit*, pp. 216-225.
16. *Ibid.*, pp. 225, 230.

11

Regional Parties in Indian Federalism after the 2014 Elections

Subhendu Ranjan Raj

Regional parties have been the distinguishing feature of Indian democracy for many decades. For some three decades of coalition governance that we have had till 2014 we witnessed their syncretic role in formation of minority governments at the centre. Observers have maintained that their efflorescence and divergence panning the whole of India and in all states shows the strength and depth of federal ethos in India. Nowadays, however instead of paeans being written about them their obituaries are being written as single majority government has been formed at the centre. Is it true that the era of glory of regional parties in India is over.The truth is that regional parties now, contrary to the prolific views being engendered, are not obliterated – they remain significant. Because electorally speaking, facts suggest the contrary. If one collects the data of the last general elections of 2014 one would realise that the regional parties consolidatedly have got the same number of seats and the same percentage of votes in the 2014 elections as in the earlier 2009 election. Indeed regional parties have not been banished out into the oblivion as some observers would want us to believe.

Regional Parties as Important Constituents of Elections and Government Formation

The last some decades have been one of constant political change– and the most significant one has been in the changing nature of party system in India. From unipolarity of the 'Congress system' of the yesteryears a bipolarity has ensued a contest between two alliances, the United Progressive Alliance (UPA) led by the Congress and the National Democratic Alliance (NDA) led by the BJP. Indeed the last decade and half has evinced a polarised polity with multi-polarised contests in many states. It has also led to the emergence of small and regional parties. These federal parties have become the *de riguer* of politics in any Indian election – be it a election at the state level or at the national level. The salience of the local factors –such as ethnicity, backward caste, linguism, religious sensitivities etc. play a major part in the formation of multi-party coalition alliances in the Indian setting.[1]

We need to go beyond on the ideological premises in the Indian context because ideology is superseded by the convolution of ethnicity based salients (based on caste-lingual-regional and other parameters, usually considered as non-political criteria) that are pre-modern traditional loyalties yet transferred to a modern setting and work within the modern space of a constitutional democracy with as much correspondence as they did in days of yore. These salients may define the ideological or other postures of parties that participate in the Indian setting of coalitions, and are much more of primordial importance than mere ideology. These are variously described as the regional or the local factors in any election perhaps erroneously so, because they have a strong imprimatur on Indian politics and have come to be seen as strong determining forces guiding the fate of any election result.[2] Interestingly, some serious political developments have been noted behind the emergence of federal political outfits known loosely as regional political parties. They are the potential *de-riguer* in any alliance formation and would remain so, barring exceptional circumstances.

The last some decades have been one of constant political change – and the most significant one has been in the changing nature of party system in India. From unipolarity of the 'Congress system' of the yesteryears a bipolarity has ensued a contest between two alliances, the United Progressive Alliance (UPA) led by the Congress and the National Democratic Alliance (NDA) led by the BJP. Indeed the last decade and half has evinced a polarised polity with multi-polarised contests in many states. It has also led to the emergence of small and regional parties. These federal parties have become the *sumum bonum* of politics in any Indian election – be it a election at the state level or at the national level.

Under their impact, in a real sense we are now witness to the emergence of federal coalitions. India has seen the emergence of such coalitions since the nineties. Box No. 1 here below mentions the different coalitional and federal arrangements in power sharing at the centre here. It is to be noted that the initial experiments at power sharing were first started in the states of the Indian union.

Box No. 1: COALITION GOVERNMENTS AT THE CENTRE

- **4 Dec 1989–10 Nov 1990**: National Front Minority Coalition -V.P. Singh was Prime Minister.

  Coalition constituents-Janata Party, Congress(S), AGP, CPM, CPI, Lok Dal, DMK. Outside support of the BJP.

- **10 Nov. 1990–21 June 1991:** Minority Government Coalition Chandrasekhar was the Prime Minister. Formed with the outside support of the Congress.
- **21 June 1991–28 July 1993–31 Dec 1993**: Congress Minority Government-headed by P.V. Narasimha Rao. It lost minority status after the Jharkhand Mukti Morcha and Janata Dal (Ajit) helped defeat the no-confidence motion and these splinter groups were inducted into the Congress (I) party.
- **1 June 1996 – 21 April 1997 – 28 Nov 1997:** United Front minority Coalition government - headed by H.D. Deve Gowda and I.K. Gujral Coalition constituents-CPM, CPI, RSP, Forward Bloc, Samajwadi Party, Janata Dal, RJD, DMK, Tamil Manila Congress etc.
- **19 March 1998– 17 April 1999**: Minority Government led by BJP without side support from the Telugu Desam, Trinamul Congress etc. A.B.Vajpayee, the PM continues till 12 Oct 1999 as caretaker PM.
- **13 Oct 1999–May 2004**: National Democratic Alliance BJP's second Minority government formed with Vajpayee as PM. Coalition constituents– 24 parties such as Shiv Sena, DMK, Biju Janta Dal, INLD, PMK, Akali Dal, Janata Dal United, HVC,Trinamul Cong. Outside support of the Telugu Desam.

- **May 2004–May 2009**: United Progressive Alliance – I with Manmohan Singh as PM, 16 Coalition constituents: DMK, NCP, Trinamool Congress, National Conference, JMM, AIMIM, Kerala Congress, SDF, Kerala Congress (Mani) Republican Party of India (Athvale); Outside support given by 4 Left parties.
- **22 May 2009 – May 2014:** United Progressive Alliance –II with Manmohan Singh as PM, with 10 prepoll party constituents such as DMK, NCP, National Conference, JMM, IUML, Kerala Congress (Mani), AIMIM, Viduthalagaichiruthaigal Katchi, RPI (Athavale) Later adhesions : Bahujan Samaj Party and Samajwadi Party (giving Outside support).

Source: Compiled by the author from various sources.

Box No. 1 confirms empirically that in India since 1990 successive governments have been a motley of political alliance formations. The regional parties have become very significant in the emergence and formation of the alliances– be it the National Democratic Alliance or the two successive United Progressive Alliance or the earlier examples of the National Front and the United Front. Under their impact, in a real sense we have witnessed the emergence of federal coalitions. They have become very significant for the functioning of democracy.

Since the fourteenth Lok Sabha elections the vote share of regional parties has hovered around 29 per cent of the total votes in all elections which is almost equal to or more than the vote share of the national parties Congress party (28.6 per cent in 2009) and BJP (25.6 per cent in 1998). An absolute new civil society organisation turned political party which can be considered a regional force loosely, the Aam Aadmi Party (AAP) has emerged and has set new benchmarks as it garnered 30 per cent vote share in the Delhi Assembly polls in Dec 2013 (competing favourably with the national parties: the BJP secured 33 per cent and the Congress secured 25 per cent merely–thus resulting in-3 per cent of BJP and-15 per cent from the respective vote shares of the BJP and Congress.) This is in conformity with the increasing trend wherein new and small parties are securing as much, if not more voting share as the established parties.

These parties have popular support and have redefined the matrices of electoral and coalitional politics. Truly the regional parties are setting the parameters of government formation, coalitional functioning, defining the rules of internal floor management in the Parliament and in state assemblies, the making of policy and balancing priorities of governance increasingly. They are espousing causes, supporting demands of people of their regions, highlighting significant issues. In some cases, as in the case of AAP they have redefined the agenda of all political parties namely, what are the issues that are needed to be focussed upon by all parties much beyond the issues of caste, religion and identity factors that generally Indian political parties have been known to limit themselves to. Issues such as crony capitalism, nexus of big business with electoral funding, rampant corruption, nepotism ... etc have become the new benchmark for electoral propaganda.

II. Analysis of National and Regional Parties

The national parties in India are not too many. According to statistics available there were only seven such parties at the time of the 2009 General Elections. Of these seven (see Table 2) which are included in the list, actually two namely the NCP and RJD were in reality regional parties which had turned national parties because they had secured 6 per cent vote share in four or more states (which is the Election Commission criteria for declaring any party national).

In the run up to the 16th General elections in April – May 2014, one of these parties namely, the Rashtriya Janata Dal

(RJD) had lost its national tag and has reverted to its regional party category as it was hitherto.

Table 1 : NATIONAL PARTIES IN THE GENERAL ELECTION, LOK SABHA (2009, 15th LOK SABHA)

NATIONAL PARTIES	
Abbreviation	*Party*
BJP	Bharatiya Janata Party.
BSP	Bahujan Samaj Party.
CPI	Communist Party of India.
CPM	Communist Party of India (Marxist)
INC	Indian National Congress.
NCP	Nationalist Congress Party.
RJD	Rashtriya Janata Dal

Source: Election Commission of India.

In every state we find the presence of a sizable number of regional/state parties, some of which have a very influential following.

(It is to be noted that since 1989 there has not been a majority single party government at the national level in India, and there is unlikely to be in the future given the dynamics of state politics. In 1989, the National Front alliance took power, ruling until 1991 when the Congress returned to power as a minority government, led by Narasimha Rao. The BJP came to power as the largest party in the 1996 elections and after 13 days conceded that they were unable to form a coalition, handing over power to a left leaning coalition, the United Front).

In addition to this there are innumerable parties which have been characterised as Registered Unrecognised Parties by the Election Commission. These number more than fifteen hundred and are spread all over India. Some of the important regional parties are the Samajwadi party, Dravida Munnetra Kazhagam, All India Anna Dravida Munnetra Kazhagam,

Shiromani Akali Dal, Biju Janata Dal, Trinamool Congress, Jammu and Kashmir National Conference, Jharkhand Mukti Morcha, Bahujan Samaj Party, Marumalarchi Dravida Munnetra Kazhagam, Shiv Sena, Janata Dal (U), Rashtriya Janata Dal etc.

Table 2: Percentage of Votes Polled in 2009

Bahujan Samaj Party	6.17%
Bharatiya Janata Party	18.80%
Communist Party of India	1.43%
Communist Party of India (Marxist)	5.33%
Indian National Congress	28.55%
Nationalist Congress Party	2.04%
Rashtriya Janata Dal	1.27%

Others (Incl. Regional /State Parties, Registered unrecognised Parties and Independents)

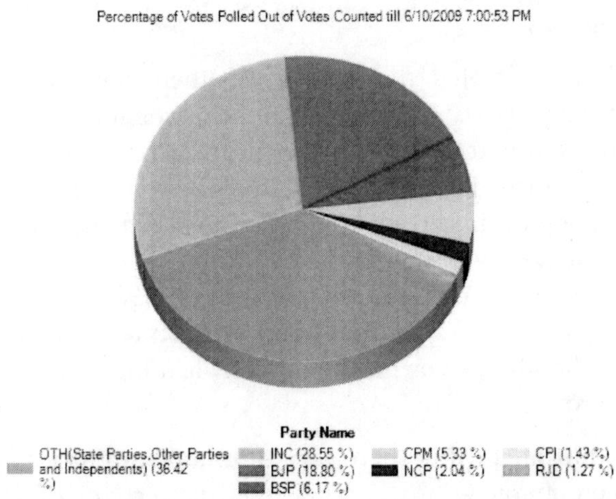

Source: Compiled by the author from various sources.

These parties have emerged in the background of typical factors in the specific context of a state or region within the state and some times spread in regions across states. Increasingly, in India they have come to play a very significant political and electoral role. Table 3 shows clearly the impact of regional parties on national level elections, namely in the context of the 2009 General Elections to the Lok Sabha. It states categorically that regional and registered unrecognised parties between themselves accounted for 36.42 per cent of votes share. This share is more than the vote share of the seven national parties individually which were in the fray in 2009.

III. The Regional Forces in Indian Federalism

For some time now the regional parties have been on the ascendancy. In fact, the importance of these regional parties can be seen even in earlier elections. Tables 4 and 5 show that in various states the regional parties are a major force in state elections and legislatures. Table 4 indicates the share of Lok Sabha seats occupied by the regional and state parties. It is seen that the Bahujan Samaj Party, Samajwadi Party, Trinamool Congress, Biju Janata Dal, DMK, AIADMK, Samata/Janata Dal(U) and Shiv Sena were major players who secured a sizable presence and traction in legislative action. Interestingly, these are the major players who have had a significant impetus in the formation, working and success of the two major Alliances that have emerged in the period spanning over the last two decades – namely the National Democratic Alliance and United Progressive Alliance I and II. No national party can overlook their legislative presence and bargaining skills.

Table 3: Lok Sabha seats Occupied by Regional/ Caste-Based parties (1989-2009)

Parties	*General Election*						
	Years						
	1989	*1991*	*1996*	*1998*	*1999*	*2004*	*2009*
Telugu Desam	2	13	17	12	29	5	6
AGP	0	1	5	0	0	2	1
Jharkhand M.M	3	6	1	0	0	5	2
J&K NC	3	0	0	3	2	2	3
Akali Dal	6	0	8	8	2	8	4
AIADMK	11	11	0	18	10	0	9
DMK	0	0	17	6	12	16	18
Sikkim Dem. F	0	0	1	1	1	1	1
Biju Janata Dal	-	-	-	9	10	11	14
Trinamool C	-	-	-	7	8	2	19
Shiv Sena	-	-	-	6	15	13	11
Pattali M. K	-	-	-	4	5	6	0
MDMK	-	-	-	3	4	4	1
Himachal VC	-	-	-	1	1	0	0
Samata/JD	-	-	-	12	21	8	20
R J D	-	-	-	17	7	21	4
Samajwadi	0	5	17	20	26	36	23
Bahujan SP	-	-	11	5	14	19	21

Source : Subhendu Ranjan Raj–Coalition Politics in India: Dimensions of Federal Power Sharing, Manak Publications New Delhi (2009) p. 32.

Thus, this represents what is considered as most important in a democratic set up- namely the vote shares of the regional parties in the state legislatures. A study of some twelve states finds that they have improved their share of votes in the respective assemblies consistently and progressively. This shows that their acceptance to voters even in the states of their origin is an accepted *fait accompli*. This gives them great bargaining strength William Riker calls this as critical for the formation of *'minimum winning coalitions.'*[2] In the 1952-1996 period, as we can see from Table 5 many states have returned the respective regional parties in their state handsomely in elections. In some cases, about 42 to 77.2 per cent of the vote share has gone to them. In Sikkim and Tamil Nadu, it was 77.2 per cent and 66.9 per cent respectively in the 1996 elections.

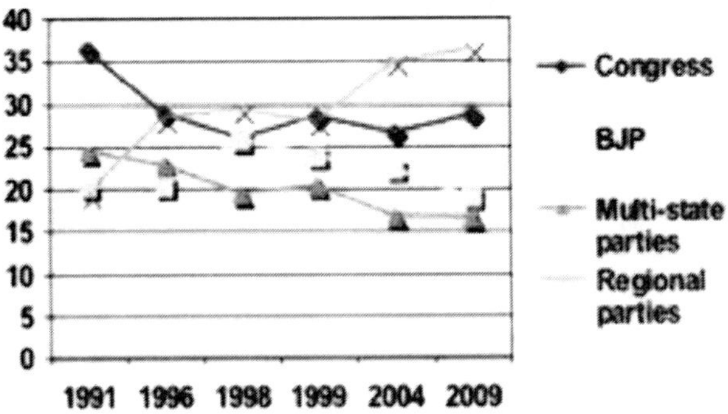

Source: Compiled by the Author.

Fig. 1. Historical shifts in terms of vote share across General Elections.

This histogram (Fig. 51) is a very important indicator of comprehensive shift of votes over a period of two decades. It graphically reveals a trend that is now quite pronounced. It shows very clearly that the BJP's curve is going downhill. The Congress curve is also showing a downward shift but after 2004 it has slightly inched towards the top. It is the regional parties which are going into stratospheric heights. In the particular case of regional parties, however different the context may be – whether there is a so called 'wave' for one national party or the other; whether single individuals are projected as national leaders par excellence and therefore increasing the winning ability factor of a political party (like it is in the context of 2014 election when Narendra Modi was touted as the adhesive that will resurrect a moribund BJP into power) or even in the face of anti- incumbency (like in the failure of the NDA – II coalition) or pro incumbency (as in the context of 2009 re-emergence of United Progressive Alliance) the tenuous importance of regional parties has sustained. In no circumstance have they become irrelevant or insignificant.

Table 4: Vote share of Regional and National parties (1984-2009)

	1984	*1989*	*1991*	*1996*	*1998*	*1999*	*2004*	*2009*
Congress	48.0	39.5	36.6	28.8	25.8	28.3	26.5	28.6
BJP	7.4	11.4	20.1	20.3	25.6	23.8	22.2	18.8
Left	9.3	10.2	9.7	9.1	7.8	7.6	7.9	7.5
BSP	0.0	2.1	1.8	4.0	4.7	4.2	5.3	6.2
Regl. Parties	11.2	27.1	21.1	26.2	29.3	29.5	29.3	28.4

Source: Sudha Pai–"*Handbook of Politics in Indian States–Regions, Parties and Economic Reforms*" OUP, N. Delhi p. 153.

Table 4 posits that the last few decades have shown a shift in voter's preference. The major national parties are facing a real challenge in terms of shifting of its support bases amongst the voters belonging to the Other Backward Castes (OBCs). Especially after the Mandal Commission these voters are politically articulate and seeking a political role for themselves independent of the Congress party's "umbrella" system which Rajni Kothari, Paul R Brass talked about in their works as existing in the pre-eighties' India. There is also a declining support for the national parties amongst adivasis. The emergence of BSP has polarised the dalit votes. The Muslim and minorities' vote has similarly changed hands. It is no longer going to the Congress party – other regional parties such as the Samajwadi Party, Samta, JD(United), Rashtriya Janata Dal have come into the field with secular credentials and they have been claiming such share of votes.

IV. The Sixteenth General Elections (2014): Towards a New Paradigm?

In seven elections from 1989 to 2009 no single party won a majority of seats in the Lok Sabha. In 1991, the Congress formed a single-party minority government (which achieved a majority half-way through its term) but in all other cases minority coalitions dependent on outside support were formed, these being large, multi-party coalitions with participation of several regional parties since 1996. It was noted by this author as also by some commentators before the 2014 elections that increasingly the results of the 2014 election will depend on alliances, both pre- and post-poll between parties in particular states. Electoral alliances between political parties operating on the basis of negotiating the number of seats a party may contest in a particular state, with the alliance partner contesting in the other seats. I had noted elsewhere in the run up to the May elections that efforts had been made by the BJP, in particular to have some pre-poll alliances as well.

The general elections of 2014, has indeed changed the scene entirely by giving single party overwhelming majority to the BJP. Has a paradigm shift in Indian politics occurred? This section focuses on the performance of the regional parties in this context and *argues that it is too early to say that the regional parties seem to have lost their importance.*

Although there are seemingly some changes brought about of a cataclysmic nature in 2014 with the BJP winning a majority, the significant fact remains that the regional parties and their importance has not been wiped out, howsoever one might think. Today, in the aftermath of 2014 elections, surprising as it may seem, *the total vote share and seat share of regional parties remains exactly the same as it was in 2009 – i.e., 46.7 per cent and 212 seats.*[3]

Moreover, the majority that BJP has garnered has been on the basis of coalitional arrangements with the regional parties. So, a rethink on the regional parties is necessary. A new think would have to examine the prevailing view that we are back to the era of single party majoritarian rule.

Party	Vote Share	Seats
BJP	31	282
INC	19.3	44
BSP	4.1	0
AITC	3.8	34
SP	3.4	5
AIADMK	3.3	37
CPM	3.2	9
IND.	3	3
TDP	2.5	16
YSRP	2.5	9
AAP	2	4
SHS	1.9	18
DMK	1.7	0
BJD	1.7	20
NCP	1.6	6
RJD	1.3	4
TRS	1.2	11
NOTA	1.1	0
JDU	1.1	2
Others	10.3	39

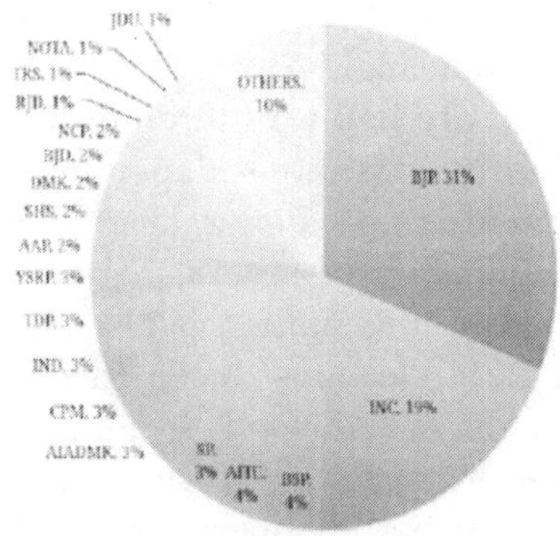

Source :http://scroll.in/article/666049/Everything-you-need-to-know-about-Lok-Sabha-Verdict-2014(Accessed on 25 .2.2016)

Fig. 2: 2014 Lok Sabha Election results-I.

Party	2009		2014	
	Vote Share	Seats	Vote Share	Seats
Trinamool	31.18%	19	39.35%	34
CPM	32.11%	9	22.71%	2
BJD	37.23%	14	44.08%	20
AIADMK	22.88%	9	44.28%	37
DMK	25.09%	18	23.58%	0
TDP	24.93%	6	29.15%	16
TRS	6.14%	2	13.93%	11
YSR Congress	0.00%	0	28.94%	9
SP	23.26%	20	22.19%	5
BSP	27.42%	23	19.63%	0
SHS	17.00%	11	20.64%	18
NCP	19.28%	8	15.04%	4
JD(U)	24.04%	20	15.78%	2
RJD	20.13%	4	20.14%	4
LJP	6.96%	0	6.40%	6
SAD	33.85%	4	26.27%	4

Source : http://scroll.in/article/666049/Everything-you-need-to-know-about-Lok-Sabha-Verdict-2014(Accessed on 25.2.2016)

Fig. 3: 2014 Lok Sabha Election results-II.

If we look at the election results on 2014 it becomes manifestly clear that the mandate for the BJP hides more than it shows. Although it can be seen from Fig. 2 and 8 that BJP has secured 282 seats with a vote share of 31 per cent in this election, my submission is that this factuality should not be construed to mean that it is a return to single party majoritarianism as it is being thought of by a majority of commentators.

I'll submit some evidences why the contrary may be more correct.

(i) Seat share and Vote percentage share of Regional parties : Looking at the actual voting percentage of the regional parties it becomes clear that manifestly the regional parties vote share has not dropped !. The combined vote share of the regional parties remains the same as it was in the 2009 elections, namely that both in 2009 and 2014 elections the combined vote share of regional parties remained constant at 46.7 per cent of the votes polled.[4]

Same is the case of the total seats gained by the regional parties. Both in 2009 and 2014 elections the combined vote share of regional parties remained unchanged at 212 seats. (See Fig. 4)

The fact that is highlighted by this table is that the regional parties remain very significantly entrenched in the Indian body politique. They could not gain a higher share of seats of the Lok Sabha for a variety of reasons such as swing factor working in favour of BJP, the dominant aspirational nature of change desired by the voters, a wave for a strong leader on the background of a lacklustre, supine and vacillating spell of UPA–II's Manmohan Singh. Despite the tsunami of change to single party majoritarianism established by the BJP, the regional parties have held out. Some regional satraps have had decrease in their share but others such as the BJD, TMC, AIADMK, TRS, YSR Congress etc have notched

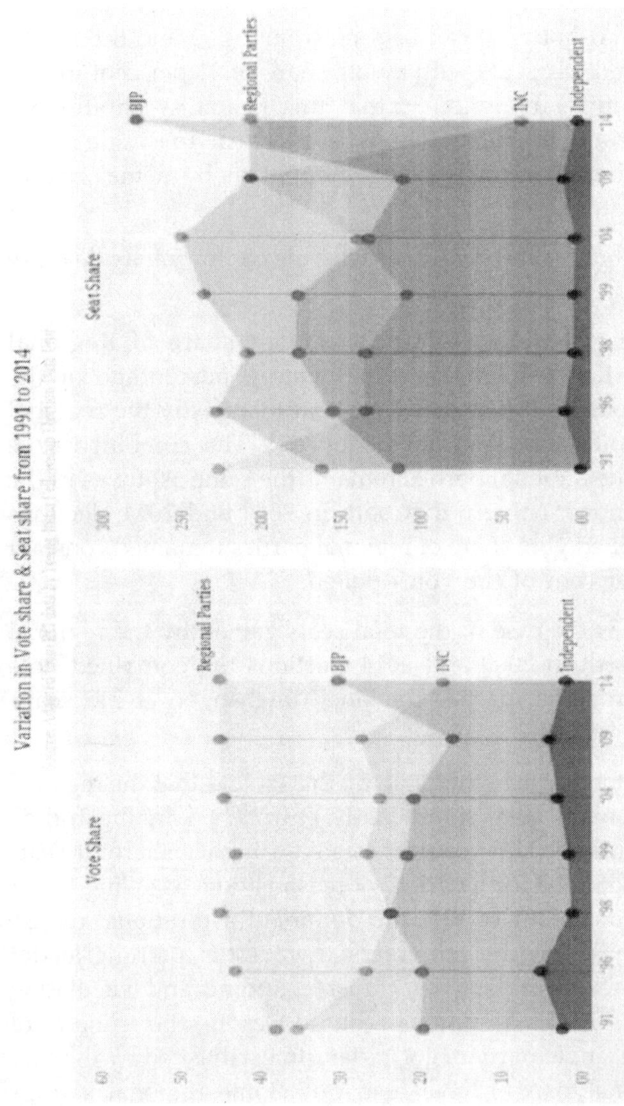

Source: http://scroll.in/article/666049/Everything-you-need-to-know-about-Lok-Sabha-Verdict-2014 (Accessed on 25 .2.2016.

Fig. 4: Vote and Seat Share Variation (1991 to 2014).

spectacular gains both in the number of seats and in their vote shares.

Thus, the regional parties cannot be written off. Especially as in this author's view the coalitional identities and formations have not been subsumed entirely.

(ii) Value of alliances: BJP's Pre-Poll alliances: We cannot assume that the era of importance of regional parties is over because of another reality. The BJP understood the significance of forging pre-poll alliances with a number of parties despite being confident of being returned to power. E. Sridharan says in 2014, the BJP had ten pre-electoral alliances compared to six alliances in 2009 in which both it and its partner(s) contested seats, of which 7 were new alliances– in the states of Bihar, Seemandhra, Telangana, TamilNadu, Haryana, Kerala and UP –and on more favourable terms. By contrast, the Congress in 2014 had 8 alliances, one more than 2009, on essentially the same terms as before (except in UP and Bihar, with an improvement over the terms of 2004). In all other states the terms remain essentially the same. What this reflects is the willingness of a range of parties to ally with the BJP in response to the perceived swing in its favour according to forecasts, as against an unwillingness to ally with the Congress, patently so in Tamil Nadu, former Andhra Pradesh and West Bengal, as it is seen to be a party in relative decline and unlikely to be able to form a government and offer a share of power at the Centre. To the extent that pre-electoral coalitions make a difference, the odds seem to be against the Congress.[5]

E. Sridharan says very perspicaciously that the BJP's alliance politics help it to win from areas where its alliance partner had a sway. For example, in Maharashtra where it had an alliance with Shiv Sena it contested 24 seats out of which it won 23; Shiv sena contested on 20 seats merely. In Bihar similarly, it had a seat sharing alliance with Lok Janshakti Party and Rashtriya Lok Samta Party and contested seven and four respectively and won six and three seats.

Thus, the alliance formation has undergone a change. Although it needs no allies BJP has maintained the power sharing paradigm of distributing ministries among its pre-poll alliance partners. This government has five non-BJP ministers in the 45-member council of ministers (four in the 23-member cabinet, of whom one each is from the Shiv Sena, TDP, SAD and LJP, and one out of the 22 ministers of state is from a minor Bihar party)." Of the 282 seats won by the BJP, as many as 57 seats are accounted for by states in which the BJP depended significantly on coalition partners. These are Maharashtra (23 seats), Bihar (22 seats), Haryana (seven seats), Andhra Pradesh (two seats), Punjab (two seats) and Tamil Nadu (one seat) the figures in parentheses indicating the number of BJP seats and principal allies in these states being the Shiv Sena, LJP, HJC, TDP and Pattali Makkal Katchi (PMK) and several minor parties in Tamil Nadu respectively."[6]

The BJP won 282 seats, a majority of the 543 elected in the Lok Sabha on the strength of such pre-poll alliances and was able to form a surplus majority NDA government with its pre-electoral coalition partners, the principal ones being the Shiv Sena, LJP, TDP and SAD,taking its majority in the Lok Sabha to 334.[7]

So the victory of BJP was also in no small measure due to value of electoral alliances.

Conclusion

The major conclusion in this paper is that a historical continuity of alliance formation of national party with regional parties will continue and help even though it may not be necessary for government formation *per se* as has been the case in the past UPA and NDA experiments. There seems to be little chance for a scenario for a formation (which may be variously nomenclature as minority government formation, third front government etc) allied with very few pre-poll but many post-poll adhesions and supported by at least one national party may also have a chance of gaining power at the centre can become a reality. This is in the context when efforts at a third front have not taken off and regional satraps (the powerful leaders/aspiring Chief Ministers heading the regional parties) have had Prime Ministerial ambitions in the past and as of now. Thus, we are headed towards a future wherein strong leaders in national parties will be able to stem the tide of multi- party government formation and coalitional alliance pattern that has set in the Indian party system due to the crisis in majoritarian party politics seen universally and in the Indian context. This thus is another momentous factor which is being underlined in bold relief – and this is, that the importance of political leadership in managing large diverse federal, regional, caste and cultural/ linguistic politics effectively has become central in the people's perception apart from taking care of the economy. The Westminister model that India follows gives effective power to the Prime Minister from whom strong leadership expected. Increasingly, it is being seen that when such leadership is not emerging, for whatever reasons, then policy paralysis, economic stasis and degeneration of political authority occurs and leads to public disenchantment and defeat of a party/ coalition. Indian public supports a strong leader. 2014 elections have thrown open the response of people in such a scenario. Their stance and approach is now focussed on prioritisation of the development agenda and apparently it seems that the era of coalitions is over. But is this really the end of the coalition era? No and neither the regional parties seem to have lost their importance.

This paper postulates however that theoretically and empirically based on the historical facts of party system, there is no paradigm shift and the relevance of regional parties is not subsumed. There is a change in the manner in which the regional parties are now germane to the changed political situation and discourse. Regional and small parties will be required for they reflect the body politique and the uniqueness of the Indian political environment and the aspirations of Indian people. There might be change in their role for now. But in the not too distant future, they may revert to the status quo, if BJP fails to deliver on its grandiose plans and designs. Single party majoritarianism may again be thrown to the winds and we may again see the recrudescence of coalitional politics and with it regional parties may again come centre stage.

NOTES

1. See Subhendu Ranjan Raj, *Coalition Politics in India–Dimensions of Federal Power Sharing,* Manak Publications, New Delhi (2009).
2. William H. Riker, The Theory of Political Coalitions, Yale University Press, New Haven (1961).
3. Gilles Verniers and the YIF "Electoral Data Unit,"VERDICT 2014 -Everything you need to know about Lok Sabha Verdict 2014 explained in 40 charts"Jun 6, 2014 http://scroll.in/article/666049/Everything-you-need-to-know-about-Lok-Sabha-Verdict-2014-explained-in-40-charts
4. Gilles Verniers and the YIF "Electoral Data Unit,"-*ibid.*
5. E Sridharan, "Pre-electoral coalitions in 2014" Ballots and Bullets School of Politics and International Relations, University of Nottingham http://nottspolitics.org/2014/04/07/pre-electoral-coalitions-in-2014 /
6. See E. Sridharan and Adnan Farooqui (2014): Is the Coalition Era Over in Indian Politics?, The Round Table: The Commonwealth Journal of International Affairs, p. 4.
7. See E. Sridharan and Adnan Farooqui (2014), *ibid,* p. 10.

REFERENCES

Subhendu Ranjan Raj, Coalition Politics in India – Dimensions of Federal Power Sharing, Manak Publications, New Delhi (2009).

Badri Raina, "An Indian General Election Like No Other" Mainstream, Vol. LII, No. 12, March 15, 2014.

Sudha Pai, Handbook of Politics in Indian States – Regions, Parties and Economic Reforms OUP, New Delhi (2013)

Sudha Pai, *Dalit Assertion and the Unfinished Democratic Revolution:The BSP in North India* Sage Publications, New Delhi (2002).

William H.Riker, *The Theory of Political Coalitions* Yale University Press, New Haven (1962)

D D Khanna and Gert W. Kueck (eds), *Principles, Power and Politics,* Macmillan, N Delhi (2002)

Paul R. Brass, *Factional Politics in an Indian State: The Congress Party in UP,* University of California Press, Berkeley (1965).

Christophe Jaffrelot, *India's Silent revolution:The Rise of the Low Castes in North Indian Politics,* Permanent Black, New Delhi (2003).

Lloyd, I. Rudolph and Susanne Rudolph, *The Modernity of Tradition: Political Development in India,* University of Chicago Press, Chicago(1967).

G. Shah (ed.), *Dalit Identity and Politics: Cultural Subordination and the Dalit Challenge,* Sage Publications, New, Delhi (2001).

Lawrence Saez, *Federalism without a Centre –the Impact of Political and Economic reform on India's Federal system,* Sage Publications, New Delhi (2002).

12

Federal Decentralisation in the Era of Globalisation and Coalition Politics

Ruchi Tyagi

Federalism refers to the advocacy of multi-tiered government combining elements of shared-rule at the Centre and regional self-rule. It is based on the presumed value of achieving both unity and diversity by accommodating, preserving and promoting distinct identities within a larger political union. Political events in various parts of the world during the past decade have attracted new attention to the strengths and weaknesses of federal solutions as means of resolving political problems. In the Twenty-first Century the development landscape worldwide is constantly being shaped and reshaped by the simultaneous processes of globalisation and localisation (conjointly called 'Globalisation'). In this scenario the subnational political units are emerging as principal actors in the global economy. With this, the location or site of governance is changing. It indicates revival of local cultural identities. Here, 'local' becomes the provider of the response to the forces that are 'global'. Globalisation reflects the growth imperatives forcing the organisations and nations to negotiate with and mediate or interrogate the global pressures. Globalisation and localisation have become the most important trends of the new century.

As a result, governments have been faced increasingly with the desires of their people to be global consumers and local citizens at the same time. Global communications and consumership have awakened desires in the smallest and most remote villages around the world for access to the global marketplace of goods and services. In other words, the global economy has unleashed economic and political factors strengthening both global and local pressures at the expense of the traditional nation state. Here, the nation-state itself is simultaneously proving both too small and too large to serve all the desires of its citizens. Because of the development of the world market economy, self-sufficiency of the nation-state is widely recognised as unattainable and nominal sovereignty is less appealing if it means that, in reality, people have less control over decisions that crucially affect them. At the same time, nation-states have become too remote from individual citizens to provide a sense of direct democratic control and to respond clearly to the specific concerns and preferences of their citizens. The foregoing trends have tended to engender a common tendency to assume that we are witnessing the beginning of the end of the nation-states and rise of supranational regional or/and global economies. This is largely true but the on closer observation of the situation is found to be more complex, for the nation-state is not in decline all over the world. In various parts of the globe it is declining in some, failing is some, and becoming stronger in some. In such a context, federalism with its different levels of government has provided a way of mediating the variety of global and local citizen preferences.

Seven components of designing decentralisation are crucial for its success.[1] These are:

1. Finance should follow function: Revenue raising authority must be linked, at the margin to the service provision responsibilities.
2. Informed public opinion: There should be local access to right information to enable the local community to develop meaningful public opinion and decide priorities.
3. Mechanisms for making local priorities known must be put in place.
4. Credible incentives for people to participate: Writers on institutional economics have long observed that people's willingness to participate varies according to their perception of how much impact such participation will have.
5. Adherence to local priorities: There should be compelling incentives for politicians to be responsive and accountable.
6. Appropriate incentives for sub-national governments to maintain fiscal responsibility: It is argued that destabilisation effects of decentralisation arose mainly from inappropriate incentives than any problem inherent in decentralisation (Spahn, 1997) including soft budget constraints.
7. Instruments of decentralisation should be designed to support political objectives. The instruments of decentralisation at the disposal of a policy maker are:
   (i) Legal institutional framework.
   (ii) Structure of service delivery responsibilities.
   (iii) Allocation of various taxes among different levels of the government.

(iv) Intergovernmental transfers.

(v) Central government controls and constraints upon sub-national borrowing.

(vi) Local government election rules.

During early 1990s, the initiation of economic reforms in India reduced Centre's role in controlling the economy and recent changes in the political configuration in the country, have broken the monopoly of the political party that had ruled at the Centre and the states in the initial 40 years after independence, and has replaced it by the coalition government at the Centre. There has been the emergence of governments in several states run by regional parties, leading to the demand for greater regional autonomy to the states and vesting of constitutional status to local bodies, consequent upon the enactment of constitutional amendments. All these developments led to the demand for **"cooperative federalism"** in the country, to guard against the emergence of monopoly at the Centre. Cooperative federalism accords primacy to lower tiers of the government in providing public services, and contemplates the most decentralised form of governance. But a change from quasi-federalism to cooperative federalism needs lot of changes - political, legal and constitutional. A Constitution Review Commission was set up by the Government of India, to consider different aspects of changes demanded in the Constitution.

Federal Decentralisation in the Era of Globalisation

The debate on decentralisation since 1990s can be seen as a final stage of the dialectical movement of the development paradigm (Sharma, 2005a:2). Till mid 1980s there was a trend in favour of more economic role for the state (this paradigm gave rise to the extreme forms of centralisation). The centralised decision-making was seen as a way to 'rationalise scarce resources and to depoliticise the masses' while decentralisation was viewed as likely to heighten cleavages; political, radical, ethnic, and religious. The second phase emerged in late 1980s and early 1990s accompanying an obsession with curtailing the economic role of the state and reducing the size of the public sector, as these were seen as major causes for financial crisis in the developing countries. The public sector far from being regarded as engine of development came to be perceived as an obstacle to it. There was a fascination with the private sector. (Privatisation is seen as extreme form of decentralisation). By mid 1990s, however, a renewed appreciation of the public sector's development role began to emerge.[2]

The economic liberalisation transformed central–regional relations unleashing unintended and unplanned decentralisation. Since the beginning of economic liberalisation and the parallel process of regional representation in national governments (that began in 1996), India's regional states now enjoy considerable political and economic autonomy, but also face intense fiscal pressures on their fragile economies. Lawrence Saez has noted that economic liberalisation policies in the 1990s prompted a change in federal relations from inter-governmental cooperation toward inter-jurisdictional competition among the states.[3] Rob Jenkins has argued that federalism facilitated the political sustainability of India's reform process displacing opposition to the state level.[4] Lloyd and Susanne Rudolph[5] have characterised the changes in the following way: "A federal market economy is fast replacing a Nehruvian centralised command economy in the country's economic imagination and practice." John Echeverri-Gent[6] has analysed significant "decentering" in the economic relations between regional states and the Centre. Pradeep Chhibber and Samuel Eldersveld[7] compared the extent of local popular support for economic reform in India and China.

The recent trends are generating tendencies in both directions (centralisation and decentralisation) with the aim of providing good governance and a stable, secure and just government. It has been argued that centralising tendencies are likely to be more salient in countries like the United States where intra-state authority was initially more decentralised, while decentralising tendencies are likely to be more salient in states that were initially more centralised like China and India.[8]

Federalisation of the Party System

These formal and informal changes in India's policy regime were accompanied by significant political decentralisation in the party system, electoral system, and the structure of coalition governments.[9] The party system in India has undergone a significant change from a one-party dominant system, what has been termed the "Congress-system," to a multi-party regionalised system. This realignment was evident in the late 1980s with the decline of the Congress party and the rise of "backward caste" based and regional parties. Moreover, minority or coalition governments have ruled India since the late 1980s. The 1989 national general elections generated a minority government, with V. P. Singh's Janata Dal supported by the Left and the Congress party from the outside. In 1991, another minority government came into power, led by the Congress party. The elections of May 1996 led to the subsequent coming to power of the United Front, a coalition of thirteen parties, many of which were regional (like TDP from Andhra Pradesh, TMC from West Bangal, DMK from Tamil Nadu, and AGP from Assam) and the swearing in of a Prime Minister, Deve Gowda, a regional leader prominent in Karnataka. Subsequently, with the fall of the United Front ministry in 1998, national elections generated another hung parliament and a seventeen-party coalition government led by the BJP, one including many regional parties, took power in April 1998. The 1999 and also the 2004 governments were yet again coalition governments with regional parties as partners.

At the national level no single party is able to accommodate in it the Indian multi-verse of the class, caste, religious, linguistic, ethnic and regional interests. Thus, the latest phase in party politics is characterised by the emergence of a two-coalitional party system, in which the two leading national parties, with more or less equal electoral strength, act as central pillars to the rival coalitions.[10] Understanding the dynamics of party coalitions has emerged as an important field in Indian politics in recent years.[11] BalveerArora describes this competitive multi-party system as "bi-nodal", a node being a centering[12] point of component parts. He sees in this process both the trends of federalisation of the party system and renewal of parties.

Small states often perceive themselves as being on the periphery of national agendas, and seek to maximise the returns from their minuscule representation. This results in the dominance of local concerns in calculations of smaller state-based parties. And that's why national level tie-ups are negotiated and justified primarily by their beneficial impact on state-level struggles. Political opportunism, therefore, has its roots in the compulsions of local political processes. There legitimate aspirations are to be taken in account while assessing their space in cohesive national fabric.

These parties sought to reconcile territorially-based identities within a cohesive frame even in the absence of shared ideologies. Politics during past three decades has proved that coalitions based on ideological affinity frequently splits or schisms (gets divided into opposing groups through a difference in belief or opinion) after quarrels over turfs between covetous allies, and bitterest contests are often between like-minded parties seeking configuration of political space. On the other hand, federal coalitions based on the accommodation of regional aspirations can arguably be converted into stable arrangements with greater ease. This is particularly applicable to coalitions with a predominance of parties in power at the state level. On the other hand, coalition with parties in opposition seeking alliance to capture power with the help of central intervention as pivotal members could prove unstable. As power to dislodge state governments under Article 356 is now subject to judicially determined norms and overtly discriminatory practices may impose heavy political costs.

The process altogether focused on reconciliation, recuperation and even reintegration of potentially secessionist movements with innovative accommodation. The system reflected toleration for difference. It not only accepted but also celebrated diversity; and considered it central to the consolidation and stability of federal coalitions.[13] Political culture, which accords a central place to accepting and negotiating differences, is considered conducive to the consolidation and stability of federal coalitions.

The new trends reflected low levels of trust in opportunistic political cultures that have reduced the time-horizons of coalition partners engaged in multi-level political combats. While each partner works towards an improved vote / seat share, efforts are simultaneously deployed to contain rivalry and prevent antagonisms that could be fatal to the coalition itself. In such context, parties that understand and seize the possibilities offered by coalition building have an advantage. Those who can make the system work are rewarded, while those who are unable to reconfigure it to their advantage are gradually marginalised.[14]

While the struggle for power between castes and classes dominates political life in the primary arena of state and panchayat politics in India, regional aspirations are significant factors in the political calculations that parties make when they enter the secondary arena, which is more concerned with national policy cohesion and federal governance.[15] Such calculations play a determining role in forging coalitions and therefore, have important institutional consequences. Ideological affinities and programmatic alliances do not preclude regional aspirations. Taken into account are the ambitions of territorial consolidation and expansion of its partners. These arrangements are not merely 'elite accommodation', instead are generally tactical calculations based on ground-level cleavages. Example of such alliance can be found in the Shiv Sena and BJP alliance in Maharashtra.

A reasonable relation between espoused national causes and regional concerns has also been observed. Because of the predominance of local concerns, leaders of state-based parties are shielded and insulated to some extent from the consequences of their actions at the national level. Occasionally there is an overriding national event or issue capable of generating a 'wave', but last such wave was arguably seen in 1984, after the assassination of Indira Gandhi. Otherwise, local issues invariably prevail in non-wave conditions, especially when questions of identity and demands for space, voice and esteem in the wider polity dominate the electoral consultation.

The era of globalisation has resulted in the merger of global capital with Indian monopoly capital resulting in steep rise in the potential and strength of corporate sector. It has also resulted in the emergence of regional business groups on one hand and regional as well as rural-urban dichotomy on the other. Most of the parties, national vis-à-vis regional, have widely accepted the GPL (Globalisation, Privatisation and Liberalisation). With no exception, all parties are inviting foreign capital, welcoming multinational corporations and seeking ways and means for economic reforms. Even voters are aspiring for quick returns in terms of infrastructure from Bijli-Pani-Sarak to employment with better salaries and better life-style. Sanjaya Baru is of the view[16] that the failure of national political parties and the Central Government to address the needs of emergent regional business groups encouraged the latter to seek political and material support from state governments and regional political parties. It is to be noted that regional political parties have been more active in the States where regional business groups have been more dynamic and assertive. Thus, according to Baru, the link between the emergence of regional capitalism and regional parties is too stark to be ignored.

The maturing of electoral politics in many states—the stabilisation of two-party systems within states, separation of national and state-level electoral logics, institutionalisation of single-state parties, and the necessity of pre-electoral alliances between national and single state parties—unwittingly contributed to sub-national policy autonomy. The "increased assertiveness" of political institutions such as the Supreme Court, the President, and the Election Commission have also magnified what John Echeverri-Gent, in a recent assessment, called the "decentering" of India's polity. In a path-breaking judgment that set the tone for a new Centre–State compact, the Supreme Court in 1994 ruled against a misuse of the provision that allows the Centre to impose President's Rule in states (Article 356). The unanimous judgment by the nine-judge constitutional bench delivered on March 11, 1994 held that any proclamation under Article 356 is subject to judicial review. The Supreme Court thus rejected the contention of the central government that imposition of President's Rule requires no justification, ruling that Article 74(2) does not bar the Court from summoning the material that formed the basis of the cabinet advice to the President in initiating dismissal of a state government. (Article 74 (2) of the Indian Constitution bars an enquiry into the question of whether any or what advice was tendered by the Council of Ministers to the President.) This ruling changed Centre–regional relations significantly, giving the federal compact a new institutional force.

From a political economy perspective, these economic, fiscal, and political changes unleashed a new logic of collective action in India's "federal market economy."[17] In the 1980s, Jyoti Basu, N. T. Rama Rao and other opposition Chief Ministers tried to build a coalition of opposition party states—of "Non-Congress CMs"—challenging the hegemony of the dominant party and what they termed "the centralised state."

They mobilised their citizens against the Centre, and held conclaves and conferences to discuss the coming together of such forces. At least four national conferences or conclaves were held in the 1980s: at Vijaywada, Srinagar (October 1983), Calcutta (1984), and Delhi (April 25, 1987) where CMs from opposition parties attended and attempted to coordinate their strategy for greater regional autonomy against a dominant Centre and a dominant party. These meetings intensified during 1987–89. In 1987 seven CMs participated in the conference held at Delhi. This was followed by more focused meetings in May 1987, September 1987, December 1987, and January 1988.[18]

But in the late 1990s, after Chandrababu Naidu replaced his father-in-law, as the Chief Minister of Andhra Pradesh, he tried to organise a different kind of coalition, the coalition of "performing and reforming states."[19] Naidu's aggressive lobbying succeeded in modifying the rules of the Eleventh Finance Commission, which inserted a system of rewards (carrots and sticks) for states that had better institutional and fiscal indicators. The central government has created an "Incentive Fund" from which fiscal performance based grants were to be made for those states that achieve a reduction of the revenue deficit. In India, central government's tax revenue as a percentage of the GDP increased from 9.0 per cent in 1980 to 10.8 per cent in 1997, while China's tax revenue in 1997 as a percentage of its GDP was as low as 4.9 per cent.

Since Sixteenth General Elections

The perspective of an emerging post-Congress polity has lately dominated the analyses of political parties in India. Since no party got an absolute majority between 1989 and 2009, the emerging coalition politics was seen as federalisation of the party system. As the one-party dominant system moved to a multi-party competition, a stable political pattern gave way to fluidity as the principle of party competition, which became all too apparent during the fifteenth general election in 2009 when a Fourth Front too came into the fray. However, multipolarity did not take shape then, indicating perhaps that the party system in India was reaching its fragmentational and coalitional limits. This became clear in the sixteenth general election with the BJP becoming the first party to obtain an absolute majority in three decades.

A look at the way national and smaller parties have been situated between 1991 and 2014 with the prevalent classification indicates that though their combined votes declined from 67.5 per cent to 47.35 per cent in two decades, the two largest parties Congress and BJP obtained over 50 per cent votes and 40 per cent seats in the sixteenth Lok Sabha almost similar to the last election. If we disregard the claim of other smaller parties to technical status, rest of the parties have had nearly 50 per cent of the space in votes and 40 to 45 per cent of seats. In 2014, they have 35 per cent of votes and over 39 per cent seats, but a decline of the smaller parties with national status is visible in 2014. Also, there has been a plateauing of state parties, in the ECI parlance, since 2004. Three significant facts:

(i) Cong+BJP's combined strength is similar to the last election and they have consistently held 55-60 per cent LS seats since 1996;

(ii) Rest of the smaller parties have continued to retain 40 per cent space and 50 per cent votes, but for one party majority, they could have leveraged this for greater bargain;

(iii) The category of other parties, classified as national but small, have significantly shrunk, raising genuine question on their categorisation as national;

(iv) BJP's majority in the same space with similar vote share that it has had with the Congress in earlier elections gives the extent of loss of the Congress to the BJP and other small parties.

A tentative putting together of the data given out by the ECI after 2014 general election creates a fascinating scenario of the emerging party system in India.

First, the BJP has clearly replaced the Congress as the main dominant party and is expanding its base across the country. Yet, it still has miles to as nearly 90 per cent of its seats have come from the northern and western states that are its stronghold. It is not past vulnerability.

Second, the Congress has very sharply lost its already shrinking space. It has reasons to worry and put the house in order.

Third, the smaller parties, whether called national or state parties, still occupy nearly 50 per cent space, which is large and indicates the limitations of the two national parties.

Fourth, those among smaller parties with a national tag such as the CPM and CPI have to reflect on their ideology, political organisation and popular imagination if they have to survive.

Fifth, the base for coalition politics at the national level has weakened due to the BJP becoming uncoalationable due to its strength and the Congress losing attraction due to its weakness.

Growing Significance of Inter-Governmental Mechanisms

Since 1990s, India has become considerably more federalised than before. This is evident in the increased political autonomy and revenue of state governments vis-à-vis the Union Government; growing maneuverability of the constitutional heads of state – President and governors; growing salience of Union constitutional agencies like the Election Commission of India and intergovernmental agencies like the ISC (Inter-State Council) and NDC (National Development Council); decline in the role of centralised planning; creation of a series of independent regulatory agencies and appellate tribunals under parliamentary status in such vital sectors of the economy as communications, electricity, insurance, finance, stock exchange, etc.; greater visibility of the Human Rights Commission, Minority Commission, Scheduled Castes and Tribes Commission appointed either under the constitution or a parliamentary statute; and the revival and constitutional entrenchment of local self-governing institutions of Panchayat and Nagar Raj, etc.

With declining investment by the state in the economy and the emerging profile of a federal regulatory state in place of the bureaucratic state, a new partnership between the state, the civil society, and the market needs to be forged. What is required is: (a) constitutional entrenchment of the NDC, like the ISC, as the major line organisations of intergovernmental 'executive federalism' (b) Streamlining of the two staff agencies of executive federalism, namely, the Finance Commission and the Planning Commission. (c) Implementation of the entire spectrum of party system reforms recommended by the Venkatachaliah Commission Report (d) Setting up of a constitutional commission on the taxation system as recommended by the Sarkaria Commission. (e) Streamlining of local self-governing institutions of Panchayat Raj Institutions and urban Municipal Bodies. India moving from a two-level federation (Union and States) towards multi-level federalism with local bodies (village councils and municipalities) at the district and below becoming the third level has made the nation a cascading federalism; a federation of federations. It may be recalled here that India has vibrant autonomous councils to meet the specific demands of the regions, as per the Constitution of India. This multi-level federalism should be seen as the structural means through which self-government goes all the way down to village councils from the Centre. Local self-governing units in such a scheme will draw sustenance from grassroots level political and democratic process as well as effective people's participation.

Since 1990s, Indian political system recorded growing significance of inter-governmental mechanisms like the ISC (Inter-State Council) and NDC (National Development Council), Zonal Councils and interstate tribunals. Accepting constitutional "emergencies" and legislations warranted in "national/public" interest (determinable jointly by the Union executive and Parliament), the constitutional scheme of Union-State relations normally expects a functional interdependence between the two orders of governments.

Article 263 of the Constitution contemplates an Inter-State Council (ISC) for harmonisation of inter-state and Union-State relations and policy coordination. The composition and rules of business of this council are left wide-open by the Constitution. The Constitution itself did not set up the ISC. Article 263 only made an enabling provision for establishing it by the Union Government if "it appears to the President that the public interests would be served by the establishment of a Council". The ISC was not set up until 1990 at all, and after that date it has not really come into its own[20]. It has either been inert, ineffective, or bypassed by such extra-constitutional intergovernmental forums such as the National Development Council (NDC) set up by the Nehru government in 1952 for intergovernmental approval of five-year plans[21] or several National Councils in some policy areas (like local self-government, health, and population)[22]. Parliamentary enactments have also set up Zonal Councils under the States' Reorganisation Act, 1956, and some inter-state tribunals under the Inter-State River Water Disputes Act, 1956. Prima facie, these enabling constitutional or legal openings have left Article 263 in splendid isolation. Instead of the Constitutional formality of this provision, the Union governments have generally preferred to set up apex forums by less formal cabinet resolutions, for they allow the Union Government a greater leeway. Besides, parliamentary creations have also been largely defunct (e.g. Zonal Councils, excepting the Northeastern Council) or overly conflict-ridden (especially Satluj and Kaveri tribunals and judicial commissions). Supreme Court have had to step in frequently to prevent the Kaveri from being on fire.

May be the Union Government finds the informality and flexibility of non-formal intergovernmental forums more convenient as well as productive, with the groundwork done by provisional secretarial and ministerial conferences of intergovernmental scope and by the Planning Commission officials.The Planning Commission, through their constant interaction with and intermediation between the two orders of governments know the minds of the Union and State governments and are able to persuade the executive heads in New Delhi and State capitals with techno-economic reason. A former Couple of former senior officers of the Government of India, who had been participant observers in some ISC and NDC meetings, have remarked that meetings of these bodies have been technically constrained by the given texts of the Constitution (in relation to Article 356) and five-year plans – the two items that have haunted their agendas. Mostly the first ministers and their delegations come with prepared speeches to be read out and there is little interactive session, if any. In contrast, the ad hoc ministerial and official conferences are more open-ended and negotiative on the day-to-day problems of policy and administration they are convened to deliberate on. Despite repeated discussion and consensus in the ISC and its subcommittees on reforming the provisions regarding President's Rule in a State for about a decade no follow-up amendment has resulted! The Srinagar meeting of the ISC (monsoon 2003) – first ever held outside New Delhi – has again reached a consensus to entrench the new regulatory case law laid down by the Supreme Court in *S.R. Bommai and others* v. *Union of India* (1994) in the Constitution by amendment. This landmark judgement made President's Rule in a State for the first time subject to judicial review and ordered that while dismissing a State government in a "constitutional emergency" the Union executive must not simultaneously dissolve the State Assembly until the presidential proclamation has been approved by the Parliament.

Despite considerable federalisation since the 1990s, the high-handedness of the Union leaves the States down and dry. For example, Punjab and Tamil Nadu have had to move the Supreme Court to oppose the unilateral signing of the World Trade Organisation (WTO) treaty in 1995 which adversely affects exclusive jurisdictions of States, e.g. agriculture. The matter is still pending in the court. Similarly, the Parliament, alone or in collusion with richer non-Hindi States, has recently (2002) partitioned some Hindi-speaking States like Bihar, Uttar Pradesh and Madhya Pradesh in a cavalier way. The same category of States have also been robbed of increased parliamentary strength that they would have gained by delimitation of constituencies after each decennial census by freezing the process in 2002 until 2026. The Hindi-speaking States that dominated the politics of the country in the era of Congress dominance have lost weight in the current phase of multiparty federal coalition governments.

In the domain of fiscal federalism, the constitutionally mandated transfers from the Union to States on the advice of the Finance Commission (appointed every five years by the President of India under Article 280 of the Constitution) have enjoyed greater legitimacy than the discretionary grants-in-aid by the Union on or without the advice of the Planning Commission (an extra-constitutional creature of the Union executive). However, going by a walkout from the NDC by the Telugu Desham Chief Minister of Andhra Pradesh around the mid 1980s and the sharp reaction of the richer states to the Eleventh Finance Commission Report, shows the need for political understanding and persuasion within the larger framework of Indian nationalism and comparative federal theory and practice.

Multi-Level Federalism with Local Bodies

During 1980s the search was on for institutional arrangements for improving the relations between the Centre and the states as well as state and the lower echelons. The choice of an appropriate federal system for India was on top of the agenda of concerned intellectuals, judicial and legal experts, social thinkers and political parties. By late 80's it was realised that the extension of the federal idea hinged on decentralisation at the sub-state level. The 73rd and 74th Constitution Amendments extending participatory democracy and popular base to the villages and municipalities can be reckoned as the turning point since independence, to reflect the social realities of a federal polity. India is therefore an evolving "Federal Nation".

In 1989 General Elections, election manifestos of almost all political parties mentioned the idea of strengthening of Panchayati Raj. After coming to power, the National Front government prepared an Amendment Bill in June 1990, in which objectionable features of earlier proposed 64th Amendment Bill were dropped and some new features were included. The Amendment Bill was introduced in September 1990, but with dissolution of the Lok Sabha, it got lapsed. The new Congress (I) government led by Prime Minister P.V. Narasimha Rao brought the fresh Constitution Amendment Bill. The Bill was introduced in Lok Sabha on September 16, 1991 and was referred to a Joint Parliamentary Committee, consisting of 30 members from both the Houses. This time efforts were made to have a consensus of all the parties. Consequently the Constitution (Seventy-Third) and (Seventy-Fourth) Amendment Bills were passed with near unanimity by both the Houses of Parliament, rectified by the State Legislatures and were assented by the President of India. Thus, on April 20, 1993, through official notification the new Panchayati Raj and Municipal Systems finally got constitutional status.

Through 73rd Constitution Amendment Act, Part IX was added to the Constitution, 16 new Articles (Articles 243, 243 A to 243 O) and an Eleventh Schedule were added in this Part. Thus, it is for the first time that the composition, powers and responsibilities of the Gram Panchayat came to be elaborately provided in the Indian Constitution.

By bringing the village councils and municipalities under Part IX of the Constitution, India has moved towards multi-level federalism to accommodate its diversity and give vent to people's aspirations. Balveer Arora and Nirmal Mukarji, have expounded the idea of multi-level federalism for the emerging Indian situation. They are of the view that in large federal systems "rising tide of pressures for participation in the political and developmental processes" and "concurrent pressures of integration and differentiation" result in multiple layering of structures. India had reached a point where it had become inevitable that without taking "cognizance of the layering of socio-political realities" the Union could not have survived. And multi-level arrangements in India are the new and ongoing search for new modes of adaptation to the pressure created by democratic development, designed to make the federal system more responsive.

India moving from a two-level federation (Union and States) towards multi-level federalism with local bodies (village councils and municipalities) at the district and below becoming the third level has made the nation a cascading federalism; a federation of federations. It may be recalled here that India has vibrant autonomous councils to meet the specific demands of the regions, as per the Constitution of India. This multi-level federalism should be seen as the structural means through which self-government goes all the way down to village councils from the Centre. Local self-governing units in such a scheme will draw sustenance from grassroots level political and democratic process as well as effective people's participation.

As a result of campaigns by civil society organisations, intellectuals and progressive political leaders, the parliament passed on December 22 and 23, 1992 two amendments to the Constitution Amendment for rural local bodies (panchayats) - 73rd Constitution and 74th Constitution for Amendment for urban local bodies (municipalities) making them 'institutions of self-government'. Within a year all the states passed their own acts in conformity to the amended constitutional provisions.

The 73rd and 74th Amendments to the Constitution have further given a new meaning to Indian federalism. A *de facto* third tier of governance, with a wide democratic base, has come into existence in the country. Till the passage of the 73rd and 74th Amendments, Parliament and Assemblies of the state and union territories of India had about 4963 elected members but today, more than three million people's representatives are being elected by this democratic process. Out of this, over one million are women. A large number of excluded groups and communities are now included in the decision-making bodies. Now there are nearly 600 district panchayats, about 6,000 block panchayats, at the intermediate level and 2,50,000 gram panchayats in rural India where 72.2 per cent of India's population lives. Urban India, with 27.8 per cent of India's population, has 101 city corporations, 1430 town municipalities and about 1,900 Nagar panchayats. Today, every five years, about three million representatives are elected by the people through the democratic process, of whom more than one million are women. Women head about 200 district panchayats, more than 2000 block panchayats at the intermediate level and about 85000 gram panchayats. Likewise, more than 30 city corporations and about 500 town municipalities have women chairpersons. A large number of hitherto excluded groups and communities are now included in the decision-making bodies. As the Indian population has 14.3 per cent Scheduled Castes (SCs) and 8 per cent Scheduled Tribes (STs), about 800,000 elected members – nearly 23 per cent of the total membership in the rural and urban local bodies – will be from Scheduled Castes and Tribes.

Multi-level federalism and widening democratic base after the 73rd and 74th Constitution Amendments

First Stratum	*Second Stratum*
Union	**States and Union territories**
Two Houses of Parliament have 800 Members (Lok Sabha: 550; Rajya Sabha: 250)	28 State Assemblies and Two* UnionTerritories have 4,508 Members

Total Elected Members at the Union and State Level 5 308

Third Stratum
DISTRICT and BELOW

Rural population: 700 Million plus	**Urban population:** 300 Million plus
594 District Panchayats elect 15 815 5 912 Block/Tehsil/Mandal Panchayats elect 1,45,412 231,630 Village Panchayats elect 2,971,446	101 City Corporations** 1,430 Town Municipalities
Total Elected Members : 3,132,673	**Total Elected Members : 68, 554**

The Third Stratum Elects 3,200,000 Members (Approx)
Of this more than 10,00,000 are women and 800 000 are SCs/STs

* only two Union Territories (Delhi and Pondicherry) out of seven have elected Assemblies.

** Population above 3,00,000.

*** Areas in transition. One-third of all the Panchayats and City Corporations/Muncipalities/Nagar Panchayats are headed by women as Presidents or Mayors. About one-fourth are headed by hitherto untouchables (Scheduled Castes) and Scheduled Tribes.

Source: Institute of Social Sciences, Panchayati Raj Research.

This marks a qualitative change in the federal character of the Indian Union. Each state has become a federating unit with three layers below it - district, block and village. This is a unique federal feature. An organic link in the democratic process has been established from *Gram Sabha* (village assembly) to *Lok Sabha* (Parliament). India has moved from administrative federalism to multi-level federalism. Of course, the elected local bodies have no legislative powers in the strict sense of the term and *de jure*, the Union and the States constitute federal India. The qualitative change that has come about in the Indian federal structure nevertheless has far-reaching consequences making the local bodies the third tier of governance.

Implications of *panchayati raj* / municipalities as the third tier of governance in India's federal structure:

- **UNION**
- **STATE**
- **THIRD TIER**
  - **Panchayati Raj**
    - ❖ Zilla Panchayat
    - ❖ Block/Taluk
    - ❖ Village Panchayat [GRAM SABHA (Village Assembly)]
  - **Municipality**
    - ❖ Municipal [WARD MEETINGS (For Municipal Areas)]
    - ❖ Municipal Council
    - ❖ Nagar Panchayat
  - **Autonomous Councils for Tribal Areas**

The decentralisation process that has gathered momentum in India in the last one decade or so has deep implications for human rights situation in India. This is particularly so for the villages in rural India. The democratic process has brought people closer in the villages, and they could now take part in the local election every five years and assert their right to vote. The elections in India are a big education process. The rights of the excluded people had been violated over the years owing to lack of democratic system of governance at the community level where they could participate effectively. The system of local self-government as manifested in the panchayati raj institutions has taken a leap forward in guaranteeing a life of dignity and respect to the citizen at the local village level. Ideals of social justice based on gender equality and liberty are best pursued at the local level.

In a formal sense, all the states have confirmed to the constitutional requirement of ensuring the participation in the PRIs to the hitherto excluded groups (women, dalits, and adivasis) through the system of reservation. The problems of the poor have been sought to be addressed by transferring some of the poverty alleviation and development programmes to the panchayats due to the constitutional obligation. By and large women have found representation in the panchayats through the one-third reservations of seats. The dalits and adivasis have been represented to the extent of their share in the population. Evidently, formal representation need not necessarily be an indication of participation. Since the new phase of decentralisation, there is evidence that some of the worst forms of exclusion that plagued the rural society in India are no longer practiced in a number of states. Elected members sit together and discuss issues in formal and informal meetings. A symbolic participation of all in the village, including the dalits and adivasis and women does take place at least as a constitutional requirement. This is due to the slow but sure changes in the larger political landscape in India.

Social transformation through a democratic process is not peaceful in India. Therefore, on the other side after India has taken bold steps to strengthen decentralisation and local governance system the human rights violations at all levels have gone up. The main reason is that all those who were enjoying the powers and privileges so far are trying to subvert the constitutional mandate overtly or covertly. Since 1993, in the new generation of panchayats, at least two rounds of elections have been held except in a couple of states. It is ironical that elections in India become an occasion for serious human rights violations. During the election period, the rich try to dominate the poor by buying their votes or keeping the poor as 'vote banks'. In many cases the upper castes stop the lower castes from exercising their democratic rights if they come to know that the poor and disadvantaged will exercise their votes independently. In the process violent incidents take place and many lose their lives. Although it happens even during elections to the states and parliament the violence is more in the local elections as the polling percentage is higher at this level.

Panchayats have, all the same, opened possibilities for bringing to surface most of the things previously swept under the carpet. No more it is hidden or secret. Although gram sabha and gram panchayat are hotbeds of manipulative politics, they provide a democratic forum to grapple with social and political issues in the open. Such a forum is now available, for the first time, with the constitutional backing.

Here, the role of political parties is crucial. The earlier concept of consensus (in effect, consent to whatever the powerful was saying or doing) is giving way to people aligning on party lines questioning every action that is less than transparent. If one political party becomes protector of the oppressed for whatever reason, another party becomes the guardian of the oppressor. In the local situation, state politics or national level ideology is of little consequence. As of now, open participation of political parties in the panchayat elections is the best way to challenge the age-old autocracy of caste or family. The dynamic multi-party political process, the widening democratic base as well as the structural changes brought about by the new panchayats and municipalities have contributed significantly towards the development of a healthy federal system. As governments at the Union level nowadays are coalitions that include state level or regional parties, the federal level cannot ignore the states politically or in other areas. In the same vein, state governments cannot ignore the *panchayati raj* institutions. If they do so there are chances of not being re-elected. A state ruling party's popularity depends on the extent of the sincerity with which it devolves power to the local bodies and strengthens them in the letter and spirit of the Constitution.

The mass media, communication technology and spatial mobility have broken the isolation of villages. Incidents even in remote village panchayats are thrown up promptly at the state and national level. The new panchayat system, with all its current weaknesses, has helped to weave the village into the broader social fabric.

The silver lining on the otherwise dark horizon is positive intervention of judiciary upholding the human rights of the downtrodden at the local level. Although, Indian judiciary is slow, the public interest litigation has been a successful tool to give meaning and content to the local bodies legislations. There was an instance where a woman belonging to a dalit community who was elected as the head of the panchayat had to face retribution by the defeated candidates belonging to the upper caste.

The Indian Federal System has been dynamic in accommodating political and societal changes since its constitutional blueprint was drawn in 1949-50. However, there has been a fundamental transformation in the operative principles of federalism particularly during the last decade or so. The rhythm and the beat of the political system, and of the federal system within it, has changed on account of a variety of socio-economic and political factors, but primarily because of a disarray of the party system, neo-liberal economic policies, and judicial decisions. The centralizing thrust of the earlier years has yielded to some kind of a 'confederal' operation of the political system, making the formulation and implementation of public policies a 'consociational' exercise between political elites at the two levels of government-central and provincial-with the third, now constitutionally entrenched level-local institutions of self-government-waiting in the wings.[23]

NOTES

1. Sharma, Chanchal Kumar, "When Does Decentralisation Deliver? The Dilemma of Design." *South Asian Journal of Socio-Political Studies* 6(1): 38-45, 2005, p. 39.
2. Sharma, Chanchal Kumar. 2009, "Emerging Dimensions of Decentralisation Debate in the Age of Globalisation", *Indian Journal of Federal Studies,* 1/2009: 47-65.
3. Lawrence Saez, Federalism Without a Center: The Impact of Political and Economic Reform on India's Federal System, New Delhi: Sage, 2002, p. 135.
4. Jenkins, Democratic Politics and Economic Reform in India, pp. 119–71.
5. Lloyd I. Rudolph and Susanne Hoeber Rudolph, "The Iconisation of Chandrababu: Sharing Sovereignty in India's Federal Market Economy," *Economic and Political Weekly,* May 5, 2001, p. 1546.
6. John Echeverri-Gent, "Politics in India's Decentered Polity," in Alyssa Ayres and Philip Oldenburg, eds., *India Briefing: Quickening the Pace of Change* (Armonk, NY: M. E. Sharpe, 2002), pp. 19–53.
7. Pradeep Chhibber and Samuel Eldersveld, "Local Elites and Popular Support for Economic Reform in India and China," *Comparative Political Studies,* Vol. 33 (April 2000), pp. 350–73.
8. Supra no. 2.
9. See Pradeep Chhibber and Ken Kollman, *The Formation of National Party Systems: Federalism and Party Competition in Britain,*

Canada, India, and the United States (New Jersey: Princeton University Press, forthcoming) for a comparative analysis of party system change and decentralisation.

10. Sheth, D.L. "The Change of 2004", *Seminar*, 545, Annual Number, January, 34-39, 2005.

11. Sridharan, E., "Electoral Coalitions in 2004 General Elections: Theory and Evidence", *Economic and Political Weekly*, 39 (51), December 18, 2004, 5418-25; 88; *Ibid.*, "The Fragmentation of the Indian Party System: 1989-99", in Zoya Hasan (ed.), *Parties and Party Politics in India*. New Delhi: Oxford University Press, 2002, 475-503; and also *Ibid.*, "Principle, Power and Coalition Politics in India: Lessons from Theory, Comparison and Recent History", in D.D. Khanna and Gert Keuck (ed.), *Principles, Power and Politics*. Delhi: Macmillan 1999.

12. Balveer Arora, "Negotiating Differences: Federal Coalitions and National Cohesion" in Francine R. Frankel and Zoya Hasan, (ed.), *Transforming India: Social and Political Dynamics of Democracy*, New Delhi, Oxford University Press, 2005, pp. 176-206.

13. Rasheeduddin Khan, *Bewildered India: Identity, Pluralism, Discord*, New Delhi, Har-Anand Publications, 1994.

14. *Supra no. 7.*

15. Francine Frankel and M.S.A. Rao (ed.), *Dominance and State Power in India*, 2 Vols, New Delhi, Oxford University Press, 1990.

16. Sanjaya Baru, "Economic Policy and the Development of Capitalism in India: The Role of Regional Capitalists and Political Parties", in Francine R. Frankel and Zoya Hasan, (ed.), *Transforming India: Social and Political Dynamics of Democracy*, New Delhi, Oxford University Press, 2005, pp. 207 – 230.

17. Rudolph and Rudolph coin this term in "The Iconisation of Chandrababu." *Supra n. 3.*

18. See "Non-Congress (I) Chief Ministers Meeting Today," *The Hindu*, April 25, 1987, p. 9; and "Six Chief Ministers Endorse Joint Front on Agreed Plan," *Hindustan Times*, April 26, 1987, pp. 1, 8.

19. "Naidu to Meet PM, Sinha on Finance Panel Report," *Times of India* (internet edition), August 20, 2000.

20. Lawrence Saez, *Federalism Without a Centre: The Impact of Political and Economic Reforms on India's Federal System*, New Delhi: Sage Publications, 2002.

21. Rekha Saxena (Ed.), *Mapping Canadian Federalism for India*, New Delhi: Konark Publishers, 2002.

22. M.P. Singh, "Federal Division of Responsibilities in India", *Indian Journal of Federal Studies*, 1/2004.

23. B.D. Dua and M.P. Singh (eds.), *Indian Federalism in the New Millennium*, New Delhi: Manohar, 2003.

13

Indian Federalism : An Empirical Study of People's Perception

S.K. Jain

The present study on "Indian federalism: An empirical study of people's perception" is the only empirical study ever conducted to capture the public perception on the emerging issues of Indian federalism in general and federal political culture and structure of India in particular. The study has the backup of a database comprising of 500 respondents covered in five states in different regions of the country during 2009-10 and has overall methodical orientation encompassing qualitative and quantitative data analysis. Four key objectives were premised to be the focus of information gathering under the study which were as follows: (1) To study the public perception or attitude of people on the working of Indian federalism in contemporary India, (2) To examine the extent of support of people at various levels of government, centre, -state and Local. (3) To ascertain how strong or weak is the public opinion on federal structure of India, (4) To study whether any federal political culture in India has emerged particularly in the era of coalition politics since 1990.

Federalism has been described as a response to the economic political and social conditions of a society. Federations have arisen in very different circumstances, each being the unique result of choices by political leaders and larger historical forces. As a matter of fact, there is no single pure model of federation that is applicable everywhere, rather the basic notion of involving the combination of shared rule for some purpose and self rule for others within a single political system so that neither is subordinate to the other has been applied in different ways to fit different circumstances. Federal systems are increasingly becoming popular all over the world. Twenty eight countries home to over 40 per cent of the world population, either call them federal or are generally considered to be federal. Even the newly emerged democracy in the sub-continent, Nepal has declared its position in favour of federal parliamentary democracy. The unitary system like United Kingdom (UK), France and Italy had shown tendencies in favour of decentralised governance if not for a federal democracy. Federalism has been adopted in post-conflict environments in Bosnia, Congo, Iraq, Sudan and South Africa. The European Union (EU) has a number of federal characteristics. However, an essence of federalism is that "there are two constitutionally established orders of government with some genuine autonomy from each other and the governments at each level are primarily accountable of their respective electorates."[1]

Throughout history India has been characterised by diverse culture, language, religions and regions. India is the most extreme plural society with 22 national languages and some 800 dialects, a dozen ethnic and seven religious groups fragmented into a large number of sects, castes and sub-castes and some sixty socio-cultural sub-regions spread over seven natural geographic regions. This union of state has 28 states and six union territories as units of federation. "The Indian constitution is generally flexible but rigid in federal matters and any change in the federal provisions requires a special two-third majority in Parliament as also ratification at least half of the legislatures of the states"[2].

Objectives of the Study

The primary objective of the study is to study the "Emerging Federal Political Culture in India" in the wake of coalition government and politics of India. However, the specific objectives of the present study included:

1. To study the public perceptions or attitudes on the working of Indian federalism in contemporary India,
2. To examine the extent of support of people at various levels of government, central, state and local,
3. To study how strong or weak is the public opinion on federal structure of India, and
4. To study whether any federal political culture in India has emerged particularly in the era of coalition politics since 1990.

Scope of the Study

As the present study was mandated to capture perceptions of people of the country as a whole, pertinently, one state from each region i.e. Bihar in the east, Gujarat in the west, J&K in the north, Kerala in the south and Delhi at the centre was selected as representative geographic sample under the study. Although it was originally proposed to include one state from the North Eastern (NE) region, but the selected state i.e. Manipur could not be covered due to disturbances in the region with blockades and agitation at the time of undertaking field work under the study. Nevertheless the universe of study comprised the country as a whole with the representative states to get the overall view of people on federal political culture and structure of India.

Methodology

To meet the objectives of the study, methodology and study design based on both quantitative and qualitative research techniques were adopted. Quantitative technique was used in preparation of sampling frame, sampling procedure, determination of sample size, collection of primary or quantitative data, whereas qualitative techniques like FGD and IDIs were employed in the process of qualitative data gathering.

Study Area and Sample

Over-all, 500 respondents in five states (Delhi, J&K, Gujarat, Bihar and Kerala) were covered under the study with a break-up of 100 in each selected state. Distribution of sample in the studied states is presented below:

Name of the State Covered	*Region*	*Sample Covered*
Delhi	Central	100
J and K	North	100
Gujarat	West	100
Bihar	East	100
Kerala	South	100
Total		**500**

The survey was conducted on random basis in one selected city or district in the selected state. While selecting the sample within the city, efforts were made to cover the city in its entirety so as to have wide representation of sample within the geographic location. The city of Bhagalpur in Bihar, Ahmedabad in Gujarat, Thiruvanathapuram in Kerala, Srinagar and Jammu in J&K and the whole city of Delhi were covered under the field survey.

Study Tools

Under the study, comprehensive semi-structured, state-specific interview schedules were designed, developed, pre-tested and finally used under the study. In the state of J and K where the field work was initiated, two different schedules for professionals and general respondents were canvassed which was later abandoned due to maintaining uniformity in data sets. State specific interview schedules were adopted to capture key issues relevant to the study and its objectives. For the purpose of collecting qualitative data under the study, question guides were purposively developed and appropriately used.

Field Data Collection

The field survey started in May 2009 in J&K followed by Gujarat, Bihar, Kerala and ended with Delhi by July 2010. In each state, the field survey was completed within two months which included canvassing of interview schedules with selected respondent categories and conducting FGDs with youth groups, students, political activists, professionals and common citizens. To overcome the language barriers in specific states like Gujarat and Kerala, help from university students or translators was sought.

Photograph-1: The Project Director in conversation with respondents in J and K

Data Analysis and Development of Study Findings

Field data were entered through FoxPro and analysis was made using SPSS (Statistical Package for Social Science) programme. Requisite tables were generated and so also the study findings. Five chapters were finalised to present the key findings of the study in the form of a Study Report. Copies of interview schedules used under the study are appended to the Study Report.

Limitations of the Study

This study bears the burden of an inherent limitation which is most common in survey research. Survey research presumes that respondent who falls in the sample has the capacity to formulate, articulate and to express his or her thoughts on questions put to them within a stipulated time frame. However, the field experience or observation suggests that while in general respondents could be able to comprehend the issues on their own, in many cases substantive probing and discussions were undertaken to get desired responses from the selected categories of respondents. Formulation of thoughts and its articulation to suit the field research objectives was not only time consuming but also too cumbersome. However, attempts were made to minimise these limitations to the extent possible under the study.

Socio-Economic Background of the Respondents

Under the present study, 500 respondents from five studied states i.e. Bihar, Gujarat, J&K, Kerala and Delhi were interviewed and based on responses received, a comprehensive profile on their socio-demographic situation has been undertaken. This chapter primarily focuses on analysis of data collected on indicators such as age, gender, education, profession, place of birth etc. of the respondents contacted over a period of one year between May 2009 and July, 2010 in different states, some of the key findings are presented below.

Age Group

Table 1 presents the distribution of respondents by their current age. Analysis depicts that more than one-third (38 per cent) respondents were in the age group of 21-30 years followed by one-fourth (25 per cent) above the age of 50 years, almost one-fifth (19 per cent) between 41-50 years and 18 per cent were between 31-40 years. It may be noted that respondents below the age of 21 were deliberately kept out of the sample under the study owing to factors such as political immaturity and lack of in-depth understanding of the subject area.

Table 1: Distribution of respondents by age group

Age Group	*Delhi*	*J & K*	*Gujarat*	*Bihar*	*Kerala*	*Total*	
						Num-ber	*Per cent*
21-30 Years	15	70	49	20	36	190	38
31-40 Years	24	10	14	19	22	89	17.8
41-50 Years	32	11	16	17	20	96	19.2
>50 Years	29	09	21	44	22	125	25
Total (N)	**100**	**100**	**100**	**100**	**100**	**500**	**100**

State-wise variation indicates that greater proportion of younger respondents participated in the survey in the states of J and K (70 per cent) followed by Gujarat (49 per cent) and Kerala (36 per cent). While in Bihar a majority (44 per cent) of participating respondents in the survey were in the age group of more than 50 years, in Delhi majority (32 per cent) were in the age group of 41-50 years.

Gender

With regard to composition of gender of the respondents it was noted that more than two-thirds (76 per cent) were male and the rest 24 per cent were female. The trend of higher proportion of male participation was evident across all states with the exception of J and K where more than 40 per cent respondents belonged to the female category. The gender data thus shows that women in J and K were more conspicuous in their participation (41 per cent) whereas they formed a minority (10 per cent) in the sample in the states of Bihar and Delhi (16 per cent). In fact, this shows that except these two states, in rest of the three states women respondents very willingly participated in the survey.

Table 2: Distribution of respondents by gender

Gender	*Delhi*	*J & K*	*Gujarat*	*Bihar*	*Kerala*	*Total*	
						Number	*Per cent*
Male	84	59	74	90	74	381	76.2
Female	16	41	26	10	26	119	23.8
Total (N)	**100**	**100**	**100**	**100**	**100**	**500**	**100**

Educational Qualification

Analysis of data with regard to educational attainment of respondents indicates that more than half of the respondents were educated up to university level (51 per cent) thus indicating that people with higher level of education and better knowledge levels had participated in the survey. This also indirectly suggests that respondents with better political maturity and comprehensive understanding on the subject area had formed part of the sample under the study.

Table 3: Distribution of respondents by educational qualification

Educational Qualification	*Delhi*	*J & K*	*Gujarat*	*Bihar*	*Kerala*	*Total*	
						Number	*Per cent*
School	00	06	09	23	12	50	10
College	21	08	23	36	17	105	21
University	65	80	35	27	46	253	50.6
Professional	14	06	33	14	25	92	18.4
Total (N)	**100**	**100**	**100**	**100**	**100**	**500**	**100**

Respondents studied up to college level were little more than one-fifth (21 per cent) followed by professionally qualified (18 per cent) and only 10 per cent of the respondents were educated up to school level. This trend was noted across all the studied states barring Bihar, where maximum (36 per cent) respondents were educated up to college followed by 27 per cent university level, 23 per cent school and (14 per cent) of the total respondents were professionals. In Delhi, all respondents were educated up to college or beyond.

Photograph-2: Focus Group Discussion (FGD) undertaken with students in Gujarat University.

Rural or Urban Representation

Under the study an attempt was made to capture perceptions of respondents staying in both rural and urban areas. The purpose of having urban as well as rural respondents on the sample was to ascertain whether the dwelling or place of stay determine their perceived notions with regard to different aspects of federalism and political processes of the country.

As can be seen from the above table, almost one third (29 per cent) respondents had rural background and the rest

(71 per cent) were from the urban areas. State wise variations indicate that in Delhi higher proportion of respondents were from the urban areas (89 per cent) followed by Gujarat (79 per cent) and Bihar (74 per cent). In the states of Kerala and J and K between 55 and 57 per cent respondents were from the urban areas.

Table 4: Distribution of respondents by place of birth

Place	*Delhi*	*J & K*	*Gujarat*	*Bihar*	*Kerala*	*Total*	
						Number	*Per cent*
Rural	11	45	21	26	43	146	29.2
Urban	89	55	79	74	57	354	70.8
Total (N)	**100**	**100**	**100**	**100**	**100**	**500**	**100**

Present Profession

The occupational composition of respondents indicates that maximum proportion in the sample (39 per cent) belonged to the category of students and common citizens followed by 37 per cent belonged to those who were employed in the government jobs. While 16 per cent respondents were self employed, only 6 per cent of the over-all sample was in private service.

Table 5: Distribution of respondents by present profession

Profession	*Delhi*	*J & K*	*Gujarat*	*Bihar*	*Kerala*	*Total*	
						Number	*Per cent*
Govt. Service	53	28	33	28	41	183	36.6
Private Service	03	08	10	09	10	40	8
Business	23	10	10	31	6	80	16
Others	21	54	47	32	43	197	39.4
Total (N)	**100**	**100**	**100**	**100**	**100**	**500**	**100**

State-wise variations indicate that in Delhi (53 per cent) was in the government jobs followed by 23 per cent in business, 21 per cent were students or common citizens and only 3 per cent were doing private jobs. In J and K on the other hand, 54 per cent were in the category of students and common citizens followed by 28 per cent in the government jobs. In Gujarat, 47 per cent were students and common citizens/others followed by 33 per cent in the government jobs and almost equal proportion (10 per cent each) was undertaking private jobs and business. In Bihar, one-third each were in the category of business and student/citizens closely followed by (28 per cent) in the government jobs. In Kerala, little more than 40 per cent each were noted in the category of government jobs and student/citizen and smaller proportion of respondents engaged in private service (10 per cent) and business (6 per cent).

Federal System in India: Constitutional Framework

Indian constitution envisages a federal mode of organisation. The process of the evolution of Indian federalism has been influenced by the interplay between the original constitutional design and changing political practices notably the relations between parties in power at different levels of government structure, rise of regional identities, end of one party dominant era and the judicial interpretation of the constitution. However, India is a federal republic with a parliamentary system. It consists of 29 constituent units (states) three of which have only been created recently (Jharkhand, Uttarakhand, Chhattisgarh and Telangana). The federal Parliament is bicameral, consisting of Rajya Sabha (Upper House) and the Lok Sabha (Lower House).

Photograph-3: The Project Director: In the midst of field survey in Bihar.

Survey of Public Perception: Findings from Five States

Across the five studied states, the opinions of the respondents on several key issues especially of different dimensions of federal political culture in India in general and ideas of respondents about federal form of government, their preference over other kind of government, levels of government that needs more power, benefits extended by the levels of government, level of government effectively representing needs of the people, discriminatory practices ever adopted by the government at the centre, aspects related to coalition government, role of the central government in carrying out development programmes in the backward regions of their states, fair distribution of central government policies regarding infrastructure and education, opinions on types of party system good for functioning of the federal system of governance, opinions on equal representation of states in Rajya Sabha, perception on Article 356 etc. were gathered. Analysis of data undertaken is described at length depicting the public perception on the key issues on federalism and some of the key findings are presented below.

Ideas and Preferences for Federal Form of Government

Respondents were asked to indicate their perception with regard to ideas on federal form of government to which little less than half of the respondents (49 per cent) indicated that by federal form of government they mean division of power at two levels followed by 47 per cent indicated that federal form of government is two levels of government and 4 per cent indicated having no idea on the same.

At the state level, while an overwhelming majority (Delhi-61 per cent, J and K-68 per cent, Kerala-76 per cent) had indicated that by federal form of government they mean division of power at two levels, in Bihar and Gujarat, a majority (85 per cent and 75 per cent respectively) had indicated that by federal form of government they mean

Table 6: Distribution of respondents by idea about federal form of government

Opinion	*Delhi*	*J & K*	*Gujarat*	*Bihar*	*Kerala*	*Total*	
						Number	*Per cent*
Division of power at two levels	61	68	25	15	76	245	49
Two levels of government	38	17	75	85	22	237	47.4
No idea	01	15	00	00	02	18	3.6
Total (N)	**100**	**100**	**100**	**100**	**100**	**500**	**100**

government at two levels. The analysis thus clearly indicates different perception of different states with regard to federal form of government.

Photograph 4: A field orientation address by the Project Director in Kerala University.

A majority of (91 per cent) respondents contacted under the study preferred federal form of government. State-wise variation indicated that while in Gujarat and Kerala about 5 per cent of the total respondents did not prefer federal form of government, their proportion was 7 per cent in Bihar and little more than 10 per cent in both Delhi and J and K.

Table 7: Distribution of respondents by preference for a federal form of government

Preference	*Delhi*	*J & K*	*Gujarat*	*Bihar*	*Kerala*	*Total*	
						Number	*Per cent*
Yes	86	87	95	92	94	454	90.8
No	11	11	05	07	05	39	7.8
No Idea	3	02	00	01	01	07	1.4
Total (N)	**100**	**100**	**100**	**100**	**10**	**500**	**100**

On being asked to specify which level of government needs more power at present, 40 per cent indicated the government at the centre followed by 30 per cent for local self government and 29 per cent stated that the state government needs more power. Majority of respondents indicating state government needing more power was evident in the state of J and K (40 per cent) followed by Bihar 36 per cent) and Gujarat (31 per cent) as compared to Delhi (16 per cent) and Kerala (23 per cent). Out of these three states, two states are being ruled by opposition parties of the UPA which is ruling at the centre.

Table 8: Distribution of respondents by level of government that needs more power

Level of Govt.	*Delhi*	*J & K*	*Gujarat*	*Bihar*	*Kerala*	*Total*	
						Number	*Per cent*
Central	48	24	33	39	53	199	39.8
State	16	40	31	36	23	143	28.6
Local	35	35	34	25	22	151	30.2
No Idea	01	01	02	00	02	07	1.4
Total (N)	**100**	**100**	**100**	**100**	**100**	**500**	**100**

The above analysis indicate a wide variance of perception with regard to idea about federal form of government that exists among the respondents across the states, preference over federal form of government has been quite emphatic and government at the centre needing more power finds favour with a majority of the respondents of the study.

Trust Deficit and Requirements

In terms of reposing trust on a particular level of government, majority (49 per cent) respondents stated it as the government at the centre followed by state (28 per cent) and local government (20 per cent) which includes the MCs or municipalities in urban areas and Panchayati Raj Institutions (PRI) including the GPs in the rural areas.

Table 9: Distribution of respondents by level of government that is most trusted

Level of govt.	*Delhi*	*J & K*	*Gujarat*	*Bihar*	*Kerala*	*Total*	
						Number	*Per cent*
Central	63	50	49	49	36	247	49.4
State	08	22	34	31	47	142	28.4
Local	24	27	13	19	15	98	19.6
No Idea	05	01	04	01	02	13	2.6
Total (N)	**100**	**100**	**100**	**100**	**100**	**500**	**100**

At the state level, in Delhi 63 per cent respondents mentioned central government is more trusted, in J and K 50 per cent stated so, in both Gujarat and Bihar 49 per cent each opined central government but in the state of Kerala only 36 per cent indicated the central government which is trust worthy.

On being asked which level of government is least trusted, over-all a majority (40 per cent) of respondents indicated it as the local self government followed by 27 per cent levelled it as state government and 26 per cent mentioned it as central government.

At the state level, in Bihar, a majority of respondents (59 per cent) indicated local government to be least trusted followed by Delhi (48 per cent), Gujarat (40 per cent), 30 per cent in J and K and only one-fourth (25 per cent) respondents in Kerala felt so. Higher proportion of respondents (42 per cent) in Kerala indicated that the central government is least trusted. Except J and K where 28 per cent respondents indicated the central government less trusted, in other state 18-22 per cent respondents stated central government to be less trusted.

Table 10: Distribution of respondents by level of government that is least trusted

Level of govt.	*Delhi*	*J & K*	*Gujarat*	*Bihar*	*Kerala*	*Total*	
						Number	*Per cent*
Central	18	28	22	20	42	130	26
State	28	38	28	20	23	137	27.4
Local	48	30	40	59	25	202	40.4
No Idea	06	04	10	01	10	31	6.2
Total (N)	**100**	**100**	**100**	**100**	**100**	**500**	**100**

Delivering Services and Representing Needs of Population

With regard to government that provided better benefits, more than half (50.2 per cent) of the respondents contacted in the study area indicated that the central government has been able to provide better benefits, 32 per cent of the total respondents stated it as state government and only 15 per cent mentioned it as local government.

Table 11: Distribution of respondents by level of government that provided better benefits

Level of govt.	*Delhi*	*J & K*	*Gujarat*	*Bihar*	*Kerala*	*Total*	
						Number	*Per cent*
Central	57	44	53	42	55	251	50.2
State	26	18	36	41	41	162	32.4
Local	15	30	10	17	04	76	15.2
No Idea	02	8	1	0	0	11	2.2
Total (N)	**100**	**100**	**100**	**100**	**100**	**500**	**100**

Only in the state of J and K, little less than one-third (30 per cent) respondents opined that the local government had served them better after the central government (44 per cent) and almost accusing the state government not delivering the right desired services. Almost equal proportion of respondents (41 per cent each) in the states of Bihar and Gujarat somewhat appreciated the state government serving the needs of the people but accorded better credits to the central government in this regard.

Further, the respondents were asked to give their opinion on the level of government that represent their needs effectively to which state government was preferred by a majority (44 per cent) of respondents followed by local government (33 per cent). Central government representing need effectively was stated by only 20 per cent of the respondents contacted under the study.

Table 12: Distribution of respondents by level of government that represents needs effectively

Level of govt.	*Delhi*	*J & K*	*Gujarat*	*Bihar*	*Kerala*	*Total*	
						Number	*Per cent*
Central	25	33	15	10	15	98	19.6
State	30	49	36	55	50	220	44
Local	40	17	44	33	32	166	33.2
No Idea	05	01	05	02	03	16	3.2
Total (N)	**100**	**100**	**100**	**100**	**100**	**500**	**100**

Except in the state of J and K where one-third (33 per cent) respondents and in Delhi almost a quarter (25 per cent) indicated that the central government has effectively represented their needs in the rest three studied states, only 10-15 per cent respondents perceived so.

Over the question of elected representatives raising legitimate demands of the local population in the State Assembly and Parliament, very high proportion (64 per cent) respondents stated that "sometimes" their demands are raised.

While 19 per cent perceived that their demands were (never) raised, 13 per cent indicated that their demands were (always) raised by the elected representatives in the State Assembly and Parliament.

Table 13: Distribution of respondents by opinion on whether elected representatives raise demands effectively in Parliament/Assembly

Opinion	*Delhi*	*J & K*	*Gujarat*	*Bihar*	*Kerala*	*Total*	
						Number	*Per cent*
Never	24	21	22	12	16	95	19
Always	04	14	07	33	08	66	13.2
Sometimes	70	54	68	55	73	320	64
No Idea	02	11	03	00	03	19	3.8
Total (N)	**100**	**100**	**100**	**100**	**100**	**500**	**100**

Central Policies and Effective Distribution

With regard to fair distribution of central government policies in all states, it was noted that half (50 per cent) of the contacted respondents opined negatively. Except Delhi, where 85 per cent and in Gujarat 59 per cent respondents stated affirmatively, in rest of the three states, majority indicated that the central government policies are not fairly distributed.

Table 14: Distribution of respondents by opinion on whether central government policies are fairly distributed among all states

Opinion	*Delhi*	*J & K*	*Gujarat*	*Bihar*	*Kerala*	*Total*	
						Number	*Per cent*
Yes	85	37	59	24	32	237	47.4
No	15	59	38	73	67	252	50.4
No Idea	00	04	03	03	01	11	2.2
Total (N)	**100**	**100**	**100**	**100**	**100**	**500**	**100**

In Bihar, a very high proportion of respondents (73 per cent) followed by Kerala (67 per cent) and J and K

(59 per cent) negatively asserted by indicating that the central government policies were hardly distributed in a fair manner.

On being asked to give their opinion on whether their states are being discriminated by the Centre, 34 per cent indicated that their states were discriminated in terms getting other packages, 17 per cent indicated discrimination in general budget and 10 per cent indicated it in railway budget. Only 6 per cent respondents in the study area perceived discrimination in all. However, 33 per cent respondents also felt that their states are not being discriminated by the centre.

Table 15: Distribution of respondents by opinion on whether your state is being discriminated by the Centre

Opinion	*Delhi*	*J & K*	*Gujarat*	*Bihar*	*Kerala*	*Total*	
						Number	*Per cent*
In General Budget	13	39	08	10	17	87	17.4
In Railway Budget	01	06	18	02	22	49	9.8
Other Packages	19	41	32	66	10	168	33.6
All Above	00	00	00	00	32	32	6.4
Not Discriminated	67	14	42	22	19	164	32.8
Total (N)	**100**	**100**	**100**	**100**	**100**	**500**	**100**

In J and K, 39 per cent respondents stated that their state is discriminated in general budget followed by Kerala where 17 per cent stated so. In railway budget, discrimination was perceived by 22 per cent in Kerala followed by 18 per cent in Gujarat but both in Delhi and Bihar, a miniscule proportion of respondents (1 per cent and 2 per cent respectively) indicated discrimi-nation. In the case of other packages, maximum (66 per cent) respondents from Bihar indicated discrimination followed by 41 per cent in J and K, 32 per cent in Gujarat, 19 per cent in Delhi and 10 per cent in Kerala.

Centre-State Relation: Coalition Perspectives

The respondents were asked to view Centre-State relation in the context of coalition politics to which 65 per cent indicated that in the coalition arrangement, state gets more bargaining power, while 26 per cent opined that state interest is less represented and 8 per cent made it clear that it is nothing better than a single party rule.

Table 16: Distribution of respondents by opinion on Centre-State relation in the context of coalition government

Opinion	*Delhi*	*J&K*	*Gujarat*	*Bihar*	*Kerala*	*Total*	
						Number	*Per cent*
State gets more bargaining power	71	75	72	44	64	326	65.2
State interest is less represented	16	14	26	54	19	129	25.8
Same as single party rule	12	11	02	02	12	39	7.8
No Idea	01	00	00	00	05	06	1.2
Total (N)	**100**	**100**	**100**	**100**	**100**	**500**	**100**

Among the states, in Bihar more than half (54 per cent) respondents however indicated that in coalition arrangement the state interest is less represented to which 26 per cent respondents in Gujarat and 19 per cent respondents in Kerala seconded. Respondents in three states i.e. Delhi, J&K and Gujarat, almost two-thirds respondents had indicated that state gets more bargaining power in coalition arrangement.

Taking the cue forward, it was asked to respondents whether central government interventions are required for development of backward areas of the state by implementing certain development programmes, an overwhelming majority

(87 per cent) indicated it to be so while 12 per cent indicated not necessarily and only 1 per cent had no idea about it.

Table 17. Distribution of respondents by opinion on whether central government interventions are required for development of backward areas of the state

Opinion	*Delhi*	*J & K*	*Gujarat*	*Bihar*	*Kerala*	*Total*	
						Number	*Per cent*
Yes	85	86	90	98	75	434	86.8
No	14	11	10	01	24	60	12
No Idea	01	03	00	01	01	06	1.2
Total (N)	**100**	**100**	**100**	**101**	**100**	**500**	**100**

Interestingly, 24 per cent respondents in Kerala had indicated that the role of the centre in developing backward areas of the state is minimal which was supported by 14 per cent respondents in Delhi and 10 per cent in Gujarat. In Bihar, only 1 per cent respondents agreed to the view that without the help of the central government the backward areas of the state could be effectively developed.

Photograph 5: An In-depth Interview (IDI) conducted by the Project Director in Kerala.

Opinion on Party System

The respondents were asked to state the type of party system which is good for the functioning of the federal system to which 44 per cent stated bi-party system, 37 per cent indicated it to be multiple parties and only 18 per cent indicated that single party system.

Table 18: Distribution of respondents by opinion on which party system is good for functioning of federal system

Opinion	*Delhi*	*J & K*	*Gujarat*	*Bihar*	*Kerala*	*Total*	
						Number	*Per cent*
One Party	09	20	15	17	30	91	18.2
Bi Party	46	33	57	70	15	221	44.2
Multiple Parties	45	47	28	13	53	186	37.2
No Idea	00	00	00	00	02	02	0.4
Total (N)	**100**	**100**	**100**	**100**	**100**	**500**	**100**

A majority of respondents in Bihar (70 per cent) and Gujarat (57 per cent) believed bi-party system, in Kerala 53 per cent and J and K 47 per cent respondents vouched for multi-party system that causes good for the functioning of federal system whereas in Delhi both bi-party system and multiple parties were preferred almost equally by the respondents for the optimal functioning of the federal system.

Role of Constituent Units in Foreign Policy Making

With regard to constituent units to have roles in making foreign policy of the country, 55 per cent across states indicated it to be so and 38 per cent did not think it to be so. Only 7 per cent respondents did not have any clue about it. All states except Bihar in which 78 per cent respondents did not support to the view that constituent units should have roles in making foreign policy of the country.

Table 19: Distribution of respondents by opinion on whether constituent units should have roles in making foreign policy of the country

Opinion	*Delhi*	*J & K*	*Gujarat*	*Bihar*	*Kerala*	*Total*	
						Number	*Per cent*
Yes	64	68	59	20	64	275	55
No	31	22	28	78	31	190	38
No Idea	05	10	13	02	05	35	7
Total (N)	**100**	**100**	**100**	**100**	**100**	**500**	**100**

Equal Representation of States in Rajya Sabha

On being asked to give their opinions on equal representation of state in Rajya Sabha, the opinions were almost equally divided as 47 per cent indicated yes and 47.2 per cent indicated no. Only 6 per cent did not have idea about it.

In states, like Kerala and Gujarat more than 60 per cent respondents had indicated that there should be equal representation of state in Rajya Sabha whereas respondents in Delhi, J and K and Bihar, majority were of negative opinion about equal representation with Bihar topping the list with 78 per cent saying no to it.

Table 20: Distribution of respondents by opinion on equal representation of state in Rajya Sabha

Opinion	*Delhi*	*J & K*	*Gujarat*	*Bihar*	*Kerala*	*Total*	
						Number	*Per cent*
Yes	41	46	61	20	67	235	47
No	52	51	32	78	23	236	47.2
No Idea	07	03	07	02	10	29	5.8
Total (N)	**100**	**100**	**100**	**100**	**100**	**500**	**100**

Opinion on Fairness of Taxes

Tax levied such as central income tax, sales tax by the state and municipal property tax by local governments were not kindly received by the respondents as only 36 per cent stated that central income tax is fair, 29 per cent municipal tax and 28 per cent opined the state sales tax as fair.

Table 21: Distribution of respondents by opinion on tax levied is least fair

Opinion	*Delhi*	*J & K*	*Gujarat*	*Bihar*	*Kerala*	*Total*	
						Number	*Per cent*
Central Income Tax	46	39	34	37	25	181	36.2
State Sales Tax	32	28	32	31	15	138	27.6
Municipal Property Tax	22	33	34	32	25	146	29.2
No Idea	00	00	00	00	35	35	7
Total (N)	**100**	**100**	**100**	**100**	**100**	**500**	**100**

Opinion on Article 356 (President Rule)

On being asked whether Article 356 should be used as last resort after exhausting actions under Article 355 or it should be deleted from the Indian Constitution, 42 per cent advocated for its deletion and 56 per cent rallied behind its continuation.

Table 22: Distribution of respondents by opinion on whether Art. 356 should be deleted from the Indian Constitution for autonomy of states

Opinion	*Delhi*	*J & K*	*Gujarat*	*Bihar*	*Kerala*	*Total*	
						Number	*Per cent*
Yes	25	99	38	17	29	208	41.6
No	70	00	59	83	68	280	56
No Idea	05	01	03	00	03	12	2.4
Total (N)	**100**	**100**	**100**	**101**	**100**	**500**	**100**

Among the states, while respondents in J&K cent per cent supported its deletion or voiced not to be used at all, as high as 83 per cent in Bihar, 70 per cent in Delhi,

68 per cent in Kerala and 59 per cent in Gujarat indicated its continuation.

Opinion on Diversity and Pluralism

On being asked whether a country should have multi-religions, ethnicity and multi-lingual composition or vice-versa, a majority respondents (85 per cent) across the states preferred diversity. Equivocal and positive responses over diversity by the respondents complimented the philosophical orientation of Indian Constitution which upholds unity in diversity.

Table 23: Distribution of respondents by opinion on whether a country should have multi-religions, ethnicity and multi-lingual composition or vice versa

Opinion	*Delhi*	*J & K*	*Gujarat*	*Bihar*	*Kerala*	*Total*	
						Number	*Per cent*
Similar	15	13	13	08	17	66	13.2
Diverse	85	86	87	92	77	427	85.4
No Idea	00	01	00	00	06	07	1.4
Total (N)	**100**	**100**	**100**	**100**	**100**	**500**	**100**

Federal Leadership: Collective vs. Individualistic

The respondents were also asked to indicate their opinion on two premises, one, whether a country should have a strong leader in the government to make decision on what she thinks or a country should have a leader who takes a decision by bargaining and negotiations with wider groups. To this effect 79 per cent respondents across states indicated that a leader taking decisions by bargaining or negotiation is preferred over a leader taking unitary decisions. This delineates the belief of respondents on leadership that is less authoritarian and more federal, tolerant and skilled.

Table 24. Distribution of respondents by opinion on whether a country should have a strong leader in the government to make decision on what s/he thinks or should have a leader who takes a decision by bargaining and negotiations with wider groups

Opinion	*Delhi*	*J & K*	*Gujarat*	*Bihar*	*Kerala*	*Total*	
						Num-ber	*Per cent*
Leader taking decisions on its own	25	21	28	16	15	105	21
Leader taking decisions by bargaining/ negotiation	75	79	72	84	84	394	78.8
No Idea	00	00	00	00	01	01	0.2
Total (N)	**100**	**100**	**100**	**100**	**100**	**500**	**100**

Conclusion

Federalism for more than two centuries has provided the Indian electorates know how to live together even as they maintain their diversities. Though federalism does not and cannot provide a panacea to every political entity, however, healthy democracy seems to demand the adoption or maintenance of an effective federal system. However, it appears that there is a co-relation between the federal structure and the federal attitude of the country. The present study which has tried to capture the public perception on the emerging issues of Indian federalism in general and federal political culture in particular observes that a vast majority of the people are aware about the federal structure of Indian political system with an idea of two levels of government and with a division of power between them. It also observes that a majority of respondents prefer federal form of government and support for federal structure or system for the country.

However, interestingly on the level of trust at different level of the governments indicates loss of trust in their respective state or local governments is a cause of concern for the federal structure of the country.

There has been abundant support for decentralised federalism for the country as a majority of the respondents under the study indicated state government representing their needs effectively.

The study also observes a reflection of pro-federal attitude among the respondents. On the vital question related to "federal culture," the overwhelming response has been extremely positive and supporting.

The first question to that effect was related to whether a country having multi-religion, multiethnic, multi-language composition is preferred or vice versa, a majority of respondents across states preferred diversity. (85 per cent)

The second question was related to whether a country should have a strong leader in the government to take independent decision or a decision based on bargaining and negotiating with wider groups of society, the overwhelming majority of respondents preferred a leader taking a decision by bargaining and negotiating reflecting a clear federal attitude. (79 per cent)

On the important question related with equal representation of states (constituent units) in the Rajya Sabha (Second Chamber), 47 per cent respondents indicated "yes" which amply reflected the pro-federal attitude.

An important observation under the study relates to the role of constituent units (state) in the making of foreign policy of the country to which a majority of respondents (55 per cent) across the studied state supported, which again reflects a very strong federal attitude in the quasi-federal structure of India.

The study observed that coalition politics and government at national level perhaps has given a better space to federal structure of the country. It has been corroborated by the fact that in the context of the coalition politics of contemporary India, a majority of the respondents (65 per cent) hold the opinion that in the coalition government at Centre, state gets more bargaining power in power sharing.

The study has also underlined the perceptions against the federal beliefs and attitudes, although there has been very supporting and positive response by the respondents on some of the federal issues or questions. Example of negativity in favour of federal beliefs has been evident from the fact that a majority of respondents contacted in the studied states favoured Central government (40 per cent) in matter related to needing more power compared to state (29 per cent) and local government (30 per cent).

The study also makes an important observation which has a direct bearing on perception of the respondents on the federal structure of the country. It notes a majority of the respondents (with the exception of J and K) rallied behind the continuation of Article 356 (56 per cent) with a poser that it should be used as a last resort after exhausting all actions under Article 355 of the Indian Constitution.

Another important observation of the study further negates the federal attitude of the respondents with overwhelming majority (87 per cent) support the view that the central government intervention is required for the development of backward areas of states".

Hence, it may be aptly concluded that India is a federal democracy with emerging federal political culture in the contemporary era of coalition politics. There has been a considerable support for pro-federal attitudes preserving federal structure and strengthening effective federalism. However, there are some negative attitudes emerged towards Indian federalism which should be seen in the context of "enormous diversity" and "one party dominant central government rule for more than two decades after the independence." However, with the onset of minority and coalition government since 1990's, Indian political system is getting more tuned towards genuine federalism owing to increased attention for democracy, development and growth of identity politics. The study presumes that there will be more pro-federal political culture in India with greater and effective decentralisation, a balanced regional growth, increased culture of tolerance and accommodation, shared identity, institutional arrangement for stability and enhanced respect for the rule of law.

14

Valedictory Address

Mahendra Prasad Singh

Professor Mahendra Prasad Singh began by pointing out that when the federal scheme was first floated by the Imperial and British Indian government under the Government of India Act, 1935, federalisation meant partly centralisation but it partly remained a centralised federal structure, as federal union was compulsory for the provinces. But the princely states were given greater latitude in the sense that the federal union was voluntary for them with the threshold of at least 50 per cent of princely rulers in the Chamber of Princes they had formed since 1920 opting to join it as the condition of the scheme being applicable to them. Moreover, the scheme was only euphemistically "federal" as even in the case of the British Indian provinces only elementary aspects of public health and education and local self-government were among the "transferred" subjects handed over to the elective ministers responsible to legislatures and more sensitive subjects like finance, police, security, intelligence, etc. were "reserved" for the bureaucratic apparatus headed by the Governors in the provinces and the Governor General at the Centre. And at the Centre the system of government remained largely bureaucratic with no pretence of any scheme of even partially elected ministerial government responsible to the Central Legislature. As is well known, the 1935 federal scheme was only partly implemented at the provincial level because the princes finally refused to join the proposed union. So at the central level, the new scheme remained unimplemented except for the establishment of the Federal Court of India for settlement of intergovernmental disputes in the context of the British Indian provinces and the Centre, with the Judicial Committee of the Privy Council in London being the final court of appeal.

Shifting his attention to the last phase of the British Raj around the time of the transfer of power by the British to the Indian hands, he briefly referred to the British Cabinet Mission Plan, 1946, which was a confederal scheme with a weak central government. It was so designed to appease Muslim League lobbying for more powers for provincial governments with the Muslim-majority provinces in mind, and to induce the princely states to agree to join the confederal union. The Indian National Congress wanted a federal scheme with greater powers for the Centre, including residuary powers, but it reluctantly accepted the confederal scheme for the sake of India's unity. However, the Muslim League finally rejected it and escalated its demand its demand for a separate homeland for Muslims first made in a somewhat vague and complicated way at the Lahore session of the Muslim League in 1940. The princely states adopted a policy of wait and watch. The Constituent Assembly of united India had already been elected under the Cabinet Mission Plan in 1946 by the electoral college of the provincial legislatures under the 1935 India Act, with the provision in place for the nomination by princely rulers of their representation in the Constituent Assembly in due course. At the early sessions of the Constituent Assembly as the leader of the Indian National Congress, Jawaharlal Nehru moved the Objectives Resolution under the framework of the

Cabinet Mission Plan, still with the hope that the Muslim League members would belatedly join the proceedings. But that was not to be. Finally, the Cabinet Mission Plan was replaced by the Mountbatten Scheme of independence in mid-August 1947 with the partition of India. Thereafter, the Congress-dominated Constituent Assembly proceeded to draft a federal constitution with a strong parliamentary Centre, which came into force on January 26, 1950.

In the early post-Independence decades, India worked a highly centralised federal polity – even more centralised than its Constitution. This was due to the hangover of the nationalist ideology, presence of tall national leaders of the freedom struggle against the colonial rule, the impact of the dominance of the Congress party at the Union level as well as practically all or most states, and the unique All India Services manning top administrative echelons at both levels of government.

With the declining dominance or even majority of the Congress party by the late 1960s at the state level and the late 1970s at the Centre as well, the political dynamics tended to become more competitive. But the erosion of the electoral and organisational base of the Congress proved to be short-term affair. The unworkable confederal intra-party power structure of the Janata Party caused the fall of its government in New Delhi in July 1979 and its governments in major north Indian states also subsequently petered out in the next couple of years. Congress party got an opening to stage a comeback under Indira Gandhi in 1980 and maintained its majority at the Centre and in a considerable number of states with declining control over state governments throughout the 1980s. But Congress under Indira and after her assassination in 1984 under her elder son Rajiv was a different phenomenon than the Congress under Jawaharlal Nehru and Lal Bahadur Shastri. It was an institutionalised democratic party in the earlier phase, whereas it turned into a pack of personal, familial, and dynastic followers sans organisational elections in the party after 1972 and intra-party democracy in general. All these changes had their own impact on the working of the federal political system in general. This impact may be summarily put as a deinstitutionalised and excessive centralisation that destroyed the democratic vitality of both the parliamentary and the federal components of the polity.

Moving on to the parameter-altering transformation in the party system in the 1989 parliamentary and some state assembly elections, Singh observed that from then on the federal features of the political system came into fuller and irreversible play. This phase has generally been characterised as the phase of greater "federalisation" of the polity. He pinpointed three major factors that brought about this larger transformation in the functioning of the political system without any substantial constitutional amendments. First, there was, as already mentioned above, the party system change from Congress dominance and even majority, especially at the Centre, to a multiparty system with decisive balancing role in formation and maintenance of federal coalition governments alternately led by the Janata Party or Dal, Congress, or Bharatiya Janata Party (BJP). Second, the accelerated pace of economic liberalisation, privatisation, and globalisation of the national and state economies, especially since 1991, increased the space for the private sector in the economy as also expanded the autonomy of state governments. Third, there also followed some unprecedented changes in judicial behaviour since the 1990s. For example, in *S R Bommai v. Union of India* (1994), the Supreme Court by a creative and constructive re-interpretation of the Constitution declared the proclamation of President`s Rule in a state under Article 356 of the Constitution open to judicial review, which until before it had treated as a "political thicket" beyond judicial scrutiny and entirely subject to the discretion of the Union Executive.

However, Singh sounded a precautionary note in uncritically celebrating the post-1989 phase in Indian polity as federalisation of the previously heavily centralised political system. For, despite some positive trends, there have been some negative features as well. For about a decade since 1989 there followed a period of extremely unstable federal coalition governments none of which could survive in office even for a full year. There has also been political blackmails and rampant corruption by the government and opposition jockeying for power and political survival. Besides, the weakening of the Congress party and failure of other national parties to regain its dominance, indeed even majority, meant the unprecedented emergence of the number and power of regional parties. Their strategic decisive balancing role in government formation and maintenance made them a factor of instability and political blackmail. To my mind, it is really a regionalisation rather than a federalisation of the Indian polity. It is regionalisation gone haywire rather than federalisation in the true sense of the term. Indeed, we never have had it so far; during the phase of Congress dominance, the political pendulum remained stuck to the extreme of parliamentary centralism, and in the post-1989 phase, it swung to the other extreme, that of regionalism gone haywire. We still await a constitutionally balanced federal governance in India. He went on to argue that what we are witnessing is the tumult of mighty disharmonies and destruction of federal spirit despite the constitutional scheme of cooperative federalism. The system has lost the capacity to take consensual decisions even in matters that are very vital to our national security and economy.

For example, for nearly five years the NDA Prime Minister Atal Bihari Vajpayee and for the subsequent five years the UPA Prime Minister Manmohan Singh kept convening Chief Ministers' conferences in order to get their support or creating consensus for setting up an National Investigative Agency (NIA), because the CBI is not a truly federal agency. The CBI is set up under a Delhi Police Act (1946) and therefore it cannot be either constitutionally or legally applicable to the state governments or a state government cannot be brought under is obligatory investigative jurisdictional control. In order for the CBI to operate in a state, it has to seek the permission of the state government concerned. Only in exceptional cases, where the Supreme Court orders CBI, it can enter into any jurisdictional area within the federal system – Union or state. So, the brief of Prime Ministers Vajpayee and Manmohan Singh for a full decade was to get a consensual endorsement of Chief Ministers to set up a national investigating agency that would have statutory power to operate in national as well as state jurisdictions and also simultaneously in cases of inter-state crime, international terrorism, and so on and so forth. However, the Chief Ministers routinely rejected. It was only after the Mumbai terror attacks of 2008 that Prime Minister Manmohan Singh and his government decided to move regardless of lack of permission from the Chief Ministers and introduced the National Investigative Agency (NIA) Bill, which was passed by the Parliament by voice vote and the Agency is now in place. No chief minister has gone to the Supreme Court against it. The Chief Ministers may have murmured but none has objected to it in public or gone to the Court.

The same story is being repeated in case of the setting up of NCTC (National Counter-Terrorism Centre). Using its understanding of the federal division of powers in the Seventh Schedule of the Constitution and its power, the Manmohan Singh, headed UPA Government of India set up the NCTC through a Cabinet decision, and thereby avoided the legislative route and the expected confrontation in the Parliament. Terrorism does not appear in any of the lists in the Seventh Schedule. Law and order is there in the state list but terrorism is not there any in any of the three lists, and therefore under the Constitution, it becomes a residuary subject and therefore under Union Parliament's jurisdiction.

That must have been the understanding of the Government of India, and therefore by executive order they set up the NCTC. However, the Chief Ministers rose up in arms including the CM of West Bengal Mamata Banerjee who was then supporting the UPA coalition government. A Chief Ministers' conference was convened with an omnibus agenda, including the NCTC, but the CM of West Bengal said that it could not be discussed in that conference and another Chief Ministers' conference had to be convened for exclusively discussing the issue. So, another Chief Ministers' conference was convened in which the Chief Ministers rejected the setting up of the NCTC. And as such, the Government of India did not proceeded with the matter. The NCTC was put in abeyance.

Singh went on to state that if the process of "federalisation" had actually taken place, the key constitutional forums like Inter-State Council, NDC, and others, could have become strengthened. These are the most important intergovernmental institutions in the Indian political system. India being a parliamentary-federal system in the British Commonwealth tradition, where "executive federalism" is the dominant mode of inter governmental relations. In presidential federal systems, there are other such forums for this purpose, such as the Senate in the United States of America, the federal second chamber, is a very powerful and is a very important federal forum. But in India which is a parliamentary- federal system, Rajya Sabha is a secondary chamber because the locus of political gravity is in the Lok Sabha. In a parliamentary system, the federal second chamber does not play that important role in intergovernmental relations as it does in a presidential-federal system. So, the most important federal instrumentalities in parliamentary-federal systems are the executive intergovernmental forums like the Interstate Council, National Development Council, CMs' Conferences, Ministerial Conferences, Secretarial Conferences, which function as sites of Union-State policy formulation, harmonisation, and monitoring of policy implementation. Sometimes the official intergovernmental forums may meet in the background like officials from the two orders of governments. In addition to these conferences, there are national councils and commissions representing both orders of governments. If we are becoming more "federalised," these forums should have become more powerful and should have become more institutionalised as sites of cooperative federalism rather than confrontation. But that is not really what has happened.

Alluding to the morning panel, Singh stated that speaker after a speaker pointed out that the intergovernmental institutions, consultative institutions are just left aside and important decisions are not taken in these forums. The Inter-State Council has a rather large secretariat but it has no work to do. The large secretariat of Inter-State Council in the Vigyan Bhawan has hardly any work to do. The most important event that it has performed during its life since 1990, when it was first set up, has been ad nauseam discussion on the Sarkaria Commission report, though most of the recommendations were never implemented. Another important function that it performed was organising an international conference on comparative federalism sponsored by the Forum of Federations, Ottawa. Then, it served as the secretariat for the second Centre-State Relations Commission chaired by Justice M. M. Punchhi. As a regular secretariat of the Inter-State Council it has hardly any work to do as the ISC since its founding has largely been ignored by all successive governments including the one that established it, i.e. the Janata Dal-led National Front government headed by Prime Minister V.P. Singh. The National Development Council is somewhat more functional but limited to the deliberation of the five-year plans. As such these forums of intergovernmental forums are hardly used for consulting the state governments and decisions are either unilaterally taken by the union government or discussed in ad hoc conferences (such as CMs'/ ministerial/secretarial conferences) which have no constitutional position.

As already mentioned above, the Inter-State Council as a constitutionally sanctioned body could and should have been used as the preeminent to discuss and create consensus on all important intergovernmental affairs. Instead of unilaterally setting up the NCTC, the Government of India should have referred the matter to the Inter-State Council, and the Chief Ministers in the Interstate Council should have and would have, in national spirit, allowed the Union to proceed with NIA or NCTC. These federal forums are, however, either left in limbo or ritualistically convened where each side states it position in a spirit of confrontation sans negotiation. By convention decisions in these bodies are not taken by vote but by consensus as sensed by the chair. Therefore, most important decisions that could have been taken on these federal forums are taken elsewhere or taken by the centre unilaterally.

A conceptual distinction that Singh made is regarding federalisation, regionalisation, and decentralisation. He reserves the word "federalisation" for the kind of institutionalised mechanism that he mentions earlier. He believes that what we are witnessing today is regionalisation. It cannot even be treated as decentralisation to the local political systems like the Nagarpalikas and Panchayat Raj institutions. Regionalisation characterises the shifting of powers from New Delhi to the state governments and decentralisation can be used properly for giving more powers to the local political systems. But what has happened is neither federalisation proper nor decentralisation proper but regionalisation gone wayward. The state governments have become politically very powerful at the cost of the Union and the grassroots political systems.

Singh further opines that in the phase of federal coalition governments there has occurred a phenomenon what may be called the situation of "divided government". For example, during this phase the President, the Vice-Presdent, the Prime Minister, and the Speaker of the Lok Sabha have often come from different political parties. During the era of one-party governments, all these key functionaries had come from the same party. Moreover, during this phase the Lok Sabha has been is under coalitional majority of the ruling dispensation and Rajya Sabha under an oppositional majority.

Furthermore, if we look to the states, we find a large number of parties in power. So a chequered political chess board is there, when chief ministers belonging to a variety of parties and coalitions are ruling in various states. The speaker does not feel this is bad; rather considers it to be a positive development and natural in a multicultural society and federal polity. Thus, today the ruling coalition in the Lok Sabha must create a consensus with opposition in the Rajya Sabha for legislation and constitutional amendments. For constitutional amendments in particular, a two or thirds majority in the Lok Sabha must be backed by a similar majority in the Rajya Sabha, and if the constitutional amendment has federal implications, it must also be ratified by at least 50 per cent of a state legislatures. That is why amendments to the Constitution have become virtually impossible today. The Constitution, which was so easily amended during the year of Congress dominance, has become virtually impossible to amend today.

The bulk of the amendments have been made either during the Nehru era or during the Indira Gandhi era and only a handful of amendments have been made in the coalitional phase. It is good because in a neo-feudal society it creates a democratic and federal compulsion for the political class. The political class must act democratically and federally if it wants to get any decisions made and as such it is a positive development. But at times it leads to political or governmental immobilism, which means a deadlock or no decision. It is in this context that the political analysts at times complain about policy paralysis and the captains of industry at times complain that the government is paralysed and cannot take any decision. It can perhaps also happen that in times of national emergency or in times of urgency or crisis, the government may be virtually paralysed and therefore it can also be a matter of concern.

The speaker opined that even in the phase of federalisation, the fact of the matter is that only a few states have real governmental capacity at the state level, even in this era of federalisation, which he prefers to call "regionalisation", only a few states can take decisions and initiatives on their own without depending fiscally on the centre. For example, Maharashtra, Gujarat, Tamil Nadu, partly Andhra, Punjab, and Haryana (although Punjab and Haryana have suffered economic decline of late). States in central and eastern India and all sub-Himalayan region states from J & K to North-East are "special category states" under the Finance Commission dispensation that are heavily dependent on federal fiscal transfers for their revenue.

State-building at the provincial level or state-capacity-building is very important today because the capacity of the Union government to help the poorer and backward states has declined, and national and multinational capital is making a beeline for investment only in advanced states and backward states are languishing without any private sector investment, either national or multinational or FDI. And, therefore, regional disparities among states and class disparities are increasing enormously since neoliberal economic reforms since the early 1990s.

The speaker mused: where do we go from here? He opines that in the period under review, over the last 20 years or more, there has been a decline and deinstitutionalisation in some cases but other organisations and institutions have either regenerated or have become reincarnated themselves in an activist mode. The Judiciary, National Human Rights Commission, Election Commission, Vigilance Commission, Comptroller and Auditor General of India, etc. have become demonstrated greater vigour and activism. He cites James Manor's article where it is argued that a good thing about India is that if there is degeneration in the political system in case of some sectors there is regeneration in other sectors; and this balances the situation. So that's a very welcome development. Moreover, some recent policy initiatives are also welcome, e.g. Right to Information Act, the Mahatma Gandhi National Rural Employment Guarantee Act, Forest Rights Act and the proposed Food Security Bill and Service Delivery Bills that are on the anvil.

The speaker concluded by making reference to the second Commission on Centre-State Relations chaired by Justice M. M. Panchi. In its multiple-volume Report, the Commission has made a number of thoughtful recommendations but he referred especially to only a few of them. In Volume 2, firstly, the commission has strongly recommended the strengthening and mainstreaming of the Inter-State Council in order to make it a vibrant forum for all the tasks contemplated in clauses A to C of Article 263. When the Inter-State Council was set up, clause A of Article 263 was omitted from the Presidential Order concerned. This was the most important power of the Council and that very power was taken away from it. The Panchi Commission recommends that this constitutional power should be restored to the Council and it should be made the key institution of executive federalism under the Constitution. The Commission also suggested that Inter-State Council should be routinely consulted through a regular convening of its sessions either on the initiative of the Union Government or on requisition of the state governments and it should be consulted in all matters of common policy making, harmonisation of policies, and foreign treaty making issues. The second recommendation that the Panchi Commission has made is that the Rajya Sabha, the federal second chamber, should give equal representation to all states - small or big. Today UP has a huge representation in the Rajya Sabha but Nagaland has only 1. This federal imbalance should be ended. As it uncritically replicates the principle of representation on the basis of population as in the Lok Sabha. This is alright for the national chamber of Parliament. But replicating it in the federal second chamber is negation of the federal principle of treating states qua state as equal. Finally, the Panchi Commission has recommended that the decentralisation of power to local political systems demands that to enhance the capability of the local governments, skills and services of the All India Service (AIS) officers should be made available to the local political systems. Because local political systems are emerging as the third tier of the Indian political system after the 73rd and 74th constitutional amendments. In the emerging scenario of multilevel governance the services of AIS officers should be available to the federal government, state governments, and to local governments alike.

Index

T